LIKE
Catching
Water IN A
Net

To Francenia.
In celebration
of a long and
wonderful friendship!
Val Webb

LIKE Catching Water IN A Net

HUMAN ATTEMPTS TO DESCRIBE THE DIVINE

VAL WEBB

continuum

NEW YORK • LONDON

2007

The Continuum International Publishing Group Inc
80 Maiden Lane, New York, NY 10038

The Continuum International Publishing Group Ltd
The Tower Building, 11 York Road, London SE1 7NX

Continuum is a member of Green Press Initiative, a nonprofit program dedicated to supporting publishers in their efforts to reduce their use of fiber obtained from endangered forests. We have elected to print this title on fifty percent postconsumer waste recycled paper. For more information, go to *www.greenpressinitiative.org*.

Printed in the United States of America

Library of Congress Cataloging-in-Publication Data

Webb, Val.
  Like catching water in a net : human attempts to describe the divine / Val Webb.
    p. cm.
  Includes bibliographical references and index.
  ISBN-13: 978-0-8264-2891-2 (hardcover : alk. paper)
  ISBN-10: 0-8264-2891-6 (hardcover : alk. paper)
  1. God. 2. Spirituality. I. Title.
  BL473.W38 2007
  202'.11—dc22
                                        2007019996

To Maurice,

in celebration

of life!

Contents

Preface   ix

1   Is Something Out There?   1

2   Metaphorically Speaking . . .   9

3   The GOD Who Is Not . . .   25

4   To Be . . . or Not to Be?   37

5   What's in a Name?   54

6   Feathers on the Breath of GOD   65

7   Where Can I Go from Your Spirit?   80

8   Nature Speaks   92

9   Divine Attributes: God Is Like . . .   109

10   The Power of the One   123

11   *Imago Dei*   136

12   In the Family Way   154

13   The Bible Tells Me So . . .   172

14   Who Do You Say I Am?   191

15   What Is Truth?   210

Notes   229

Index   243

Preface

I do not know if I will ever encounter God, So I live as though divine sounds and smells are enough.[1]

This book might never have been written. I nearly said "never have been finished," but that is a given. The book is not finished. It might appear in book format with a front and back cover and a last page, but that says more about publishing rules than about the end of the subject. It might not have been written because of the roller coaster of experiences it contains within. One morning, I would rush to the computer before breakfast with an incredible thought to record for posterity and then wander around the house the following day performing unnecessary tasks and arguing with myself, "Scrap the whole project. What can I know about God? What can anyone know about God? Isn't that exactly what I hate—people who claim to know whom or what God is?" With every new book I read on God, I wanted to give up all over again as more and more angles and qualifiers were introduced—the only cure was to stop reading. After years of such internal debate, the "you can say something" reluctantly won over "the impossible, arrogant attempt at human construction," and the book is in front of you, not an exhaustive summary of the topic but the struggles of one traveler.

What kept me going on good days is what keeps Japanese artists painting. Despite the satisfaction of faithfully reproducing a milky full moon dawdling behind spindly charcoal trees, such painting within the lines (as if a hovering Spirit raps naughty fingers that stray) confines creative imagination. Japanese artists listen instead to hints and intimations of what is not there, or certainly not center-stage—a pregnant bud not quite open, light gradations as the moon flees before dawn, and the possibility of creating a mountain with just a few wavy brush strokes. Such teasingly fleeting "intimations of immortality" open the door just a crack to whet the appetite for the hidden. Yet, the search for the Real is no simple matter. The more we succeed in pulling aside the curtain shrouding Divine Mystery, the more questions arise.

Japanese artists also favor asymmetry, believing that life is not boringly predictable, and that impermanence and surprise are more real than permanence. Our Western Greek heritage carved their eternal ideas and all-encompassing philosophies into chilly statues, yet Eastern thought celebrated the rich transience of existence—life as a verb, not something to grasp onto and hold. Buddha taught that all was transient—chopsticks are discarded, paper walls need replacing, and the noblest human body decays. A delicate tapestry-veined flower is overwhelming, not because it inspires artists to capture it on canvas, but because its clinging to life with fragile tentacles demands our attention and wonder. As Japanese artists work with hints, suggestions, sounds, and smells, I take courage and claim permission from such ambiguity and immediacy to write about the Divine with equal lightness and nonpossessiveness, not needing to add it all up and make it come out exact, to describe it for all time, or ensure all the lines are straight or even. The mystic Meister Eckhart (1260–1328) once wrote, "*Only the hand that erases can write the true thing.*"[2]

○ ○

As the title *Like Catching Water in a Net: Human Attempts to Describe the Divine* suggests, this project is both elusive and compelling. Chapter 1 examines why people through the centuries have suspected there is Something More. Chapter 2 proposes that anything said about the Divine is metaphorical, and outlines how metaphors and theology work together. Chapter 3 looks at the difficulty of describing Mystery, introducing God-talk that either says nothing or describes what the Divine is not. Whether God is not *at all* is discussed in chapter 4 with a summary of arguments for and against Divine "existence" across the centuries. Chapter 5 opens the discussion of what *has* been said about the Divine, beginning with Divine Names. Chapter 6 moves to the earliest images of Formlessness, Breath, Wind, and Sound, while chapter 7 concentrates on Spirit, both as free Agent and enclosed in a Trinity. Chapter 8 considers nature as a vehicle for Divinity, highlighting prominent metaphors drawn from the natural world. Chapter 9, acknowledging a hesitancy to describe the Divine in anthropomorphic form, speaks of Divine attributes, one of which is described in chapter 10, where different models of Divine power are examined. Chapter 11 looks at humans made in "God's image" (*imago Dei*) and the reversal of describing God in human forms, including King, Judge, and Warrior. Chapter 12 discusses Divine metaphors from the patriarchal family and gender issues that arise. In light of the Christian claim that Jesus is God, Chapter 13 discusses how the Bible, on which this claim was built, evolved through its history and, therefore, the type of authority that can (or cannot) be ascribed to it. From that discussion, Chapter 14 traces the evolution of Jesus from Jewish man to God in human form, a development that influences any discussions of God and challenges Divine images in religions other than Christianity. Chapter 15 views the contemporary world with its challenges from science and interfaith dialogue and examines God-language that may (or may not) sit comfortably with today's worldviews.

An ongoing theme through the book is the metaphorical nature of anything said about the Divine, and the resulting distortion and constraint when certain anthropomorphic metaphors become reality, including those surrounding Jesus as Messiah (*Christos*). The "existence" of the Divine is not assumed, as this is a faith statement, an individual choice to include (or not to include) Something More in one's worldview. While not exhaustive in any way, wisdom from various religions has been woven into the discussion, acknowledging the scope, similarities, and differences of human attempts to describe the Divine, and also introducing useful Divine metaphors that may be beyond the reader's current repertoire. "*Theology is like a garment we have produced, not a universal truth,*" theologian Marjorie Suchocki says. "*The garment, like all garments, will fit some, and not others. Should garments be thrown out then, because they do not fit everyone? Ah, then we should freeze in the winters of our loneliness! Better we should simply adjust the fit and see to helping others as they, too, weave their mantles.*"[3]

The New Revised Standard Version of the Bible is used throughout (unless otherwise indicated) and sources of the Islamic, Hindu, and Buddhist texts are indicated in the notes section at the back of the book. Gender-specific terms such as "he, his, him" for the Divine and "man, men" for humanity in quotations from other writers do not sit well with me; however, multiple "[sic]s" or bracketed feminine alternatives scattered through such texts considerably disrupt the flow of ideas. I hope that such gender-exclusive terms will sound awkward and anti-quated to you as well, thus highlighting the problem with their usage. As explained in chapter 2, I have used "GOD" from then on simply as a three-letter symbol, nothing more, and I have capitalized it to jolt us into reading it free of gender, doctrinal attributes, or form, allowing it to take on multiple meanings in different contexts and not any one spe-cific meaning.

A worldwide web of people and experiences created the inspiration and material for this book—friends, family, colleagues, book authors, students, and the many who influence me without my knowing it. A few need special mention, however. Frank Oveis, Senior Editor at Continuum, graciously retained interest in this endeavor, despite delays between proposal and manuscript due to family illness, and then nego-tiated the transition from manuscript to book with wisdom, humor, and a friendly professionalism greatly appreciated by the author. My chil-dren and their spouses, Helen and Steve, Paul and Alexis, Karen and Sean, listened patiently far beyond the call of duty to my verbal ponder-ings on the topic over time, and I hope these thoughts, now on paper, will contribute in some way to the world my grandchildren, Daniel, Rhys, Kyle and Calvin, inherit. As for my husband Maurice, his enthu-siasm for this topic kept the book idea alive over several years and also supported its extended gestation period and birth, despite his own seri-ous illness and recovery during that time. This book is dedicated to him as the one whose life, shared with mine, grounds me in love and helps me to soar.

Is Something
Out There?

A Pacific island chief was being bullied by a missionary about his beliefs.

"Have you, my dear sir, no conception of a deity?"

The chief replied, "We know that at night-time someone goes by amongst the trees, but we never speak of it."

From earliest times, people have asked the same questions: Who are we? Why are we? Where did we begin? What are the human limits? Why do bad things happen to us? Why is life not fair? These are questions about the nature of things—philosophy. The human being is by nature a philosopher, according to theologian Paul Tillich (1886–1965), *"because he inescapably asks the question of being. He does it in myth and epic, in drama and poetry, in the structure and the vocabulary of language."*[1] The child who asks "why?" and the Enlightenment's famous son Immanuel Kant (1724–1804) differ only in the form and intensity of their questions and answers, and when the "why" questions include Who or What is greater than us, does Something pull the puppet strings of life, and can we manipulate this Something for our benefit, we are moving from philosophy to religion.

Who knows which came first, the questions or the answers, but ancient people certainly sensed Something bigger than themselves within their world, calling It different names and attributing to It different characteristics and intentions. The gigantic faces on Easter Island, the cave and rock paintings of Australian Aborigines, and the miniature clay figurines found in ancient regions of Europe all represent primal estimations of a Something More. In the same way, the oldest Indian Vedic texts spelled out their questions and tentative answers about the Mysterious One:

> In the beginning this (One) evolved,
> Became desire, first seed of mind . . .
> Who knows truly? Who can here declare it?
> Whence it was born, whence is this emanation.
> By the emanation of this the gods
> Only later (came to be).
> Who then knows whence it has arisen?
> . . . Only he who is its overseer in highest heaven knows.
> (He only knows), or perhaps he does not know![2]

There is a difference between knowing that Something exists (or doesn't) and knowing what It might be (or not be). The former comes through experiences of awe, presence, or fear in unexplained events that on reflection seem orchestrated from beyond, the core of any religion. The latter is a second-hand knowing—human explanations of a Something that then become the doctrines and rituals of the clan. In ancient times, this Experience was described as an amorphous, enigmatic force, like mana in the South Pacific or Brahman in the Hindu Vedas. Others personified this Presence into fanciful forms of jinns, angels, little people, and mimi spirits, while others described anthropomorphic Beings who "spoke" and could be petitioned for help, like Earth Mothers Inana, Tiamat, or Ishtar, or High Gods Zeus, Allah, or Yahweh. Some simply cried out, not knowing whom or what to address, like the Queen in Euripides' *Trojan Women* (fifth century BCE)—"*Whoever thou art, beyond our mind's poor grasp, whether Zeus or Fate or spirit of men, I implore thee.*"[3] The difference is language, the choice of words and images to describe Something experienced but not seen.

To accommodate this Something into their world, our ancestors envisioned different realms: the human realm of ordinary reality full of limits, powerlessness, scarcity, and uncertainty, and a Divine realm of extraordinary reality free of all conditions and limits, everything that humans were not. These two realms usually shared the same physical space, Divine Beings and humans interacting on the same turf, as it were, and breathing the same air. The Vedic Gods lived, loved, and battled in the human plane of identifiable places; Sacred Beings of central

Australia emerged from the ground to leave their form in mountains and rivers; and Hebrew beginning stories pictorially describe a segregated neighborhood after the Divine garden became a gated community, even though God still came and went, getting involved in human everyday life outside the Divine walls. The Hebrew word for "heaven" had two meanings—the physical firmament or dome of sky that covered the earth, and the presence of God, never restricted to that dome but present everywhere in the created world and beyond. When dedicating the first temple in Jerusalem, Solomon said, *"But will God indeed dwell on the earth? Even heaven and the highest heaven cannot contain you, much less this house that I have built!"* (1 Kings 8:27). In John's Gospel, the two realms sharing space were differentiated as "earthly," the human realm, and "heavenly," the Divine realm. Only later in Christian history was the "heavenly" realm (and God) removed to that dome of sky by a sleight of language that merged the two Hebrew meanings for "heavenly" and added a dash of Greek concepts.

The two big questions for ancestral clans were "How can we penetrate this wall between the Divine and human realms?" and "Who/What is/are on the other side?" Subquestions proliferated. Can the Divine Beings see us and, more importantly, could we see them? Are they friendly toward us, or do they ignore our existence, amuse themselves with our foibles, or zap us with fickle whims? Can we influence them with rituals, sacrifices, and prayers? Can they visit us, and can we visit their realm, either now or after death? At this mysterious, amorphous wall between the two realms, religion (from the Latin *religio,* to bind) formed—binding the ordinary to the extraordinary, the profane to the sacred, humans to the Gods. *"Any religion,"* theologian Charles Bayer says, *"is only a signpost, a hesitant way to talk about what God is doing . . . all human institutions, creeds, hierarchies, systems, religions and formulae are fragmentary ways to talk about that which is beyond them all."*[4] Many people today call themselves spiritual, rather than religious or belonging to a particular church or temple. They talk about their personal relationship with the Sacred rather than joining a religious group where the Sacred is named for them. In ancient worlds where our religions began, however, the group posed the religious questions and shaped answers with the group's welfare in mind. Whether it was a desire to live forever like the Gods, or a need for Something Powerful fighting in their corner, or a guarantee for more reliable benefits here or later, human beings have always been obsessed with penetrating that boundary between the two realms to grasp Divine attention and enlist Divine assistance. Religions are our different stories of how this assistance might be found. Hundreds of creation stories across cultures explain how humans are different and separated from Gods, and how they can reestablish relationships with the Gods and live in harmony with them through prayer, rituals, and deeds.

When our generation faces crises such as the HIV/AIDS epidemic, we consult doctors and scientists, knowing their answers will reflect current knowledge that may differ twenty years from now. When our ancestors faced similar crises, they consulted their shamans and healers, who also responded according to their knowledge and worldview, with answers revolving around cosmic events, Divine intervention, and demons. Yet the questions that lit such fires in ancient primal hearts still burn in our hearts today despite all our technology, medicine, and psychology. When someone I love slips away with each faltering breath, or a phone call tells me my daughter is missing in a strange country, fear rolls over me like a suffocating blanket and I am helpless and distraught. My first reflex is to cry for help from Something beyond myself, like the psalmist: "*No refuge remains to me; no one cares for me. I cry to you, O Lord; I say, 'You are my refuge, my portion in the land of the living'*" (Ps. 142:4–5).

"Oh my God" is a response today for anything from mustard on a T-shirt to a ten-car highway collision. It is entirely possible to conduct a meaningful conversation with nothing more than successive "oh my Gods" uttered with alternating enthusiasm and horror, with no thought of a Divine Being. Yet the first "oh my God" tossed at mysterious powers against which our ancestors struggled exploded, no doubt, off panicked lips as something went madly wrong or out of control. Stumbling amongst the uncertainties of being human, where even birth was a rude shock that continued throughout life, our ancestors must have longed many times to return to the womb where all was safe and provided for. Did they despair at talking to the Unknown, unsure whether anyone or anything was listening? Did they perform complicated rituals all the while doubting their efficacy in the eyes of the Beholder, or did they simply cry "oh my God" into the wind and take their chances, not knowing if human life was of vital concern to the Gods or mere entertainment, if that?

What has made the human race over many centuries, in all its diverse forms, believe there is Something out there or deep within? Some say it is because, in ordinary moments of every day, we find extra power, courage, or endurance to do things that amaze even ourselves, or experience feelings or emotions that seem beyond human capabilities to generate. I clipped a newspaper story once about a man who avoided picking up heavy things after a heart attack. One day, he found a small boy trapped under an eighteen-hundred-pound cast-iron pipe in a freak accident, and without thinking, he leapt out of his car and lifted the pipe while two women dragged the boy free. When the man tried to move the pipe later, he could not budge it, nor could his grown sons, a young police officer, or the newspaper reporters. This is what assures Rabbi Harold Kushner that God is real, *"the fact that people who pray for strength, hope, and courage so often find resources of strength, hope, and courage that they did not have before they prayed."*[5]

Some folk are convinced of Something more because they read it in nature and the world around them, whether in the astounding complexity of the human body or the wasteful beauty of a miniscule iridescent beetle. No amount of scientific explanation can disperse the awe that comes with staring into the night sky and watching stars multiply by the second as eyes adjust to "seeing." *"With all your science,"* naturalist Henry David Thoreau (1817–1862) wrote, *"can you tell me how it is, and whence it is, that light comes into the soul?"*[6] Poet William Wordsworth and some of his nineteenth-century contemporaries had an answer—souls were not formed in the womb but already existed in heaven with God, thus we arrive at birth *"trailing clouds of glory,"* those memories of the Divine now mislaid or let go like a kite snapping its string in the wind: *"Turn wheresoe'er I may, by night or day, / The things which I have seen I now can see no more."*[7] These ever-diminishing *"intimations of immortality,"* so startlingly fresh in infancy, still invade our minds at rare, unplanned intervals, arousing a desire for what has been lost.

Some people accept a Dimension beyond themselves because they feel being human needs an opposite, something to give us reference points. How can we define the term "human" if there is nothing that defines what we are not? We could say we are not rocks, plants, nor animals, but is there not a tendency to assume that Something stands beyond us? In human history, no matter how remote, tribes "religiously" set up stones, sang sacred songs, or fenced off special spaces to worship that which was "not them." Susan Howatch in one of her novels wrote this need into the mouth of a dissipated Anglican priest trying to deal with the suicides of a gay priest and a disturbed parish worker: *"Human beings need some kind of God in order to feel whole,"* he said, *"and if they lose touch with The God, the right God, they can't rest until they've put something else in his place and elevated it into a false god. The spiritual vacuum always has to be filled."*[8] Nineteenth-century philosophers Ludwig Feuerbach, Friedrich Neitzsche, and Karl Marx spring to mind with such claims that humans need a God and so create something that is not there, yet needing something does not necessarily mean it is not already present. One of Fyodor Dostoevsky's characters says, *"I want to be there when everyone suddenly understands what it has all been for. All the religions of the world are built on this longing, and I am a believer."*[9]

Although we might be hard-pressed to find someone who will admit to this reason to believe in God, many do so because they find a Something potentially useful—Aladdin was not the only one fond of his genie of the lamp. Professor James Leuba (1867–1946), the first psychologist to write a book on religious consciousness, said:

> God is not known, he is not understood; he is used—sometimes as a meat-purveyor, sometimes as moral support, sometimes as friend, sometimes as an object of love. If he proves himself useful, the religious consciousness asks for no more than that.[10]

Consider some of today's television purveyors of God. They sell benefits, not the product itself—healing for your cancer, a way to get rich and be successful, or a guardian angel at your beck and call. Those who respond are told very little about God except what God can do for them. Because we all face death and are afraid both of what happens before and after, one of the biggest benefits is assurance in face of *"the terrors of death"* (Ps. 55:4). We want Someone to help us through this process and Something on the other side, a Divine afterlife insurance policy that we, rather than our beneficiaries, collect.

Many people simply live for the religious quest, whether a Native American vision quest, cycles of rebirth toward Nirvana, following the Five Pillars of Islam, or the mystic's journey to the Center. For them, this quest is not a choice but an integral part of what it is to be human, something written in their genes. According to thirteenth-century Sufi mystic Rumi, who founded the order of the Mawlawiya (Whirling

Dervishes), "*God has planted within you the desire to search for him . . . By planting within you the desire to search, God is guaranteeing the strength and wisdom you need.*"[11] Books to sink a continent have been written on this search in every religious tradition, every language, and with every conclusion. For Dag Hammarskjöld (1905–1961), once Secretary-General of the United Nations, it was simply a matter of saying "yes":

> I don't know who—or what—put the question. I don't know when it was put. I don't even remember answering. But at some moment I did answer "Yes" to Some One—or Something—and from that hour I was certain that existence is meaningful and that, therefore, my life in self-surrender had a goal.[12]

But is certainty always the outcome? Historian of religion Karen Armstrong described entering the convent as an adolescent nun, "*convinced that I had embarked on a spiritual quest, an epic adventure, in the course of which I would lose the confusions of my adolescent self in the infinite and ultimately satisfying mystery that we call God . . . God would no longer be a remote, shadowy reality but a vibrant presence in my life.*"[13] Even when the convent let her down and her adolescent God proved impotent and absent, her longing for "*the sense of heightened intensity and transcendence that the convent had promised to give me*" remained. She asks, "*Was I still a nun, living in the world and yearning for a deity that did not exist?*"[14] Are we yearning for a Deity that does not exist? Huston Smith, who has studied many religions, says, "*Whether we realize it or not, simply to be human is to long for release from mundane experience, with its confining walls of finitude and mortality. Release from those walls calls for space outside them.*"[15]

And what does it mean anyway to say "I believe (or not believe)," whether in Shiva, Amida Buddha, Yahweh, or Allah? What if we never find a "made by God" label on a certain basket of miracles, never feel our heart "strangely warmed" like the eighteenth-century founder of Methodism, John Wesley, or never say with ninth-century Sufi Akhbar al-Hallaj, "*You have unveiled yourself to me so openly that you are in my soul itself*"?[16] Do we simply believe in the Divinity others describe as true, like Alice in Wonderland believing "six impossible things before breakfast," or do we continue the search? For a long time, I let others believe for me, accepting their certainties in place of my doubts, but it didn't work, because we live with the consequences of what we believe, or don't believe. There will always be a moment, or many moments, when we have to ask "What, if anything, is the Divine for me?" with an honesty that goes beyond blind or secondhand belief, or nonbelief. The aim of this book is to explore, across wastelands and fertile plains, deserts and cities; across Islam and Buddhism, Hinduism and Christianity; across scholars and lay people, monks and mystics; what has been said about the Divine, in the hope that it might offer us a wider perspective within which to search. Just as atheists say God does not exist and agnostics say they are not sure, some people say true love is a fallacy and yet they don't stop looking. I recently found this poem I had written in one of my old notebooks:

> Perhaps I will know some day where God is
> or who God is or whether God is.
> It is the question I most often ask, even as the answer
> moves further away with each asking.
> Sometimes I almost forget where and how and whether to ask.
> I wonder if anyone knows where God is
> or who God is or whether God is.
> Is it the one question everyone asks, even as the answer
> moves further away with each asking?
> Sometimes God seems to forget
> where and how and whether to answer.

Metaphorically
Speaking . . .

Since God is necessarily infinitely larger than any human definition, we need all the stories, all the words, images, patterns, and forms we can get, even if only to show up their shallowness in the face of the infinite God we say we can believe in. The concept of legal blasphemy seems to me theologically stupid.

—*Sara Maitland*[1]

A writer is nothing else: a person alone in a room with the English language, trying to get human feelings right.

—*John K. Hutchens*[2]

Why attempt yet another book about God, I asked myself often, and the answer I always gave myself was "because our descriptions of the Divine matter." It makes no sense to say we believe, or don't believe in Something, without having some image in our mind of That to which we refer—how It appears and acts toward us, how we act toward It, and how we define ourselves as human beings as a result.

If we imagine God as a wrathful judge on a high-flying cloud, sizing up our every thought and action to punish or reward, we will spend our lives cowering before such scrutiny, constantly fearful of overstepping the line. As a child, I remember being bothered by a newspaper cartoon depicting a church service. Halfway into the sermon, a word balloon appeared above every head in the congregation revealing their wandering thoughts—the sexy dress on the woman in front, what to cook for dinner, how to resolve a business deal, and other less mentionable fantasies. This was my image of a private-eye God who knew all I ever thought or did and from whom I could never hide, the perfect Orwellian Big Brother to keep a child's mind pure and good. A woman writing about her life under communism described the few rooms in her tiny apartment as her only secure space, her hidden cave—everywhere else, she felt watched by people who would punish her if she broke the rules. When she read George Orwell's novel *Nineteen Eighty-Four*, what scared her most were descriptions of television screens acting as cameras in people's most private spaces, the ultimate situation of powerlessness and vulnerability.

If, on the other hand, God is described as a lover, then I am also a lover, loved by and in love with God. Such love does not depend, as in the previous scenario, on obedience or submission, but on the mutual, reciprocal relationship that Rumi described: "*When you are a lover, you want your beloved to be a lover also. God is humanity's greatest lover; and we, his beloved, must become his lovers.*"[3] The Hebrew people experienced Yahweh as lover because they included among their sacred writings a book of erotic descriptions of the consummation of young love, reminding them of their relationship with God:

> As a lily among brambles,
> so is my love among maidens.
> As an apple tree among the trees
> of the wood,
> so is my beloved among
> young men.
> With great delight I sat in his
> shadow,
> and his fruit was sweet to
> my taste.
> He brought me to the banqueting
> house
> and his intention toward me
> was love. (Song of Sol. 2:2–4)

Such an image paints an entirely different picture of how I can respond to the Divine, compared with always being afraid of being caught out.

Many people have no useful Divine images. They have walked away from their religious tradition because its God was unbelievable or alien or because their churches, synagogues, or mosques were unable to offer new ways to talk about the Sacred. Deities still described in prescientific worldviews, breaking natural laws to punish some and not others, no longer engage our technological age. One hundred and fifty years ago, social reformer and theologian Florence Nightingale (1820–1910) upset her Church of England friends by claiming that since Divine descriptions evolved with civilization, those people with God-concepts stuck in outdated worldviews made *"the same sort of mistakes as the man who fashions an idol with his own hand."*[4] If questioned why she believed in God, she would reply, *"Which of the ideas of God do you mean?... The God of the Old Testament, who commanded the extirpation of the Canaanites? Or the God of the New Testament, who commanded submission to the yoke in many things in which, as we worship Him now, we believe that He commands the struggle for freedom?"*[5]

Our fledgling ideas about God usually come from family. If our parents rejected a Supreme Being, the One they rejected will come to mind whenever God is mentioned. If our family was God-oriented, we probably absorbed this God with our first solid food, if not before. We all have some inherited religious experience, even if it is a reaction against, or a dismissal of, religion, and we all spend a lifetime, overtly or unconsciously, cultivating, repeating, ignoring, avoiding, or rejecting this inheritance. Religious clichés and moralizing make us angry, uncomfortable, challenged, or comforted, depending on how they operated in our youth or still do. Even long after arguing ourselves beyond childhood images, the mind quickly spirals back to old fears, guilt, or comfort when certain words are said or sung. When I was flying between Minneapolis and Los Angeles a month after September 11th, I couldn't help wondering what those ill-fated passengers did in their last few minutes. No doubt some took comfort in an active religious faith while others struggled to reconnect with a God they had ignored for years, mouthing snippets of childhood prayers or half-remembered words of confession and absolution. Those resigned to their own (or God's) impotence in the situation may simply have grabbed a nearby hand so as not to be alone when the fiery end came.

The story of three blind people describing an elephant appears in many cultures. Each described the part they felt—a rope (the tail), a cement wall (the side), a tree trunk (the leg). We know the moral of the story—we each describe what we know through our various senses and particular knowledge pool, and while this may be "true" for us, it may not be the whole "truth." In Central Bouganville (in the southwest Pacific Ocean), the Willy Wagtail bird lays its eggs in a visible nest, yet the Golden Plover nests are never found. According to the explanatory story, an evil spirit once asked Willy Wagtail to watch for the dawn and wake him so that he could go fishing. It was a full moon, and Willy Wagtail nodded off, only to wake and see the light. He woke the evil spirit, who went fishing and caught nothing because it was not yet dawn. The spirit asked the Golden Plover to watch the following night. All went well and the spirit caught lots of fish. Later, he summoned both birds, telling Willy Wagtail that because he failed his task, he would have to build his nest in a place where everyone would see it and where children would steal the eggs. The Golden Plover, on the other hand, would lay its eggs where no one could find them. To this day, no one has seen a Golden Plover nest in the North Solomon Islands. This wonderful tale was "true" for those people, but they did not know that the Golden Plover never nests in the Solomon Islands because it breeds in the Artic before flying south. They created their story within the limits of their knowledge and observation, but they lacked one vital piece of "truth."[6]

So it is with our descriptions of the Divine. We are limited to our own small grasp on the world, which is fine as far as it goes, but we cannot hope to know the totality of Something beyond our human experience or comprehension. My five-year-old grandson recently commissioned me to draw a number of things for him to color. After the usual dog, cow, and monster, he asked for his favorite television action hero, naming a character I had neither seen nor read about. I did not know if it was a robot, animal, person with green hair, or a fantasy being with antennae and hairy legs, but he knew what it was like and would not be satisfied unless I produced something vaguely recognizable. When I said I couldn't begin unless he described the character to me, he got frustrated. "Just do it, Grandma. Just draw it." The image was a large part of his experience and so he couldn't understand why I didn't know it as well. To claim that our particular, limited view of God is the correct and only view, the extent of all that is important to grasp, is, like the Golden Plover story, problematic.

By now, you may be calling through the page at me, "Just go to the Bible—that tells us all about God." While this seems an obvious and simple solution for knowing about the Divine, it is also rather tricky. The Bible is a collection of books covering almost four thousand years of a segment of human history, each written with its own literary style, agenda, symbols, and context. The various books do not always use the same term for God nor describe the Divine with consistency, as several recent books have pointed out.[7] The Yahweh of the Hebrew scripture evolves, hardly a formula for an unambiguous portrait, and the fact that such variations existed side by side indicates the reluctance of biblical compilers to confine Yahweh to any strictures of uniformity. Some people have also argued that the New Testament God is different from the Hebrew Bible God—the second-century theologian Marcion claimed that the Hebrew Creator God had nothing in common with the God of love taught by Jesus, and many still want to make much of law versus gospel, old versus new, as reflected in "Old" and "New" Testament terminology.

Theology (*Theos*, God; *logia*, sayings) means talk or discussions about God. Its classical application was eighth-century BCE poet Homer's talk about Olympian and pre-Olympian Gods, but once Greek philosophy became well-developed, theology became the subsection of philosophy that dealt with Divine Beings. For Greek-influenced early Christianity, theology was the study of the nature, attributes, and will of the revealed God, expanded in medieval Christianity to include doctrines about God's work in the world (systematic theology or dogmatics, the systematic study of Christian dogmas and doctrines), often ordered by the categories of creation, fall, and redemption, or creation, redemption, and sanctification.[8] The doctrines about God taught in church or read in Christian literature are not spelled out as such in the Bible, but come from centuries of theologians interpreting the scriptures within their own particular philosophical worldviews, using their church traditions and their own reason and experience. As new knowledge came to light or worldviews changed, so did ideas about the Divine. If such evolution in theology were not the case, clergy would simply need one slim book and a couple of weeks' training. Before people knew about bacteria, they attributed illness to various causes—Divine judgment, position of the stars, miasmic vapors from decomposing matter, and lack of sanitation, but once the microscope was invented and bacteria could be seen as causing disease, these other "causes" lost favor. In the same way, without microscopes to "see" the Divine Essence, we can only observe manifestations and speculate on what might or might not be the cause. Such speculation (theology) is always limited by current knowledge and open to new information. _"Theology is the study of God and his ways,"_ theologian and author Frederick Buechner said. _"For all we know, dung beetles may study man and his ways and call it humanology. If so, we would probably be more touched and amused than irritated. One hopes that God feels likewise."_[9]

To demonstrate to students the subjectivity and tentative nature of organizing ideas about the Divine into all-encompassing, eternal systems, I produce a stack of paper cutouts of different sizes, shapes, and colors and ask students to organize them into some system. The first few students arrive at four or more piles according to different properties—size, shape, texture, or color. When I ask others to organize them into fewer piles, they have to sacrifice some of the variations and therefore put all circles together regardless of size and all squares together regardless of color. There is always a student who makes one pile of "all paper," onto which I then throw a plastic shape. What does all this demonstrate? First, that subjective, personal choice decided the criterion or organizing principle for each of their systems, whether color, shape, size, or materials, and that there was always more than one way to organize the information. Second, in order to create only one pile, that is, one system into which all the shapes fit, diversity of shape, size, and color had to be sacrificed, and the few pieces that did not fit into the chosen system (like my piece of plastic) simply discarded.

Over the centuries, talk about the Divine has been organized into various doctrinal systems depending on the organizing principle chosen, whether it be the creeds as normative statements of the church, a specific theme such as sixteenth-century reformer Luther's "justification by faith through grace," or a specific understanding of the person and work of Jesus the Christ. Certain biblical texts (shapes) are blended with philosophical concepts of the day and interpreted through the lens of the theologian's cultural and personal convictions. Such organizing is only made possible by leaving out, or explaining away bits that don't fit, which is what systematic theologians have done for years. For example, a traditional theological system for Divine activity has been creation, fall, and redemption, categories once subjectively chosen by theologians and repeated by others down the centuries. This system was based on the interpretation of the Adam and Eve story as the beginning of sin in the world, even though this story was not so used by Hebrew people, nor did Jesus mention the first couple as originators of sin. Now that modern scholarship has challenged the interpretation of this story as "sin" and a "fall," the creation-fall-redemption "system" also comes into question and has to be reexamined. Doctrines have evolved at a certain time and place within the knowledge and philosophical framework of that time, yet the systems have become chiseled into stone (dogma) as if the system itself was written down by God. Interestingly, "doctrine" and "dogma" both derive from the Greek *dokein*, meaning opinion, belief, or "to seem good," a much more flexible approach than what dogma has become and how doctrines have been used and still are used to control others with the "truth." We need to be constantly vigilant as to whether our human God-talk says more about us than the Divine. Speaking about massive changes in our contemporary knowledge and worldview, theologian Matthew Fox says:

> As we change our understanding, which you do during a big cultural shift like this, whole new images of God are going to flood out. If [Meister] Eckhart is right and the names we give to God do come from understanding ourselves, then if we can broaden, deepen and make more beautiful our names for God, we'll be making ourselves deeper, broader and more beautiful as well. [10]

Many traditional images of God and their accompanying doctrines are crumbling today because people realize that many of the metaphors used and explanations offered were formulated within outdated cosmologies using obsolete philosophical arguments and based on theological assumptions now proven incorrect—the Golden Plover story sounds remarkably like some of our past theological conclusions. It has taken the poor of the world questioning their oppression as part of God's plan, the church's lay folk questioning their exclusion from certain privileges and sacred spaces, and women questioning their subordination as a Divine "order of creation" to challenge doctrines written by and for those with the power to do the writing. Any theological constructions are *"houses to live in for a while, with windows partly open and doors ajar,"* theologian Sallie McFague says. *"They become prisons when they no longer allow us to come and go, to add a room or take one away—or if necessary, to move out and build a new house.*"[11]

A jigsaw puzzle is perhaps a better metaphor for organizing and interpreting Divine "sounds and smells." While we will never complete the God picture on the puzzle box, we give individual puzzle pieces (hints of the Divine) equal weight in the emerging Divine vision. We cannot throw away pieces that don't seem to fit because all are important if the puzzle is to progress and ever become clear—and even then we may find that we do not have all the pieces. However, that does not stop us working on the puzzle, watching a Divine image or images develop as pieces lock together, not only from our religious tradition but from others who also speak of the One, images forged in different cultures and circumstances to add to the Whole. "*Everything that exists is a mirror for the Divine,*" religion scholar Abd al-Hakeem Carney says, "*but the Divine Effulgence is colored and shaped, we can even say distorted, by the imperfections and irregularities inside each particular mirror.*"[12] We each describe our God as Love, Justice, Power, Mystery, in terms that answer our needs. Does this mean we create the Divine with our descriptions? In one way, "yes" in terms of language, but the flip side is that what we describe in our faltering metaphors as a result of our ambiguous experiences may equally be interpreted as the Veiled One reaching out to us and others. We cannot say how God should appear to another, and so we must also tolerate and respect Divine images as they appear in other religions and other people. "*Do not attach yourself to any particular creed exclusively, so that you may disbelieve all the rest,*" the twelfth-century Sufi Ibn al-Arabi said. "Otherwise you will lose much good, nay, you will fail to recognize the real truth of the matter. God, the omnipresent and omnipotent, is not limited by any one creed, for, he says, 'Wheresoever ye turn, there is the face of al-Lah'" (Surah 2:109).[13]

The most important thing to take from this book is that anything we say about God is a metaphor, a construction of language. No one has actually seen God face-to-face, so no one can describe the Divine as is. "Knowledge" about God has been deduced over centuries from events within our world that have been ascribed to Divine activity and character, "*necessarily approximate, provisional, corrigible and mainly wrong,*" according to historian of religion John Bowker. "*But they point, nevertheless, to the One who evokes these words and pictures, but remains beyond the verbal net in which we try to catch our fish.*"[14]

For those scratching their heads to recall the definition of a metaphor, it is a word picture used for clarity and impact to describe, not itself, but something else hard to describe or indescribable. (For the purists, I acknowledge that I should also talk of simile, analogy, and allegory here to be fully nuanced, but there is a long way yet to go with this book and much to cover before I, and you, sleep.) "I stopped when I heard a ghostly howl echoing across the moonlit moors" is a seriously under-stated description of terror arising like bile in my throat. "I froze on the spot" expresses the petrifying fear much more powerfully, even though you and I both know there was no actual drop in temperature. "Froze" is metaphorical, a visual image to describe my feelings when ordinary words fail. My brain has scanned its collective memory for something the thing being described might resemble, checking especially compar-isons of taste, sound, color, texture, and feel. For a metaphor to work, the word picture selected must be an experience shared between speaker and hearer. To say I am about to burst after a particularly large meal would not be a suitable metaphor to use with someone who has known little but starvation. Holocaust survivor Primo Levi, describing the dread of his concentration camp companions at the approaching winter (seven out of ten had died the previous year and the rest suffered severely), could find no adequate words for what they experienced together:

> Just as our hunger is not that feeling of missing a meal, so our way of being cold has need of a new word. We say "hunger," we say "tiredness," "fear," "pain," we say "winter" and they are different things. They are free words, created and used by free men who live in comfort and suffering in their homes. If the Lagers had lasted longer a new, harsh language would have been born; and only this language could express what it means to toil the whole day in the wind, with the temperature below freezing, wearing only a shirt, underpants, cloth jacket and trousers, and in one's body nothing but weakness, hunger and knowledge of the end drawing near.[15]

If metaphors are useful to describe elusive but known objects and experiences, they are extremely useful for describing the Unknown experienced in many ways by different people, religions, and races. We all choose our metaphors to describe Divine Mystery from our culture, traditions, and worldview, always limited and always expressed, how-ever imperfectly, in the words available at that time. When we say God is wise, good, and trustworthy, we are actually talking about respected human values which we then apply in perfect form to God, even while admitting God is not human—as Greek philosopher Xenophanes (570–480 BCE) pointed out, if cows and lions fashioned Gods for themselves, they would also do it in their own forms.[16] We don't even know whether our human metaphors are appropriate for the Divine realm. Should we apply human characteristics writ large to Something that may well be more like an amorphous energy surging within us and the expansive universe beyond our imagination? Technological metaphors from our scientific world may well be more suitable, or equally further from the "truth," and to those who resist such technological images because they are not in the Bible, theologian Elizabeth Johnson says:

> It is not necessary to restrict speech about God to the exact names that Scripture uses, nor to terms coined by the later tradition. So long as the words signify something that does characterize the living God mediated through Scripture, tradition, and present faith experience, for example, the divine liberating action or self-involving love for the world, then new language can be used with confidence.[17]

The difficulty with metaphors from biblical desert culture, early Greek philosophy, or ancient Asian worldviews is that some of these metaphors became cemented into traditions as sacred, despite a very different worldview of origin from ours. Jewish rabbis and early Christian fathers for the most part recognized the allegorical and metaphorical nature of Divine descriptions, but over time, anthropomorphic images of God as warrior, ruler, father, and judge became the norm once Christianity became established as a major religion with male political and religious hierarchies. By the Middle Ages, the ancient metaphors had become literal descriptions—God was literally a warrior, king, judge, and father, and human beings were literally soldiers, subjects, sinners, sons, and daughters. Christian art bolted this imagery into place. On monastery, church, and museum walls, an old man with a white beard sat beside a younger, beardless clone as a bird fluttered between them to represent the Divine Trinity. Nonanthropomorphic biblical metaphors such as Spirit, Breath, and Love paled into insignificance or were exiled to ecclesiastical margins.

Many Divine metaphors are not only irrelevant today, but downright harmful and need to be retired and replaced by ones that work in contemporary experience. We sing in cozy suburban churches about God our Sword and Shield, having rarely seen an ancient Israelite sword, let alone felt the metal in our hands, or was it wood? Most of us cannot imagine how it sounded or felt going to battle on foot with nothing but sword and shield between us and death. And what would happen in our tenuous global relations today if Israel or the West seriously invoked the biblical God who delighted in destroying the enemies of Yahweh's favored people—"*The righteous will rejoice when they see vengeance done; they will bathe their feet in the blood of the wicked*" (Ps. 58:10). Such aggression would draw severe censure in our international courts of law. Our world could use today more of the ancient *Tamil Veda Tiruvaymoli's* respectful vagueness:

> He [the One] is beyond our knowledge,
> He is this and not this,
> He comes in the form those seek
> Who truly turn to him,
> And yet that may not be his form.[18]

Because metaphors are multisymbolic, the hearer needs to make the symbolic connection intended by the speaker. If I call someone a ferret, meaning that her research methods always uncover well-hidden pieces of information, my metaphor would be disastrous if interpreted as ferretlike characteristics of sneakiness or tenacious cruelty in hunting. If such misreading can happen between people of similar cultures and circumstances, how much more difficult is the transplanting of metaphors from ancient biblical worlds into today's context with any assured accuracy of meaning. Ancient Hebrews sitting around the fire would have nodded in comfortable recognition as the Divine was described as rock, shield, high tower, and fortress, yet this original metaphorical impact is lost in our everyday world and experience. We continue to teach high-tech city children about ancient shepherds, believing we must preserve the biblical metaphor of Divine Shepherd, yet as author George O'Brien notes, "*A God who travels only on camels may end up as a subject only for tourists, not for life's daily commuters. How is the modern commuter to engage his or her imagination with that Biblical narrative so overstocked with sheep and figs?*"[19] "Shepherd" is neither sacred nor a literal picture of God but something conjuring up Divine protection for sheep-herding tribes on unforgiving Palestinian hills. Church school pictures of a neatly groomed, serene shepherd surrounded by cute, play-ful lambs may be someone you might like as your suburban pastor, but it bears no connection to the original, a rugged and odiferous loner fighting wild animals at night with sticks, not from self-sacrificing hero-ics but as economic survival, protecting what little livelihood his family possessed. Even the adjective "good" meant a shepherd who did this job successfully as opposed to an irresponsible, careless shepherd, yet this was interpreted in later Christianity as a moral category—good versus evil, pure versus sinful.

There has never been only one metaphor for God, even though some traditions have zeroed in exclusively on one or two, ignoring the others. As a focus for Islamic devotion, ninety-nine beautiful names for God curve and curl in decorative calligraphy across arches and walls of mosques in place of the humanlike Divine images preferred by Christianity. Hindu temples drip with whole worlds of fanciful charac-ters from the ancient epics, embodied metaphors or avatars of the One Brahman. The Hebrew Bible overflows with Divine metaphors drawn from everyday culture and experience—eagle, lion, hen, rock, and wind from nature; gardener, builder, potter, wise woman from human life; shield, fortress, hiding place, and high tower from military encounters; and ruler, prophet, patriarch, and law-giver from religious and political society. None were intended to describe the Divine in actuality (that could not be known), and using so many reminded people that no sin-gle metaphor was the definitive or preferred description. Multiple metaphors allow us to say more, not less, about the Divine, each adding to the composite of what is essentially unknowable while not supersed-ing previous images. These metaphors or "models of God" are to be judged, according to Sally McFague,

> . . . not by whether they correspond with God's being (the face is not avail-able to us), but by whether they are relatively adequate (in other words, more adequate than alternative models) from the perspective of postmod-ern science, an interpretation of Christian faith, our own embodied experi-ence, and the well-being of our planet and all its life forms.[20]

Even the word "God" is used metaphorically. It is a word borrowed from the English language to describe Deities in general and, as such, conjures up different images for a Sikh and an Anglican. For many years, I met with a group of people from various professions to read new books on religion together. We soon became highly sensitized to the difficulties of ascribing any image-laden term to the Sacred. One woman's delightful Southern accent still rings in my ear as she began each of her comments, "If God—or whoever or whatever we call Him, Her, It, or Nothing . . ." Our desire to avoid the problem of traditional doctrinal assumptions accompanying the term "God" produced another problem—our inability to function unless we could agree on a term all could comfortably hear and conveniently use without tying the Named to associations we no longer espoused. We finally agreed on "God," but as a tool, a symbol of three letters to enable communication while in no way reflecting a particular set of doctrinal arguments. This worked only because of our shared understanding and agreement—another group might use the same term with an entirely different, even opposing, set of meanings tucked into its belt. "*No man of faith*," Jewish philosopher Martin Buber (1878–1965) once wrote, "*imagines that he possesses a photograph of God or a reflection of God in a magic mirror. Each knows that he has painted it, he and others. But it was painted just as an image, a likeness. That means it was painted in the intention of faith directed towards the Imageless whom the 'Image' portrays.*"[21]

Having now revisited metaphor, an overly simplistic course in semiotics, the study of signs and how they work, is called for. Three things are important in semiotics: the sign, what it signifies, and the people who use it. A sign is something that refers to something other than itself, and its effectiveness depends on the same association being made by user and hearer. If I raise my arm at a bus stop (sign), indicating that I wish to catch the bus (what it signifies), the bus driver stops because she knows what my sign means (people using the sign, the driver and me). Communication has taken place. If I did this in a country where that sign had a different meaning, the bus would not stop, and communication would not have taken place. Signs can be of three types in relation to what they signify—an icon, an index, or a symbol. An icon looks like what it signifies, for example, my photograph is an icon because it looks like me, the thing signified. An index does not look like the object signified but has some direct, recognizable connection with it, for example, if I tell you to look for someone with red hair and a blue shirt, the hair and shirt are not an image of that person but are recognizable connections to that person. A symbol, the one that concerns us here, is a sign that looks nothing like the object it signifies and has no recognizable connection but works because a community has agreed that this particular symbol will refer to some particular thing. Letters, words, and numbers are symbols. The number 3 looks nothing like three things, yet we learn very early to read this curly squiggle as the symbol for three of anything. In the same way, the letters CAT look nothing like a furry animal—we simply accept in the English language that these three shapes in this particular combination mean a feline. If we were in France, the letter combination CAT would not work because they have a different cultural agreement, CHAT. Symbols get even more complicated when the same symbol means different things in different languages. In English, FORT signifies an enclosed structure protecting a city, yet in French it is an adjective meaning "strong." Furthermore, agreed-upon meanings of letter symbols can evolve over time within a culture. One hundred years ago, everyone was GAY and happy in romantic novels, quite different from what GAY signifies today.

The point of all this is that a symbol as an arrangement of letters has no eternal or intrinsic meaning but acquires meaning through agreement within a particular group. Likewise, the letters GOD arranged in this particular order (DOG means something quite different) have no intrinsic meaning but take on a meaning assigned by a community. GOD loses this meaning in another language—GOD in English refers to DIEU in French, DIOS in Spanish, and GOTT in German—and even within the one language, different meanings are assigned to the symbol GOD by different groups, making its transfer between groups difficult and causing incredible conflict throughout the world. Furthermore, because of a humanly constructed rule of the English language, the letter symbol GOD, as opposed to GODDESS, indicates both masculine gender and the generic human male or female, suggesting, with the help of centuries of religious art, that the Signified is male, as a student once informed me on the first day of a Women and Theology course: "Of course GOD is male because the Bible calls him He." How much theology has been shaped by arbitrary language rules!

By whatever symbol we name the Divine, it is simply that—something that, in itself, in no way resembles or says anything about the Divine but simply indicates the One about which we speak. Without a symbol, it is almost impossible to speak at all. In this book, whenever I use the letter symbol GOD, it is simply a symbol for any talk about the Divine and not a particular doctrinal package about, or a description of, the Signified—such specifics are indicated by descriptive labels attached to GOD, such as Mother GOD, Almighty GOD, Savior GOD, and GOD the Judge. Some theologians today will not use the letter symbol GOD because of its masculine specificity over against the feminine GODDESS—they use G*D, S/He, GOD/ess, and other derivatives. Having identified the way I am using it, however, I prefer to use GOD and ask that you read this three letter symbol thus, a symbol free of any doctrinal or gender baggage. I have also capitalized the symbol from here on (except in quotations from other writers), an irregularity that should continually jolt our minds, reminding us that the symbol remains open and free. I also capitalize the first letter of any word I use for the Divine, the One, Something More, another language convention that indicates these terms be read, not in their mundane meaning, but as words about GOD—we live by signs and symbols without even thinking about it.

If I were to borrow a metaphor to illustrate this discussion of divine metaphors and symbols, I would use Uluru, the great rock monolith sacred to Aboriginal people that rises red-brown from the central Australian desert. When you walk around its massive circumference, the view of the rock is different at each stopping place. Aboriginal people tell different sacred stories about each of these points. If you only tell the story about where a thin sliver of rock forms a kangaroo tail, this will not describe the whole rock—even a helicopter view does not adequately describe the rock, because it does not show the underside. Every sunset, hundreds of cameras recording the rock's changing colors produce images, not of "rockness," but of the interaction of light with the rock's elements. Uluru could simply be called a rock or described in one arbitrary metaphor that excludes all others. So it is with the Divine. GOD could simply be described in one image for convenience or control, but the totality of the Divine cannot be captured even in a million metaphors. Our metaphors for GOD matter because they can bind us in prisons of despair or set us free to live. They determine whether or not a Divine Presence can authentically be part of our understanding and experience of life. Much theological gymnastics has been performed over the centuries to retain outmoded metaphors and theological worldviews that either don't make sense or else negate our own experiences of being human. We need to search our own experience and find ways and words, albeit limited and always evolving, to describe the Something that crosses (or doesn't cross) our path in our time and place.

The aim of this book is to introduce a multitude of Divine metaphors and images that people over the centuries and across different religions have found inviting, useful, and believable for the One whose center is everywhere and whose circumference is nowhere. Hopefully they will encourage us to continue the search or at least confirm for us that we have given it our best try. "*The purpose of a book,*" according to twentieth-century Catholic monk Thomas Merton, "*is to teach you how to think and not do your thinking for you. Consequently if you pick up such a book, and simply read it you are wasting your time. As soon as any thought stimulates your mind or your heart you can put the book down because your meditation has begun. To think that you are somehow obliged to follow the author of the book in his own particular conclusion would be a great mistake.*"[22]

The GOD
Who Is Not . . .

What if everything is an illusion and nothing exists?

In that case I overpaid for the carpet.

If only God would give me some clear sign: like making a large deposit in my name in a Swiss Bank.

—Woody Allen[1]

How can we make contact with Something that cannot be seen and that has made a career of obscurity and silence, or maybe even doesn't exist? We pride ourselves at comprehending the known, but the unknown always hovers on the edges, beckoning like the sirens' song. We have no idea how large it is or whether, by expanding what we know, we can even reduce the infinite unknown ("infinite" being that catch-all term for the continuum of existence weaving its way beyond our horizons). Furthermore, we can only ask questions about what we can surmise from human experience, which may be a very shabby amount of knowledge. Even to say GOD is omnipotent, omniscient, and all-benevolent is fudging it because, while those attributes may make sense in human culture, how do we know what they mean in Ultimate territory—and what of the questions we can't even know to ask? Cartoonist Bill Keane, penciling in a cartoon draft, was asked by his son, "Daddy, how do you know what to draw?" Keane replied, "God tells me." The boy said, "Then why do you keep erasing parts of it?"

For the ancients, to exist was to encounter the Sacred—you could not set religion off from everyday life and experience as something separate. In fact, there was no specific word in Hebrew for "religion"—it was simply part of life. Ancient Hebrew people were aware of the mystery surrounding Something above and beyond thought, an absolute Reality that could only be signified. It was blasphemous for mortals to think they could know all about GOD: "*He has made everything suitable for its time; moreover he has put a sense of past and future into their minds, yet they cannot find out what GOD has done from the beginning to the end*" (Eccles. 3:11). Since Yahweh was always disguised in clouds, thunder, or burning bushes, people had to depend on Divine voice messages through various media or the evidence of Divine activity around them. They did not make idols of Yahweh, either human or animal, nor claim to see the Divine face—didn't Yahweh tell Moses, "*You cannot see my face; for no one shall see me and live*" (Exod. 33:20)? They did, however, speak of the Yahweh they encountered in everyday metaphors, even while knowing such descriptions were symbols that in no way represented all of Divine reality. Job ranted and railed as if to another person, using the logic of human justice when he thought Yahweh had been unfair: "*Therefore I will not restrain my mouth; I will speak in the anguish of my spirit; I will complain in the bitterness of my soul . . . Why have you made me your target? Why have I become a burden to you?*" (Job 7:11, 20). The Divine answer came, not in a few disciplinary words, but a hundred and twenty verses of "Can you do this" challenges ranging from catching the sea monster Leviathan with a fish hook to naming the second when mountain goats calve to describing the heavenly constellations and throwing lightning across the earth. While admitting inferior abilities, Job at least had the satisfaction of pulling the veil a little further off the mysterious Face: "*I have heard of you by the hearing of the ear, but now my eye sees you*" (Job 42:5).

Early Christian theologians also struggled with the Divine's unknowable essence (*ousia*). According to St. Basil (330–379) from the Eastern church, "*It is by his energies that we know our GOD; we do not assert that we come near to the essence itself, for his energies descend to us but his essence remains unapproachable.*"[2] They spoke of this unknowable *Ousia* as active in the world as three *hypostases*—Source, Word, and Spirit, a poetic Trinity that translated into the Western church as three *personae* (masks) used by an actor in a play, a metaphor that would, in time, be rendered anthropomorphic in the English language as "*God in three persons, blessed Trinity.*" Church theologian St. Augustine (354–430), despite saying that "*when you begin to experience God you realize that what you are experiencing cannot be put into words,*"[3] still tried, interpreting the Triune metaphor in human characteristics of memory, understanding, and will. Much later, Dominican theologian Thomas Aquinas (1225–1274) acknowledged that human knowledge could not understand the Divine because of the different substances of the human and Divine mind: "*Hence the supreme knowledge which we have of God is to know that we do not know God, insofar as we know that what God is surpasses all that we can understand of Him.*"[4] He went on, however, to offer five proofs for GOD's existence. The concept of Divine Mystery in the Western church became limited to what of the Sacred could not be explained by human reason, what German theologian Rudolf Otto (1869–1937) later called the Numinous, "*that aspect of the Deity which transcends or eludes comprehension in rational or ethical terms.*"[5] There is a problem with this, however, which Blaise Pascal spelled out in the seventeenth century:

> If one subjects everything to reason our religion will lose its mystery and its supernatural character. If one offends the principles of reason our religion will be absurd and ridiculous ... There are two equally dangerous extremes, to shut reason out and to let nothing in.[6]

Islam's founder-prophet Muhammad (570–632) was also overwhelmed by the unknowable mystery of Allah, the GOD who had been sending revelations since the beginning of time and who finally sent one to the Arab world in the Qur'an. "*Allabu Akhbah!*" means "Allah is greater," distinguishing the Divine from all other reality and removing Allah from human description. In Islamic art, intricate patterns of calligraphy, geometric designs, and natural forms represent the Divine names, the Universal Architect and the Creator of the natural world, but never is there an image of the One beyond imagining. When Islam became more established and focused on following its laws, the Sufi movement emerged as ascetics and proponents of *mahabbah*, the inner path of "knowing" Allah through a loving union rather than intellectual knowledge. Al-Ghazali, the eleventh-century master of rational theology, stood speechless one day in front of his students, realizing that, although he knew about Allah, he did not know Allah. Distraught at the impotence of his reason in the face of Mystery, he took to the road to discover the Sufi way. "*As we travel closer to God, we begin to desire him,*" said Rumi. "*We can feel his attraction drawing us onwards. This attraction is proof of his existence. Does dust rise up without a wind? Does a ship float without a sea?*"[7]

Al Ghazali's writings inspired the great Jewish Talmudic scholar Moses Maimonides (1135–1204), who was struggling in twelfth-century Egypt to reconcile Jewish scriptures with rational philosophy. In his book *Guide to the Perplexed*, Maimonides rejected assigning any attributes to GOD, even though the Hebrew Bible was full of such pictorial descriptions to help people understand and approach the Divine. "*Whatever we say with the intention of praising and extolling God,*" Maimonides said, "*contains something that cannot be applied to God, and must always be saying of God less than God is.*"[8] Even to call GOD good was problematic because Divine goodness would be far more than anything human could ever conceive—all that could be said was that "*God's existence is absolute, and is not composed of anything. Therefore we can know only the fact that God exists, not what God essentially is.*"[9] Yet even talk about existence worried Maimonides because the Divine was absolutely different from creaturely existence and imagination and could not even be called a Being, since this implied that the Divine essence could be classified in human categories of existence and mortality, things that begin and end.

Some who have realized the impossibility of describing who or what GOD is have resorted to "apophatic" or negative theology, saying what GOD is not. "GOD is not impotent" can be said with more confidence than "GOD is all-powerful," since we cannot know the scope or nature of Divine power beyond our own experience. "GOD is not ignorant" can be said more confidently than "GOD knows everything," since we cannot know what GOD knows or even if Divine knowing is anything like what we understand as knowledge and comprehension. This may come as a shock to those who trade on long proclamations about the Divine, but if we stop to think about it, our claims about Divine will and purpose can sound pretty puny and childlike compared with what a Universal Mind might be: "*For my thoughts are not your thoughts, nor are your ways my ways, says the Lord. For as the heavens are higher than the earth, so are my ways higher than your ways and my thoughts than your thoughts*" (Isa. 55:8–9). Saying what GOD is not does not limit the totality of Divine possibilities in any way, and it reminds us that even our greatest images are inadequate and probably misguided, purely because of the limits of human imagination. A niggling question lingers, however. Can we even know authoritatively what GOD is not?

By now you will have realized that attempts to talk about Something beyond human conception are as much about language as about Divine elusiveness. GOD has to be confined within our linguistic rules and terms and there lies our problem. Even to say "GOD" is limiting, because it simply regurgitates in hearers' minds whatever humanly constructed images they hold for that word rather than Reality-in-itself. I once owned an art gallery in Minnesota, and one year, I hung an exhibition of religious art. I remember well an etching of a fire and brimstone preacher clutching his pulpit as he shouted out his message, visually represented as a stream of sentences coming out of his mouth all composed of the one word "WORDS," repeated over and over in different lettering and sizes. Religion is about language, explanations of GOD's thoughts and ways that, in the end, may be nothing more than letters strung together with little reference to, or knowledge of, what they signify. In the English language, if something is not a being, it is a thing (which actually may describe the Divine more accurately than grey beard and wrinkles), but this less-than-human designation "It" was thought demeaning for the Divine when the Bible was first translated into English. "He" was used instead, even though the translators agreed that GOD was not a human being. However, if GOD is neither a Being as we know it nor a Thing as we know it, GOD is No-one or No-thing (Nothing).

What therefore can we say about the Divine? Nothing, Maimonides finally concluded. "*It is therefore better by far to be silent and to be, simply, before God with the intention of your mind, as the Psalm again says: 'Ponder upon your beds, and be silent'*" (see Ps. 4:4).[10] In this silence, one comes to know the Something, not a cerebral knowing, but a deep, intuitive unknowing that GOD is rather than what GOD is. Martin Buber would much later describe this as moving from the impersonal I-It to the relational I-Thou:

> It is not necessary to know something about God in order really to believe in Him: many true believers know how to talk to God but not about Him.

> If one dares to turn toward the unknown God, to go to meet Him, to call to Him, Reality is present. [11]

This is what mystics do—close their eyes and mouths in order to deal with That Which we cannot see or speak about, Something rooted in silence and darkness. Rather than visualizing the Sacred in word or image, they meet the Ground of their being in a silent, concept-free place, communicating *"without words, without discursive thoughts, in the silence of our whole being,"* according to Thomas Merton. *"When what we say is meant for no one else but Him, it can hardly be said in language."* [12] The Buddha also knew the value of silence, of emptying ourselves of the externals, of craving and desire and, not surprisingly, Merton spent much of his life in dialogue with Buddhism. *"If you can only rid yourself of conceptual thought,"* ninth-century Zen master Huang Po advised, *"you will have accomplished everything."* [13] The Buddha, however, was not searching for a GOD within, since anything said about a Divine Being was, to him, speculative, and such "knowledge" erected as the Truth became an obstacle to understanding, like ice blocking a stream. By clinging blindly to such "Truth," we will not recognize Truth when it knocks on our door, and thus will not open the door.

Mystics also talk of illumining darkness as well as silence—*"the Word unspoken in the darkness that veils the ground of my being."* [14] A devout and scholarly Italian Catholic friend, when I asked him how he imaged the Divine, said "Mystery." With more probing, he added, *"Darkness—not as a negative but a positive, something hard to see, like St. Paul seeing though a glass darkly."* We are so used to hearing about Light chasing away darkness that it takes time and concentration to see darkness as Something all-inviting and safe. *"By an undivided and absolute abandonment of yourself and everything, shedding everything and freed from everything,"* fifth-century theologian Pseudo-Dionysus said, *"you will be uplifted to the light of the divine darkness which transcends everything that is."* [15] Yet is Divine Darkness something graspable by the majority of us raised in cultures where progress has been measured by emerging from darkness into light, whether through education, religion, or electricity? Is darkness a safe place or a place of paralyzing fear in the night where anything can be hiding in the wings? And what of the inherent racial context of such imagery when Victorians talked of Africa as the "dark" continent and the West as "enlightened?"

Hurrying down a hallway at a religion conference, I overheard a sliver of conversation, "I heard a rumor that God is going to retire and go to . . ." The sentence faded as I passed out of range. Of course, it was not GOD the person had said but some similar-sounding name, perhaps Bob, but the mistake made me wonder, what if GOD did decide to retire from the world and go off somewhere else? This was the Deists' argument in the late seventeenth century when it got more difficult to talk rationally about a Divine Providence that pulled our puppet strings and sent rewards and punishments. They proposed instead that the Creator began it all, installing a trusty set of laws, then left us to get on with it. The Divine Absence of which mystics speak, however, is very different from this. They mean that we cannot point to something obvious and say "There is GOD," or capture Something in our camera lens of dogma or butterfly net of absolute Truth. The psalmists regularly bemoaned Yahweh going absent on them: "*My God, my God, why have you forsaken me? . . . I cry by day, but you do not answer; and by night, but find no rest*" (Ps 22:1–2). Hindu *Bhakti* (devotional) poems yearn constantly for *Viraha* (Divine Absence): "*What is this thing they call a meeting? The night goes in wait, the day is spent in waiting.*"[16] Thirteenth-century mystic Mechtild of Magdeburg absolutely reveled in the "*blessed absence of God, how lovingly I am bound to you,*"[17] and Martin Luther's GOD refused to appear, as the arrogant human mind would expect, but was "hidden" in everyday life:

> The more I sought and the nearer I thought I was to him, the further away I got. No, God does not permit us to find him so. He must first come and seek us where we are. We may not pursue and overtake him. That is not his will.[18]

Pope Gregory the Great (540–604) was not so joyous, however, about such "obtuseness," talking of the fog, darkness, hiddenness, and unknowability of GOD as something painful and distressing—only after tremendous struggle through impenetrable darkness did one receive perhaps a fleeting taste, a moment of joy and peace.[19]

The absence of a Supreme Being in Buddhism is more a pragmatic agnosticism. Since one cannot know, the Buddha avoided speculative statements and concentrated on how human beings should live and take personal responsibility. *"Be ye lamps unto yourselves,"* he said to his followers as he lay dying, *"betake yourselves to no external refuge . . . Look not for refuge to anyone besides yourselves . . . Decay is inherent in all component things! Work out your salvation with diligence!"*[20] The outcomes of such working out, guided by the four Noble Truths, are Enlightenment and Nirvana (*Nibbana*), best described as "nothing-ness." According to Buddhist scholar U Thittila of Burma, *Nibbana* is not a negative concept *"because it is the cessation of craving, a 'blow-ing out,' for it is a blowing out of man's desires, and that blowing out of desires leaves a man free. Nibbana is freedom, but not freedom from circumstances; it is freedom from the bonds with which we have bound ourselves to circumstances . . . cravings. Such a man's binding emotions have been blown out like so many candles. That man is free here on earth. He has reached Nibbana in this world."*[21]

GOD as No-thing, No-one, darkness, absent, hidden, silent, blown out? Really? This may satisfy the mystics whom seem to be able to peek around the normal veil of the senses, but what about ordinary people like us who don't find such chinks in the wall? What use is a GOD who is silent, absent, nothing? What if *viraha* (absence) does not resolve itself in reunion? What about those who pray and feel they are simply spit-ting into the wind, like the psalmist who cried *"Why have you, God, forsaken me"* as his adversaries taunted him *"Where is your God?"* (Ps. 42:9–10). People become theologians *"not because we are particularly religious,"* Jürgen Moltmann said, *"but because we miss God's presence in the world and want to know where God is."*[22] With psalms like *"How long, O Lord . . . will you hide your face from me?"* (Ps. 13:1), we tend to scroll down to the final verse, looking for the happy ending, assuming it would not be in scripture unless the lamenter eventually did hear from GOD. Why do we do this? Because we are uncomfortable with the idea that GOD might be hiding or deaf, or worse still, not there at all. We jump to defend Divine absence as acceptable, logical, and ben-eficial, but the truth of the matter is that GOD is not there for many people or else remains in obscurity, despite prayers tossed like overripe tomatoes on the Divine doorstep. At a time when I sorely missed that Presence in my world, I confided in my journal:

To want so much to be in communion with God, this Being whom I cannot see, cannot hear, cannot explain. To be prepared to give everything to God, to live for God's cause, but to be so unsure of it. I can see why people cling to rules and guarantees of salvation. There is no pain in weekly confession, in saying the rosaries, if it comes with an assurance that this mechanical, measurable action will guarantee the goods. It was so easy the other way of dos and don'ts, truth and heresy, for now I am alone, even in the middle of a church committee, a worship service, a barrage of God talk. I feel as alien as a blond in a Middle Eastern bazaar. What also worries me is knowing that there are others hiding in this sea, swaying internally to the same drum music as I am, but still dancing to the music of the crowd on the outside . . . dancing so well, like me, that it is impossible to fault their steps, to spot an unfamiliar move, a hint that they too are wired to a call of a different kind.

Dancing so well . . . So often, our verbalized doubts about Divine elusiveness and absence are thrown back at us as inadequacy or lack of faith.[23] Theologian Mary Jo Meadow accepted the many life blows she received, believing they were all the Divine will, until the day she could no longer believe, and yet blamed herself for this ambivalent "hell" into which she was sinking, deeper and deeper:

> Briefly I dared to get angry with God: "If you're up there, at least make it possible for me to believe in you since I need you so much." But I backed off quickly, and asked again what flaw in myself made me unable to believe as others did.[24]

A presenter expounding on Luther's hidden GOD at a religion seminar I attended was challenged by a Jewish theologian, *"Don't let God off the hook like that! A hidden God says nothing to the Holocaust survivor. Such a God is useless. If God was hiding there and did nothing, who wants such a God?"* Elie Wiesel also questioned GOD as a child of the Holocaust. He witnessed the hanging of another child, who did not die immediately because he was too light, but struggled for half an hour in a slow death. Wiesel wrote later:

> This day I had ceased to plead. I was no longer capable of lamentation. On the contrary, I felt very strong. I was the accuser, God the accused. My

eyes were open and I was alone—terribly alone in a world without God and without man. Without love or mercy. I had ceased to be anything but ashes, yet I felt myself to be stronger than the Almighty, to whom my love had been tied for so long. I stood amid the praying congregation, observing it like a stranger.[25]

The silence. What if the silence is a dead silence, an eternal silence? What if the Something is nothing but an echo, the empty shell of our cry returning unheard? If the Almighty was so anxious to communicate with humanity, why has it been so unsuccessful, so vague? As a child, I was sure that if I tried hard enough I would be able to see, hear, or feel GOD. I would lie on the cool grass, staring at cottonball cumulus clouds in a faultlessly blue Australian sky, waiting for a spelled-out message like a sky-writing plane, a GOD face . . . even a wink. When the sun's rays beamed to earth around the edge of a cloud, I would scan them for Divine messages riding on their tracks. At night, with my mosquito-net tent tucked tightly underneath my mattress, I would concentrate almost to tears, pleading with GOD to say something, give me a feeling, a whisper, a feather touch of assurance. Nothing. Yet even in silence GOD held the winning straws as my religious teachers made excuses for such Silence, blaming it on me. Was a puny sign so unreasonable to expect from One billed as unconditionally loving and aware of my every need? Are those who claim to receive such signs better people? Do they have more faith? Perhaps they are weaker in faith, and therefore need the signs—didn't Jesus praise those who believed without seeing? Yet again I created an "out" for GOD, apologizing for the Silence when I could have desperately used a sign—a burning bush, writing on a wall, anything.

What if the Divine is silent and hiding because It is not, does not exist, is no such thing? Primal people living in symbiosis with the earth believed they encountered Divinity in every moment of the day. GODS moved clouds across the sky, sent rain and earthquakes, and controlled female fertility, and when something happened, people knew who to praise or blame. Yet they never questioned Divine existence. That is a modern question posed by people like us whose yardsticks are longer than the elemental forces whirling around us and whose laboratories can answer the scientific questions with more precision. What if, in all our GOD-talk, we are simply hanging on to the last fragments of a story whose use-by-date has long passed? In twentieth–century philosopher Anthony Flew's parable, two explorers stumbled into a jungle clearing where many flowers and weeds grew. One explorer said, "Some gardener must tend this plot." The other disagreed, "There is no gardener." They pitch their tents and set up watch. No gardener is ever seen. "Perhaps he is invisible," they wondered, so they built a barbed-wire fence, electrified it, and patrolled it with bloodhounds. No cries suggested an intruder receiving an electric shock, the wire never moved to betray an invisible climber, and the bloodhounds never barked. The believer was still not convinced, "There is a gardener, invisible, intangible, insensible to electric shocks, a gardener without a scent who makes no sound, a gardener who comes secretly to look after the garden he loves." Finally, the despairing skeptic replied, "But what remains of your original assertion? How does what you call your invisible, intangible, eternally elusive gardener differ from an imaginary gardener or even from no gardener at all?"[26]

"The GOD who is not" has multiple meanings: the GOD who is not this or that; the GOD who is not present, not listening, not speaking, not acting; the GOD who is not at all. All these possibilities have to be taken seriously before we can talk about what the Divine is said to be, the grist for later chapters. For an increasing number of people, "the GOD who is not" means that there is nothing out there, or anywhere. So many books give a brief nod in the direction of this possibility as if they have to acknowledge a no-GOD-at-all option, but then go on to assume an Ultimate Reality discoverable if only we try hard enough or wait long enough. Nineteenth–century Hindu teacher Shri Ramakrishna believed in such success through patience:

> If a single dive into the sea does not bring to you the pearl, do not conclude that the sea is without pearls ... If you fail to see God directly you have finished a few devotional exercises, do not lose heart. Go on patiently with your exercises, and you are sure to obtain Divine Grace at the proper time.[27]

Yet Nothing-greater-at-all must be part of any serious discussion about the Divine since this possibility haunts more thinking people deep down than any faulty description of what GOD might be like. Many who label themselves atheist or agnostic are, in fact, great religious seekers aching for a GOD they cannot find no matter how they search, yet not prepared to live the lie of belief.

"I waited patiently for the Lord," the psalmist said,
"He inclined to me and heard my cry."
I wait . . . but hear nothing.
Tears flood my being and regrets float by
still bickering about what might have been.
Didn't Job shout against the rules?
"GOD is not a mortal as I am that I might answer him.
There is no umpire between us!"
I cannot shout because I am not sure
GOD approves of such shenanigans.
And I am not yet able not to care.
Elijah heard a still small voice whispering
after the earthquake and the fire.
For me, it is always . . . nothing.
My soul is crazed like the desert floor in drought
since there are no more tears to moisten
let alone to nurture life.
Surely it cannot end this way . . .
Not without a sound from the merciful GOD.
"I cry aloud to GOD that GOD may hear me.
In the day of my trouble I seek the Lord;
My soul refuses to be comforted."
Nothing. Still nothing.[28]

To Be . . . or
Not to Be?

A woman asked Bertrand Russell what he would say to GOD if Russell's atheistic convictions turned out to be wrong. His reply? "GOD, you gave us insufficient evidence!"[1]

"Does GOD exist?" is a modern question. It was not an issue for people of the Hindu Vedas or the Hebrew and Christian scriptures—they lived amongst what they perceived as ever-present Divine activity. Their concern was not whether GODS existed, but "Which should I worship?" Even into the Middle Ages, Divine existence reigned pretty much unchallenged but augmented, when necessary, by John of Damascus's (676–749) type of argument that would raise howls of protest in many camps today—"*the knowledge of God is naturally implanted in all. Therefore the existence of God is self-evident.*"[2] Despite, or perhaps because of such blanket confidence, St. Anselm of Canterbury (1033–1100) felt it necessary to flesh out this self-evidence in the eleventh century in a more scholarly way, defining GOD as "*a being than which a greater cannot be thought.*"[3] In other words, if we can imagine a Reality so perfect that nothing more perfect can be conceived, it must exist because a Nonexistent could never be the most perfect and real conceivable being. This seemed to satisfy the curious, in part no doubt because the Divine's existence was not really in question, but there are problems—can you deduce something exists simply because you can conceive of it? We can conceive all sorts of things in our imagination, as Steven Spielberg so regularly proves. Besides, Anselm's argument limits the Divine that it tries to prove to his generation's human comprehension, both of GOD-like perfection (whatever that means) and of Divine existence.

Once GOD's existence was added to the theological smorgasbord, many scholars got into the act, some swinging the pendulum wide to claim all sorts of knowledge about GOD. By the time of the Enlightenment, the pendulum had reached a full triumphant arc, dropping rapidly when Immanuel Kant put the stopper on Divine-gazing by declaring that anything said about GOD's essence was purely guesswork. Mere mortals are limited to human reason and even then, much of what we take as reality is only appearance—if ordinary things are ambiguous, how much more ultimate things?

> The concept of a supreme being is in many respects a very useful idea; but just because it is a mere idea, it is altogether incapable, by itself alone, of enlarging our knowledge in regard to what exists . . . We can no more extend our stock of (theoretical) insight by mere ideas, than a merchant can better his position by adding a few noughts to his cash account.[4]

Kant was not questioning whether GOD existed but shifting the discussion back into the human sphere of practical or moral reason (what humans can know), maintaining, however, that something must necessarily presuppose our human experience of practical and moral reason—GOD.

Chastened now to stick with arguments from human experience, the cosmological argument for Divine existence became popular—the universe is unintelligible without a First Cause, as the sacred texts tell us. According to the Qur'an:

> In the creation of the heavens and the earth, and the difference of night and day, and the ships which run upon the sea with that which is of use to men, and the water which Allah sendeth down from the sky, thereby reviving the earth after its death, and dispersing all kinds of beasts therein, and (in) the ordinance of the winds, and the clouds obedient between heaven and earth: are signs (of Allah's sovereignty) for people who have sense. (Surah 2:164)

Despite superlatives flung wide about nature's beauty and intricacy as proof of Divine creativity, this argument is hardly proof as it can equally be said, as many have, that the universe is just there and that's all. What physical evidence is there to make the connection, without pause, that, because the universe is this or that, GOD exists, let alone to deduce Divine characteristics of love and justice from it? Attractive though this cosmological argument was, and still is, it came face-to-face with the scientific advances of the nineteenth century that offered alternative answers to that previously assigned to Divine Design and Providence. To say GOD is the First Cause was, and is, a faith statement for those wishing to go in that direction, but that direction was no longer the only viable option.

With such difficulties, probability language became useful. From the complexity of the universe, it is more probable that there is a Grand Designer than that there is not. As one who paints as well as writes, I have been known to wax lyrical (and still do) about the overwhelming beauty and complexity of nature with its mechanisms for survival and reproduction, intuitively feeling, like those who argue probabilities, that such perfection must signal a Creative Hand, but then I am reminded again that nature does not uniformly proclaim a Designer-above-reproach. Under the beautiful rose hides a spider whose poisons are lethal, with the blessings of rain come the horrors of floods, the synchronized strides of a lion result in the cruel slaughter of the innocent antelope, and cancer strikes the very good as well as the very bad. The Divine Good encountered in nature could equally be interpreted as the opposite, and as philosopher David Hume reminded his eighteenth-century audience, we may not be dealing with a First Cause but a pantheon of Causes, some not entirely competent, an idea equally as offensive to the devout as no Cause at all.[5]

In protest against such challenges, William Paley's *Views of the Evidences of Christianity* (1794) was designed to bring England back to the straight and narrow. If we picked up a watch in the forest, Paley argued, we would assume a watchmaker because of its intricate design. In like manner, when we look at nature's intricacy and beauty, we assume it also had a Watchmaker. Paley's book became compulsory reading for Oxford and Cambridge students, but doubt had been unleashed, and Victorian poets and novelists carried it to the world.[6] William Wordsworth, after his brother's death, claimed more signs of love in human nature than in Divine nature; Alfred Lord Tennyson opted for blind faith, *"believing what we cannot prove"*;[7] and Matthew Arnold bemoaned the bleakness of it all, that sea of faith once so full but *"now I only hear Its melancholy, long, withdrawing roar."*[8] Parliamentarian John Stuart Mill (1806–1873) also challenged inconsistencies in Paley's proofs of a Benevolent Creator—nature turns not one step from her path to avoid trampling us to destruction, and we should not expect that it should:

> Nature impales men, breaks them as if on the wheel, casts them to be devoured by wild beasts, burns them to death, crushes them with stones, like the first Christian martyr . . . All this nature does with the most supercilious disregard both of mercy and of justice, emptying her shafts upon the best and noblest indifferently with the meanest and worst.[9]

Theologian Benjamin Jowett (1817–1893) from Oxford's Balliol College, in light of the explosion of scientific knowledge in Victorian times, agreed with Mill that Paley's argument for a Benevolent Design *"fixes our mind on those parts of the world which exhibit marks of design, and withdraws us from those in which marks of design seem to fail. We collect, in short, what suits our argument, and leave out what does not."*[10]

All the while, Charles Darwin (1809–1882) was quietly gathering evidences on the HMS *Beagle* that would rock Paley's secure religious world and offer alternative explanations for the universe's design and order. The similarities between the "savage" of Patagonia and himself, between exotic live animals in foreign lands and extinct specimens in London's museums, led Darwin to speculate that all living things must have descended from a few primordial forms, a theory that *"accords better with what we know of the laws impressed on matter by the Creator."* Darwin did not see this as diminishing creation but rather ennobling it: *"As natural selection works solely by and for the good of each being, all corporeal and mental endowments will tend to progress towards perfection."*[11] These ideas severely challenged prevailing theories that, although recognizing some adaptation within designated species, argued that species were created separately and from scratch by the Creator in a great chain of being. Humans were the top of this chain with an "impress," according to Victorian scientist William Whewell's speech to the geological society, *"stamped upon the human mind by the Deity Himself, a trace of his nature, an indication of His Will, an announcement of His Purpose, a promise of His Favor."*[12] In *The Origin of Species,*

Darwin had not included humans in this common descent. That came later in *The Descent of Man*, where he denied that the Creator miraculously inserted a soul into the human body, giving special providence to humans: *"I would give absolutely nothing for (the) theory of natural selection if it required miraculous additions at any one stage of descent."*[13] In fact, he thought the appearance of the human being nothing compared to the *"first thinking being . . . (even) the appearance of insects with other senses is more remarkable."*[14] Others before Darwin had recognized similarities between humans and apes but halted long before suggesting an ape-to-human evolutionary step. Besides, England had had little contact with monkeys until the chimps Tommy and Jenny were brought to London in the mid 1830s. When Queen Victoria saw Jenny's antics, she unwittingly sided with Darwin, describing Jenny as *"frightful, and painfully and disagreeably human."*[15]

Darwin was not denying a Creator: *"The impossibility of conceiving that this grand and wonderful universe, with our conscious selves, arose through chance, seems to me the chief argument for the existence of God."*[16] Instead, he was suggesting that the Creator might work through the laws of nature, bringing new beings into the world through natural selection. He did, however, abandon the idea of a Providence manipulating individual fates—pain and suffering were natural and often cruel events, not some divine intervention. Of his own evolutionary journey from Paley's happy world and infinitely good Creator to an agnosticism of a shadowy, inscrutable GOD and *"the clumsy, wasteful, blundering low and horridly cruel works of nature"* where even the most beautiful evolved from *"the war of nature, from famine and death,"* Darwin wrote, *"disbelief crept over me at a very slow rate, but was at last complete. The rate was so slow that I felt no distress and (I) have never since doubted even for a single second that my conclusion was correct."*[17]

Atheism and agnosticism are terms casually thrown around, depending on where the name-thrower stands. In Greek, atheism is *a theos* (no GOD), which has meant many things. The Greek Xenophanes was labeled an atheist for criticizing poets Homer and Hesiod for *"ascribing to the gods all things such as are held a reproach and a disgrace among men—theft and adultery and mutual deceit."*[18] "Atheist" Anaxagoras of Clazomenae (fifth century BCE) was exiled for denying that the heavenly bodies were GODS—he called them glowing stones.[19] Seventeenth-century Franciscan Marin Mersenne claimed there were fifty thousand atheists in Paris, yet all the ones he named believed in GOD.[20] The term was popularized in Victorian times to apply to those who argued, not that GOD did not exist, but that Divine existence could not be proved or empirically verified. When Harriet Martineau's *Letters on the Laws of Man's Nature and Development* was published in the mid 1800s, Charlotte Bronte called it *"the first exposition of avowed atheism and materialism I have ever read; the first unequivocal declaration of disbelief in the existence of God or a future life I have ever seen."*[21] The label later became reserved for those who denied any supernatural being or transcendent order at all, like French philosopher Jean Paul Sartre. Of his "atheism," George O'Brien wrote:

> The absence of God for Sartre is, as Sartre said, like going to a café to meet Pierre. He is not there. The café therefore becomes the place where Pierre does not emerge. The same with God. The world is the ground on which the figure of God does not appear, even though we search, believing we had a prearranged appointment.[22]

The twentieth century continued the habit of labeling as atheism anything that differed from orthodox Christian theism, that *"belief in the existence of a cosmic reality—whether literally infinite or merely vastly beyond human conception—of whom religiously important personal attributes like knowledge, purpose, action, goodness, or love can be at least analogically or symbolically affirmed."*[23] Paul Tillich acquired the label in the 1950s for rejecting a theistic Being over against us, advocating instead a Ground of Being within things, an Ultimate Concern not expressed in literal representations. The British Death-of-God theologians in the 1960s also earned the title, and more recently, Bishop John Shelby Spong has been described "atheistic" by some for his non-theistic GOD, and theologian Don Cupitt for his Religious Ideal. Yet, according to philosopher Frederick Ferré, the challenge of atheism is healthy for religions:

> Atheism is the rejection of some specific sort of God-talk, whether by disbelief or dismissal. As long as such rejection is encouraged to be clearly articulated, theological dross is subjected to cleansing fires of criticism, and

the human project of relating cognitively and practically to the most high and the most real is advanced.[24]

Agnosticism (Greek *a gnosis*, not knowledge or not knowable) is, on the other hand, an unwillingness to claim that GOD does or does not exist because of insufficient evidence—either we haven't found convincing enough "proof" yet, or we believe the subject to be essentially unknowable. T. H. Huxley, Darwin's enthusiastic disciple, coined the word for the nineteenth-century debates between the church and Darwinian ideas to describe those whose intellectual integrity positioned them between the poles of theism and atheism. "*It is wrong,*" Huxley argued, "*for a man to say he is certain of the objective proof of a proposition unless he can produce evidence which logically justifies that certainty.*"[25] The category "agnostic" was handy then, but it has less use today because atheism, whether as active conviction or casual indifference, is no longer shocking, and a cautious reluctance to claim definitive things about the Divine, the old agnosticism, has become mainstreamed in much contemporary theology. As nineteenth-century poet Emily Dickenson said, "*We both believe, and disbelieve a hundred times an hour, which keeps believing nimble.*"[26]

What began as a seemingly straightforward question "Does GOD exist?" has become much more complex. If a student asks this question at the beginning of class, I know it's going to be a long night. It is not one question but many: "What do you mean by GOD?" or "Which GOD?" and "What do you mean by existence?" Even then, if we take the question seriously, it is not a yes/no answer, as we also need to define and defend our authorities. Our dilemma springs from what has already been discussed, that any description of Something More is a metaphor, and metaphors emerge in specific cultures and eras, despite desperate efforts by religious institutions to keep them breathing and eternally true for all times. Theology is not eternal truth but human, finite explanations, useful tools for a particular time and experience that allow us to talk together. While theological arguments may make sense of human questions in a particular era, they are limited by that era. Anselm understood this in the eleventh century, even as he tried to devise proofs for a Divine Being using the intellectual notions of his time:

> I do not try, Lord, to attain your lofty heights, because my understanding is in no way equal to it. But I do desire to understand your truth a little,

that truth that my heart believes and loves. For I do not seek to understand so that I may believe; but I believe so that I may understand. For I believe this also, that unless I believe, I shall not understand. [27]

Many GODS have died through the centuries as their descriptions became woefully inadequate, demanding that people living in one era leave their minds behind in another—the pre-Copernican GOD, the pre-Enlightenment GOD, the predestining Victorian GOD, the vengeful warrior GOD, to name a few. These deaths said that such humanly created GOD-claims no longer worked. Feminist, black, and liberation theologians have asked questions about a white patriarchal, colonizing Divine Being, while others have wondered about a GOD so exclusively Christian that all other religions are considered devoid of truth and eligible for extinction. For many Jews, the pre-Holocaust GOD died because any Divine image after the Holocaust had to make sense in the presence of burning children. Holocaust survivor Elie Wiesel never renounced his faith in GOD:"*I have risen against His justice, protested His Silence and sometimes His Absence, but my anger rises up within faith and not outside.*" However, he says, "*I will never cease to rebel against those who committed or permitted Auschwitz, including God. The questions I once asked myself about God's silence remain open. If they have an answer, I do not know it . . . Perhaps God shed more tears in the time of Treblinka, Majdanek, and Auschwitz, and one may therefore invoke His name not only with indignation but also with sadness and compassion.*"[28]

Can Something that allows or causes such things be called a Comforter, a loving Father, or a Keeper of the Covenant, or has humanity pushed past the old barriers into an era where such GOD-ideas are no longer viable, outgrown like Santa Claus? Huston Smith called history "*a grave-yard for outlooks that were once taken for granted. Today's common sense becomes tomorrow's laughingstock; time makes ancient truth uncouth.*"[29] But it is more than a laughingstock. Some GOD-images created in tribal or medieval times are not only outdated or irrelevant, but have become downright dangerous in the hands of religious fanatics, and we need to remove such weaponry from them. When harmful or inadequate Divine images are killed, others can mercifully be born as fresh images for a new world, yet we have to check constantly if the GOD-idea is still useful or relevant at all. Playwright

George Bernard Shaw (1856–1950) did not like this picking away at the Divine images, removing bits that no longer made sense, because it left nothing to call GOD. But that is the whole point—talking about GOD is a language event since no one has seen the Divine (John 1:18), and any descriptions are simply attempts to say something about what one experiences, wishes to experience, or does not experience.

The Death-of-God movement of the 1960s was unintentionally launched in Britain by Bishop John A. T. Robinson's explosive little book *Honest to God*, in which Robinson argued that the Book-of-Common-Prayer GOD "out there" who sent floods as punishment and miraculous healings and prosperity as rewards, needed to die because that image had become *"more of a stumbling block than an aid to belief."*[30] According to Robinson, the GOD "up there" was dislodged with the first onslaught of science (although one questions how completely this image has disappeared), and now it was necessary to take further scientific discoveries seriously and dispose of the GOD "out there." Robinson was not alone—a generation of new theologians had been nurtured on the writings of theologians Dietrich Bonhoeffer, Rudolf Bultmann, Paul Tillich, and others who had set about to reassess Christianity in light of two World Wars, the Holocaust, and a tyrannical, all-powerful transcendent GOD celebrated by three monotheistic faiths: Judaism, Christianity, and Islam. *"What is there about belief in one God,"* Robinson's colleague William Hamilton asked, *"that makes persons and cultures evil? If it is the case that belief in but one God leads to the destruction and dehumanization of those not so believing, is it not the case that Christian justice and love require the elimination of that God as a source of evil?"*[31] Paul Van Buren, an American Episcopal priest-scholar and another of this new breed, went further, arguing that Christianity was fundamentally about what it is to be human based on the life of the man Jesus, and that its language about GOD was simply a way of talking about humanity.[32]

Fourteen years after *Honest to God*, a similar group of well-respected English churchmen set off another controversy with their book of essays for the public, *The Myth of God Incarnate*, questioning whether Jesus was, in fact, GOD incarnate.[33] For Don Cupitt, one of these essayists still writing today, religion is not about supernatural myths and an afterlife but about hope in this life—guiding myths to help people live and create a new heaven here on earth. Religion is thus needed as much as ever as a "human value–creating activity" for our contemporary world so dominated by technology and unadventurous political thought:

> There is only this life and true religion is an affirmation of this life. We must say "Yes to life" in full acknowledgement of its contingency and transitoriness; and we must work towards establishing "tomorrow's god"—the creation of a just, peaceful and equitable world for all—both human and creatures alike . . . [Life is a] joyous acceptance of the way everything turns out, or just happens to be . . . It is eternal happiness, briefly, in and with the here and now . . . This life is all there is and we must love it now, before it ceases to be.[34]

Another essayist, Michael Goulder, has moved even further, rejecting Cupitt's religion-without-a-belief-in-GOD (atheism in disguise) as "a ship sailing without its topmast," just as Nietzsche in the previous century said it was inconsistent to cling to a Christian morality after abandoning the Christian GOD. When Goulder resigned from the Anglican ministry, he claimed that churches and organized religion were simply *"locked forever in the ice-floes of theological contradiction."*[35]

Bishop John Shelby Spong, a modern-day disciple of Bishop Robinson, has killed the theistic, external-to-the-world Being once again in our day, drawing crowds of disenchanted church alumni with him. Unlike Cupitt, Spong still engages with Something that calls us from the depth of our being, a GOD-presence called Love which is

> . . . boundless, eternal, passing beyond every limit and calling us to follow this love into every crevice of creation. We journey into this God by being absorbed into wasteful, expansive, freely given love . . . like swimming in an eternal ocean of love. It is also like interacting with the unperceived presence of the air . . . When I try to describe this reality, words fail me; so I simply utter the name God. That name, however, is no longer for me the name of a being . . . It is rather something as nebulous and yet as real as a holy presence. It is a symbol of that which is immortal, invisible, timeless.[36]

While many like to call Spong's rejection of the theistic GOD "atheistic," he has simply returned to the Formless Immanence of the Hebrew Bible and the Divine Love of the New Testament. Spong is not alone in speaking of the Divine as pervasive of all nature, omnipresent with everything in every moment, coeternal with the world and not separate from or other than it, and the ground of both order and freedom. Process theology (more of this in chapter 15) says that *"God is involved in the world process in such a way as to influence, lure, persuade, empower it, but not to control, coerce, or manipulate it . . . God may be thought of as the universal Eros that draws all things to Godself."*[37]

Such Death-of-God discussions are not only Protestant property. The Second Vatican Council was called by Pope John XXIII in the early 1960s to renew the life of the church and bring its teaching, structure, and discipline up-to-date. Enthusiasm for renewal inspired many progressive younger Catholic scholars, including Swiss Hans Küng and Flemish Edward Schillebeeckx. Although many steps taken at Vatican II did not become full reality, Küng, Schillebeeckx, and others continued to challenge traditional thinking despite censorship by the church. Making Death-of-God arguments against a trouble-shooter Divine Being acting from outside the world, Küng dispensed with attempts to harmonize biblical statements about the beginning and end of the world with scientific theories. "Yes" to GOD is a matter, not of rational proof, but of trust on reasonable grounds:

> Human beings are faced with an alternative. They have to decide whether they are prepared to assume, in their lives and in the history of mankind and the world, that there is ultimately no basis, no support and no meaning—or that everything has after all a fundamental basis, a support and a meaning; that, to put it more concretely, there is a creator, a guide and a fulfiller.[38]

Schillebeeckx's GOD-talk was also located in human experience. GOD was not Something external to be sought when extreme situations made humans impotent, but rather experienced in ordinary, everyday moments when people try to make sense of life. Using GOD-language to name these human experiences is a faith statement—what nonbelievers might call being *"thrown on our own into an alien world"* can be called by a believer *"being held in God's hand."*[39] As for concrete Divine descriptions, Schillebeeckx's elusive responses include Pure Positivity, and the Promoter-of-all-that-is-good, experienced and mediated by humans in the world, rather than traditional images of Divine Grace descending from heaven without historical or human mediation: *"That absolute character of faith in God is revealed in what is particular, historical and relative—in this or in that particular praxis, for example, the praxis of giving a glass of water to a man who is thirsty.*"[40] Despite serious conflict with his church, neither man has left. If all those who criticize the church leave, Schillebeeckx says, problematic teachings will simply be strengthened, and besides, the church, despite all this, is still the community of GOD. "*What 'Rome' would have liked most of all, I suspect,*" Schillebeeckx said, "*is that Hans Küng had become a Protestant. He didn't and was excluded as a Catholic theologian. But he continues as a Catholic and is a thorn in the flesh of the Catholic Church.*"[41] This is also the stance of Catholic feminist theologians Elisabeth Schüssler Fiorenza and Rosemary Radford Ruether who have "dethroned" the traditional anthropomorphic Father-GOD in favor of rebirthing Spirit-Sophia, the endlessly creating, formless Spirit of the Hebrew Bible, Sophia-Wisdom made flesh in the man Jesus and Sophia-Comforter indwelling the world. Since the Divine is encountered in human experience, it is important to include women's experiences and Divine feminine imagery. "*The tenacity with which the patriarchal symbol of God is upheld,*" Elizabeth Johnson says, "*is nothing less than violation of the first commandment of the Decalogue, the worship of an idol . . . Whenever one image or concept of God expands to the horizon thus shutting out others, and whenever this exclusive symbol becomes so literalized that the distance between it and divine reality is collapsed, there an idol comes to being.*"[42]

Today's most common demise of GOD is the turn to spirituality, a catchall phrase for any religious experience that may or may not include a Deity. Seekers of spirituality unsatisfied with the religious beliefs offered still cherish that feeling "*which cannot, strictly speaking, be taught, it can only be evoked, awakened in the mind; as everything that comes 'of the spirit' must be awakened.*"[43] On my desk as I write the first draft of this chapter is the September 5, 2005, *Newsweek* with its cover story on "Spirituality in America," a seventeen-page analysis across religions. Apparently almost 80 percent of Americans call themselves spiritual rather than religious and usually pursue spiritual practices on their own, not in a house of worship. Eighty percent believe salvation is available beyond their religious tradition, and an increasing number are exploring other faiths, whether for a personal relationship with the Sacred, help to be a better person, or peace and happiness. While some people call these nontraditional contemporary movements nebulous or alien, such adventurers see themselves as *"pilgrims on solid ground, joining all the others on the paths of the never-ending, newly prospering spiritual journey."*[44] The article's subheading reads, *"Move over politics. Americans are looking for personal, ecstatic experiences of God and, according to our poll, they don't much care what the neighbors are doing."* There is nothing new under the sun. Leo Tolstoy, equally disenchanted with organized religion in mid-nineteenth-century Russia, also searched elsewhere for answers:

> The essence of any religion lies solely in the answer to the question: why do I exist, and what is my relationship to the infinite universe that surrounds me? . . . Religion is the relationship a person recognizes himself to have with the external world, or with its origin or first cause, and a rational person cannot fail to have some kind of relationship with it. [45]

This is where many of us find ourselves today, caught between the failure of old GOD-talk and an unwillingness to let go of what has given meaning and sense to our lives. While we can exit the door of organized religion, there may not be a verandah on which to stand, let alone another room.

There have always been those who have never questioned GOD's existence and go to great lengths to defend it, even without solid evidence. For many, the Divine exists because their sacred texts "tell them so." Again, this is a faith statement based on the belief that their sacred text is the Truth, even though written thousands of years ago by unknown authors at different times and places. To argue that GOD exists because the Bible says so is also a circular argument. GOD exists because the Bible says so. Why is the Bible to be believed? Because GOD says so. Where? In the Bible. There is nothing wrong with living life by faith—we do it all the time when choosing friends, morals, and refrigerators—as long as we recognize these are faith choices, not empirically provable and not to be forced on others. Nor should we argue, as theologian Alasdair MacIntyre suggests, that such lack of empirical proof is advantageous:

> If the existence of God were demonstrable we should be as bereft of the possibility of making a free decision to love God as we should be if every utterance of doubt or unbelief was answered by thunderbolts from heaven.[46]

Defending Divine elusiveness gives little comfort to millions who seek and don't find, and downgrades thoughtful scholarship and authentic questions in preference to "just believing," regardless of whether or not something makes sense. "*Religion attracts more devotion according as it demands more faith—that is to say, as it becomes more incredible to the profane mind,*" nineteenth-century Swiss philosopher Henri Frédéric Amiel wrote. "*The philosopher aspires to explain away all mysteries, to dissolve them into light. Mystery on the other hand is demanded and pursued by the religious instinct; mystery constitutes the essence of worship.*"[47] Yet there is Mystery and mystery—the Mystery that invites and lures us beyond the limits of our human reflection, and dogmatic claims about Divine Mystery that tell us to stop thinking or asking questions at all.

The second part of the question "Does GOD exist?" is "What do we mean by existence?" In the twelfth century, when there was no question as to the existence of Something greater than, Maimonides came up with a statement infused with the philosophy of his day:

> Because there is One who exists absolutely, all other existence, dependent on that Being, becomes possible. That One Being is God, the Life of the Universe . . . Our existence is contingent made up of bits and pieces— atoms, bones, hair etc., but God simply exists and is not made up of anything at all. [48]

Yet since talk of "existence" indicates a finite realm where things appear and disappear, are born and die, can we use this descriptive term for the Infinite that, by definition, is not finite? Despite metaphorical images of Yahweh seeing, speaking, shooting arrows, and fighting enemies, the Hebrew Bible insisted that Yahweh was neither human nor finite: "*God is not a human being, that he should lie, or a mortal, that he should change his mind*" (Num. 23:19).[49] Paul Tillich argued that we could not even ask the question of the existence of That which is, by nature, above existence: "*It is as atheistic to affirm the existence of God as it is to deny it. God is being-itself, not a being.*"[50] When an interviewer asked Australian biblical scholar Barbara Thiering whether she believed in the existence of GOD, Thiering pointed out how the question defined and limited the answer by supposing that GOD could be explained in human categories of existence that assumed a time when one ceased to exist:

If an atheist, in saying there is not a God, really means, "I refuse to postulate the existence of God and God is, in Buddhist terms, the beyond or the ultimate," . . . then I go along with the atheist, as do all theologians, because the whole job of theology is to stop the objectification, to stop the making of God in one's own image. Another atheist might say that there is nothing greater at all. Then, of course, I would disagree . . . As soon as you think of God, you need to put brackets around it because you're only thinking in your own terms and your own language. [51]

In the end, however, even if the vital question "Does GOD exist?" is a nonquestion, we still want to be able to say something about the GOD experience (or lack of it), whether real or wistfully longed for, whether logical or illogical, whether permanent or fleeting, in order to explain it or explain it away. While some have definitely decided there is no GOD, most know deep down that this negative conclusion is as much a faith statement as saying there is a GOD. We are simply deciding on the worldview in which we will live, religious or nonreligious, and even then there is straying between the two because the question is more than a rational argument, especially in times of crisis. *"This quest for God was not a debate but an emotion,"* Leo Tolstoy wrote, *"because it did not arise from my stream of thoughts—it was in fact quite contrary to them—but from my heart. It was a feeling of fear, abandonment, loneliness, amid all that was strange to me, and a sense of hope that someone would help me. Despite the fact that I was utterly convinced of the impossibility of proving the existence of God . . . I nevertheless searched for God in the hope that I might find Him, and reverting to an old habit of prayer, I prayed to Him whom I sought but could not find."* [52] Christian writer Philip Yancey also admits that he "sticks around" in the Christian tradition because of the lack of a good alternative to meet his needs: *"The only thing more difficult than having a relationship with an invisible God is having no such relationship."* [53] Unexpected moments surprise even the most hardened skeptics. Australian novelist Patrick White (1912–1990), hardly labeled religious, slipped in the mud once when carrying food to his dogs in a downpour. Laughing and swearing, he began to curse GOD, when the thought came to him—how could he curse what didn't exist? In that moment, he experienced a moment of ecstasy and *"apprehended God in all existence around him*," beginning his lifelong search for that fleeting Presence. Struggling later to describe this experience, White wrote:

> I think it impossible to explain faith. It is like trying to explain air, which one cannot do by dividing it into its component parts and labeling them scientifically. It must be breathed to be understood. But breathing is something that has been going on all the time, and is almost imperceptible. [54]

Many theologians who wrote expansive arguments in the past for the existence of GOD have given up and/or changed the question. John Hick suggests the better question is whether the biblical faith-awareness of GOD "*is a mode of cognition which can properly be trusted and in terms of which it is rational to live.*"[55] Gordon Kaufman, who analyzed various Western arguments for GOD twenty years ago, believes such confidence is no longer viable:

> The symbol "God" has always functioned . . . to call attention to that reality believed to be of greatest importance for ongoing human life . . . In our use of the word God . . . we humans are attempting to direct attention to what can be called the "ultimate point of reference" of all action, consciousness and reflection. [56]

While we might sense what Kaufman calls "serendipitous creativity," the question can no longer be "What can we know about GOD?" but "How shall we live in face of such Mystery?" Rabbi Harold Kushner made a similar change of direction—what is important is not the existence (or not) of GOD but the importance (or not) of GOD, that is, "*what kind of people we become when we attach ourselves to God.*"[57] Historian of religion Karen Armstrong agrees:

> The experience of an indefinable transcendence, holiness and sacredness has been a fact of human life . . . I don't think it matters what you believe in—and most of the great sages of religion would agree with me. If conventional beliefs make you compassionate, kind and respectful of the sacred rights of others, this is good religion. If your beliefs make you intolerant, unkind and belligerent, this is bad religion, no matter how orthodox it is.[58]

And so we are back where we started. What we say about Divine existence is a faith statement and a choice, subject to our need for Something and our experience (or not) of a Dimension (real or imaged) beyond/within ourselves. Our "yes" or "no" is not necessarily for all time—in reality, atheism, agnosticism, and belief are different points on a spiraling rather than a linear life journey, with many interim "what-I-believe-now" moments of clarity and confusion along the way. While Bertrand Russell did take a final step into atheism, his words still offer assurance for those on the journey: "*If there were a God, I think it very unlikely that he would have such an uneasy vanity as to be offended by those who doubt his existence.*" [59]

What's in a Name?

He is Allah, the Creator,
the Originator, the Fashioner,
to Him belong the most beautiful names.

—*Qur'an, Surah 59:24*

○ ○

To what is one [Brahman],
sages give many a title:
they call it Agni, Yama, Matarusvan.

—*Rig-Veda 1:164*

○ ○

God said to Moses,
"I AM WHO I AM"
[or "I AM WHAT I AM"
or "I WILL BE WHAT I WILL BE"].

—*Exod. 3:13–14*

According to a Chinese proverb, the beginning of wisdom is to call things by their right names, but how can we know the right name for the Divine? In previous chapters, we have pondered whether there is a Divine about which to speak, what sort of a Divine exists, and whether anything can be said with any authority about that Divine. Some of us may be comfortable to simply leave it at that and close the book now, but for those who struggle to name the One about which they do (or do not think), we can delay the inevitable no longer. What has been said about It in the past and what can we say about It today? As we have seen, most religions trod cautiously in their early days, and many still do, making a distinction between the essence of the Divine—what can never be comprehended by the human mind—and Its attributes or energies, the things we experience as human beings and choose to name as divine indicators or actions. Lao-tzu (Lao Tze) cautioned his sixth-century BCE followers that nothing could be said about the *Tao* (*Dao*, Existence): "*The Tao that can be expressed is not the eternal Tao; the name that can be defined is not the unchanging name.*"[1] Rumi also shied away from naming the Sacred experience: "*The form of a thing is a gate; the name of a thing is a title inscribed on the gate. Pass through the gate into the meaning within.*"[2] While Rumi's highly developed spiritual sensitivities may have been able to do away with both nameplate and gate, some of us ordinary folk need both, even if it does not tell us much more about what is being named. "*It is not a human being, in so far as we know what man is; nor is it any other known thing so let us call this unknown something: God,*" Danish philosopher Sören Kierkegaard wrote. "*It is nothing more than a name we assign to it. The idea of demonstrating that this unknown something exists could scarcely suggest itself to the Reason. For if God does not exist it would of course be impossible to prove it; and if he does exist it would be folly to attempt it.*"[3]

As already discussed, GOD is not a personal given name like Tom, Dick, or Mary, but the generic term in English for any or all Deities as well as the specific term for masculine Deities, as opposed to Goddesses. In the Hebrew Bible, GOD translates both the generic *El* and its plural *Elohim*. Under these generic umbrellas, particular Deities were afforded personal names such as Yahweh and Baal. The children of Abraham are recorded as originating from Mesopotamia, a polytheistic world of many Deities with different functions, mythologies, and personal names. Each tribe or city-state had its particular Deity, often absorbed when one tribe was conquered by another. In Canaan's pantheon of Deities (where the Israelites finally settled), El was both the name for the high GOD and convener of the council of GODS and also the name for a specific Deity. Baal, Anath, and Athirat were particular Deities within this pantheon and appear in Hebrew stories located within Canaanite territory. According to Hebrew Bible scholar Mary Mills, there is evidence to argue for a Hebrew Divine Pantheon with a royal couple Yahweh-El and Asherah at the top; Deities like Baal, Shemesh, Yareah, and Mot below that; and the "slaves" of the Divine realm, angelic messengers, at the bottom.[4] Interestingly, the first Divine name in Genesis and the most common name throughout the Hebrew scriptures is the generic plural Elohim—"*Let us make humankind in our image, according to our likeness*" (Gen. 1:26), the same term used for "*all the gods of Egypt*" (Exod. 12:12) suggesting, if not a Divine Pantheon, at least a Divine Court. The plural is also used of the Creator in the Qur'an, even though Islam is monotheistic through and through:

> Have they not then observed the sky above them, how We have constructed it and beautified it, and how there are no rifts therein? And the earth have We spread out, and have flung firm hills therein, and have caused of every lovely kind to grow thereon. (Surah 50:5–7)

The first eleven chapters of Genesis tell a generic once-upon-a-time story unattached to dates or locations of how the world and human beings were created by in-the-beginning Deities, and how humans ended up separate from these Deities, a story with parallels in ancient Mesopotamia where Hebrew history began. By rejecting the rules in the garden of immortal beings, humans were sent out to inhabit their own mortal world. When the immortal-mortal lines of separation became threatened once again with sons of GOD having sex with human women, the Creator regretted inventing humans and redefined the boundaries with a horrific flood. The generic in-the-beginning story ceases in Genesis 12 when the Hebrew Bible settles down to track the specific story of Yahweh, the tribal Deity with whom Abraham covenanted and followed out of Mesopotamia.[5] As Moses told the Hebrews, "*When the Most High apportioned the nations, when he divided humankind, he fixed the boundaries of the peoples according to the number of the gods; the Lord's own portion was his people, Jacob his allotted share*" (Deut. 32:8–9). This is henotheism rather than monotheism, their one GOD among the many. While other GODS were very real and powerful and, it seems, quite attractive when Yahweh seemed to let them down, Yahweh was the One for them, the One whom Moses encountered in the burning bush and who liberated them from Egypt. To worship another was a critical offense: "*You shall have no other gods before [besides] me*" (Exod. 20:3). The Hebrew Bible is full of stories of the Israelites being tempted to worship neighboring Deities, "*the Baals and the Astartes, the gods of Aram, the gods of Sidon, the gods of Moab, the gods of the Ammonites, and the gods of the Philistines,*" and of getting into trouble for it (Judg. 10:6–7). Even on his deathbed, Joshua reminded them that Yahweh was a jealous GOD not be messed with:

> Now if you are unwilling to serve the Lord, choose this day whom you will serve, whether the gods your ancestors served in the region beyond the River or the gods of the Amorites in whose land you are living; but as for me and my household, we will serve the Lord. (Josh. 24:15)

Yahweh evolved in the Hebrew Bible. After the Babylonian exile (sixth century BCE), radical monotheism became Israel's banner—only one Deity at all. When Jesus was asked what the first commandment was, he began with "*Hear, O Israel: the Lord our God, the Lord is one,*" to which the scribe answered "*You are right, Teacher; you have truly said that 'he is one, and besides him there is no other'*" (Mark 12:29, 32). Since "Lord" (*Adonai*), a title of dignity and honor for masters or owners, was used instead of "Yahweh" to protect the Divine Name, the Jewish Jesus was saying "Yahweh, our El, is the One, the only El," a variation on the original commandment "*You shall have no other gods [Elohim] before [besides] me*" (Exod. 20:3). Christianity inherited Judaism's One GOD, and as Christianity's influence spread across the Mediterranean world under fourth-century Roman emperors, so did its exclusive claim on the term GOD, now no longer a generic name for Deities, but the personal or "Christian" name for the One and Only, as described by Christianity. References to other GODS were written with a lowercase "g," identifying them as lesser, false, or pagan, paper cutouts rather than the real thing. I remember concentrating as a child to make the "big G–little g" distinction in Sunday school in order not to incur Divine wrath in the form of floods, frogs, or a contemporary equivalent. Even today, the first task in any introductory World Religions course is to challenge this long-engrained habit in students of honoring their particular description of GOD with a big "G" and all others with a small "g."

While Moses asked "Which El are you?" and received the name of a specific One, monotheistic religions cannot have different GODS. So the question becomes "Are you the true GOD?" If someone disapproves of my theology, they may tell me I am talking about a different GOD, meaning that my GOD is false. Wars have been fought and individuals tortured, even within the same religion, over such disagreements.

Martin Buber was reading aloud the draft preface of his book when his friend, listening with growing amazement, interrupted:

> "How can you bring yourself to say 'God' time after time? How can you expect your readers to take the word in the sense in which you wish it to be taken? What you mean by the name of God is something above all human grasp and comprehension. What word of human speech is so misused, so defiled, so desecrated as this! All the innocent blood that has been shed for it has robbed it of its radiance. All the injustice that has been used to cover has effaced its features. When I hear the highest called 'God,' it sometimes seems almost blasphemous."

Buber sat awhile before agreeing with his friend that the word had been defamed, mutilated, misrepresented, died-for, and exalted, and that the symbol GOD could never even begin to capture what it represented:

> "Certainly, they draw caricatures and write 'God' underneath; they murder one another and say 'In God's name.' But when all the madness and delusion fall to dust, when they stand over against Him in the loneliest darkness and no longer say 'He, He' but rather sigh 'Thou,' shout 'Thou,' all of them the one word, and when they then add 'God,' is it not the real God whom they all implore, the One Living God, the God of the children of man? Is it not He who hears them? And just for this reason is not the word 'God,' the word of appeal, the word which has become a name, consecrated in all human tongues for all times? . . . We cannot cleanse the word 'God' and we cannot make it whole; but, defiled and mutilated as it is, we can raise it from the ground and set it over an hour of great care."[6]

And so back to the Chinese proverb with which we began, that the beginning of wisdom is to call things by their right names—what are the right names for what we symbolize by the letters GOD? Naming a crab is easy, as we can see it and describe it as a finite something with a form, but these are not options when naming GOD, and besides, the very act of naming assumes there is such a thing that can be identified and described over against other things. *"How is one to speak about that which is neither a genus nor a differentia nor a species nor an individuality nor a number?"* Church father Clement of Alexandria said back in the second century. *"If we do give it a name, we cannot do so in the strict sense of the word: whether we call it 'One,' 'the good,' 'mind,' 'absolute being,' 'Father,' 'God,' 'Creator,' or 'Lord,' it is not a case of producing its actual name; in our impasse we avail ourselves of certain good names so that the mind may have the support of those names and not be led astray in other directions.*"[7] Seventeen centuries later, Martin Buber concluded that we should simply address the Divine as "You," refusing any third-person descriptions: "*Even 'he' is still a metaphor, while 'you' is not . . . we reduce the eternal You ever again to an It, to something, turning God into a thing, in accordance with our nature.*"[8]

Naming a Deity in ancient times was unsettling because names were never random choices but of great significance, actually incorporated into the life force to denote character and identity and signify one's existence, reputation, and history—how much more the trepidation in naming the One. Naming was also an act of possession, of claiming power over the thing named, and thus instigating a relationship with it. In the second creation story, the Creator brings the newly formed animals to Adam, who had been given dominion over them, in order for him to name them (Gen. 2:19–20). Knowing someone's personal name or saying it aloud gave power to the knower, and so knowing the Divine name was huge, which is why taking Yahweh's name in vain featured in Hebrew law, not as a warning against swearing as some claim today, but about profaning Yahweh's dignity and reputation with a false or frivolous oath. When Jacob wrestled all night with a "man" (Yahweh), he refused to let his Combatant go until a blessing was bestowed, and once received, he asked his Assailant's name only to be rebuffed with the reply "Why is it that you ask my name?" (Gen. 32:29).

Power associated with naming also applied to changing a person's name—someone with the power to change your name could also demand your allegiance. Yahweh was always changing people's names when recruiting them to the Divine cause or celebrating some significant change in their situation: Abraham to Abram (Gen. 17:5), Jacob to Israel (Gen. 32:28), and Saul to Paul (Acts 13:9). Name-changing also applied when someone was promoted to an important office or was taken possession of by another—when Daniel and his friends were selected for service to Babylon's King Nebuchadnezzar, the palace master gave them new names to signify their new allegiance (Dan. 1:7). This custom is not only ancient. When my friend's grandfather arrived in the United States as an immigrant from Dahl, Norway, his strange-sounding Norwegian name was changed to Fromdahl (from Dahl). Grandfather was not too perturbed because, as a farm laborer in

Norway, laborers had to take their employer's name, and his name had already been changed three times. A more gruesome example of possessing another's name comes from the once headhunting Tugeri tribe of New Guinea who captured their victims, cajoled their names out of them, and then beheaded them in order to transfer these names to their own newborns.[9] And what of the tradition, unchallenged until recently, of a wife taking her husband's name in marriage, an ancient remnant of the notion of a wife as property and her subordination to the man? Fanny Mendelssohn, a talented composer in her own right, could not be published as a woman, and when finally published under her brother Felix's name, she had a heart attack and died in the middle of conducting her first work.

Sir James Frazer's classic book on religions, *The Golden Bough*, says that *"to obtain from the Gods a revelation of their sacred names"* in Egyptian culture meant a person actually possessed the very essence of the Divine Being and *"could force even a deity to obey him as a slave obeys his master."*[10] Was this in the Egyptian-raised Moses' mind when he asked his burning (sorry) question of the Voice addressing him from the bush: *"If I come to the Israelites and say to them, 'The God of your ancestors has sent me to you,' and they ask me, 'What is his name?' what shall I say to them?"* The Voice replied, *"I AM WHO I AM . . . This is my name forever, and this my title for all generations"* (Exod. 3:13–15). Those who learned this story with their mother's milk may not have examined this strange request, but the question was loaded. First, it recognized Moses' polytheistic environment—which of many GODS was addressing him? Second, he was asking for more than a name—what are your characteristics and credentials, what skills do you have, in comparison with other Deities, to free these people from slavery and provide them a land of their own? The name given in Hebrew was *Yahweh*, whose meaning is still debated but derives from the verb "to be." The Divine postscript, *"The God of your ancestors, the God of Abraham, the God of Isaac, and the God of Jacob,"* was what the Hebrew people wanted to hear. According to Karen Armstrong, *"I am"* was an ancient idiosyncratic expression of vagueness, meaning *"Don't you mind, it's not your business, you cannot control me with a name."*[11] By giving out the Divine Name, however, a relationship or covenant was being offered.

Although Yahweh is the common rendition, the more accurate is YHWH. Since Hebrew people did not write out the full name, given the Divine prohibition on erasing, defacing, or demeaning it, no one really knows the original vowels. By the third century CE, Hebrew people had also stopped saying the name, using instead the descriptive title *Adonai* (Lord) and other names. Even then, letters were substituted to avoid pronouncing the sacred Name and thus claiming power over the Unnamed—a One you could name was not truly transcendent but an idol or substitution, forbidden in Hebrew law. Hebrew people also combined Yahweh and El with other words expressing Divine activity to reduce the impact of using the Name by itself—for example, Yahweh *Shalom*, the Lord is Peace (Judg. 6:24); El *Olam*, the Everlasting God (Gen. 21:33); and El *Elyon*, Most High (Gen. 14:18).

A similar hesitancy around naming the Unknown and thus claiming to know or possess It exists in African tribes. The Lunda tribe talks of *Njambi-Kalunga* (the GOD of the unknown), the Ngombe of *Endalandala* (the Unexplainable), and the Massai of *Ngali* (the Unknown). In order to be more specific, they describe Divine attributes or manifestations: the Ngombe, for whom the forest symbolizes agelessness, talk of "the everlasting One of the forest," and the Baluba, who celebrate the enduring nature of the sun, speak of "He of many suns."[12] In Hindu traditions, Brahman (from "to strengthen or grow") emerged in the ancient Vedas as the Name for the mysterious Divine Force *"beyond thought and invisible, beyond family and color. He has neither eyes nor ears; he has neither hands nor feet. He is everlasting and omnipresent, infinite in the great and infinite in the small."*[13] Unspeakable and uncreated, Brahman could not be known, only named; and to say anything more was to speak of something less than Brahman:

> Both name and form are the shadows of the Lord . . . The form is of less importance than the name, for without the name you cannot come to a knowledge of the form, but meditate on the name without seeing the form, and your soul is filled with devotion.[14]

The Name was not only the letters of a word but also the sound. *Om* (*Aum*) is the eternal Hindu symbol for Brahman said or sung: *"When that sacred Word is known, all longings are fulfilled. It is the supreme means of salvation: it is the help supreme."*[15] Without sound formed into words, however, humans could not communicate with each other or with the One, and so later in Hindu history, descriptions of Brahman's attributes and activities evolved as many incarnations or avatars "making flesh" the One. The Rig-Veda speaks of thirty-three, but there are millions in Hindu lore, probably remnants of local village Deities later incorporated within Hinduism's umbrella.

The Name is highly significant in Islam as well. "Islam" means submission or surrender to the total will of Allah, not the name of a GOD but of "The GOD," the one and only of the Greek philosophers, the Jews, the Christians, and the Muslims. This is why Islam preserved the writings of Greek philosophers when Christianity denounced and destroyed them as "pagan," making them available again to Christianity after what was called its "dark ages." The first pillar of Islam, recited in Arabic from minarets five times daily, says, *"Allah is great! Allah is great. There is no God but God."* Like other traditions, Muslims cannot know all about Allah, since anything said must necessarily be incomplete and limited, but we can know Allah's attributes by seeing what Allah's Divine messengers have said over the centuries. The many references to Allah's attributes in the Qur'an make up the ninety-nine beautiful Names: *"The most beautiful names belong to God: so call on Him by them and leave the company of those who blaspheme His names"* (Surah 7:180). These names, Ar-Rahman the Compassionate, Ar-Raheem the Merciful, Al-Malik the King, and Al-Khaliq the Creator, to name a few, are also compound words linking an attribute with the Divine Name. When Sikhism evolved in sixteenth-century India as a synthesis of Islam and Hinduism, it also promoted the worship of one GOD called by many names, but not limited to any one of these particular or sectarian names. Their emphasis was again on the *Nam*, the "True Name" (*Sat Naam*) of the One, the essence of which lies far beyond any approximate names: *"How can Nam be known? Nam is within us, yet how can Nam be reached? Nam is at work everywhere, permeating the whole of space."*[16] Just as Hindus chant *Om*, the sound of the Nam repeated as a mantra brings worshippers into union with the Formless, Colorless One.

This brings us full circle back to the "I am," to Being Itself regardless of our religious tradition. *"I do not believe in God's naming himself or in God's defining himself before man,"* Martin Buber wrote. *"The word of revelation is: I am there as who I am there. (Ex 3:14)*

That which reveals is that which reveals. That which has being is there, nothing more. The eternal source of strength flows, the eternal touch is waiting, the eternal voice sounds, nothing more."[17] Although this open-ended "I am who I am" comes from the Hebrew story, it expresses the findings of most religions that search for the Divine Name in order to make sense of things, to explain life's mysteries, or simply to have a handle with which to talk. Even Buddhism, agnostic about a Something, says, "*There is an unborn, an unbecome, an unmade, an uncompounded, therefore there is an escape from the born, the become, the made, the compounded.*"[18] "I am" offers unlimited possibilities for finishing the sentence—I am angry, destructive, protecting, eternal, evolving, forgiving, vengeful, liberating, healing, holy, hopeful, hospitable, joyful, just, loving, patient, perfect, powerful, ruling, suffering, trustworthy, wise, warlike, creating, jealous, mysterious, silent, absent, cruel, and predestining. These are human characteristics, but "I am" can also be "I am food, light, storm, smoke, fire, voice, rainbow, music, mountain, water, river, gateway, length, breadth, height, width, energy, and spirit." Are these descriptions exhaustive? Never. "I am" invites each of us to complete the sentence from our own experience and in our own culture.

The three-letter symbol GOD has packed into itself over the centuries a plethora of meanings and images like grains of sand on a beach, all trying to nail down the Something we yearn to name. In choosing a baby's name before it is born, with no idea what it looks like, let alone its personality and abilities, we choose a multilettered symbol, whether Sven, Jessica, or Kyle, an arbitrary name from current fashions and famous identities, and somehow the one named begins to grow into this symbol of itself even though we know nothing else of the named as yet. In the same way, if we are going to talk about GOD, we need metaphors and images from our own worldview to finish the "I am . . ." sentence, even if it is to deny a GOD. Leo Tolstoy wrote in his mature years:

> Despite the fact that I did not acknowledge any such "someone," who might have created me, this concept of there being someone playing a stupid and evil joke on me by bringing me into the world came to me as the most natural way of expressing my condition. I could not help feeling that out there somewhere somebody was amusing himself by looking at me and the way I lived for thirty or forty years, studying, developing, maturing in

mind and body. And how now, with a fully matured intellect, having reached the precipice from which life reveals itself, I stood there like an utter fool, believing so firmly that there is nothing in life, that there never has been, nor ever will be. "And he laughs . . ."[19]

The dilemma remains, however. As soon as we finish the "I am . . ." sentence, even with new images or even by saying "I am not," we have limited GOD. The very nature of language is to limit and specify, and when we use language and concepts, we are basically inventing how things are by the ones we choose. We can't avoid using such tools, but we must realize what they are, limited and limiting. Our urge to say something in the presence of awe and wonder, tragedy and despair, mystical experience and nothingness, comes from our need to organize, classify, or control the Experienced, to make it ours; but as soon as any word leaves our lips it sounds puny, trite, and inadequate. "*Man has addressed their eternal You by many names,*" Martin Buber said, "*but all names of God remain hallowed—because they have been used not only to speak of God but also to speak to him . . . For whoever pronounces the word God and really means You, addresses, no matter what his delusion, the true You of his life that cannot be restricted by any other and to whom he stands in a relationship that includes all others.*"[20]

Feathers on the
Breath of GOD

Since you saw no form when the Lord spoke to you at Horeb . . .
take care and watch yourselves closely, so that
you do not act corruptly by making an idol for yourselves,
in the form of any figure—the likeness of male or female,
the likeness of any animal that is on the earth,
the likeness of any winged bird that flies in the air,
the likeness of anything that creeps on the ground,
the likeness of any fish that is in the water under the earth.
And when you look up to the heavens and see the sun,
the moon, and the stars, all the host of heaven, do not be led astray
and bow down to them and serve them.

—Deut. 4:15–9

∘ ∘

Water is round in a round receptacle and square in a square one,
but water itself has no particular shape.

—The Teachings of the Buddha[1]

As I outlined in the preface, the plan of the next few chapters is to develop metaphors that have been used for the Divine, beginning with the most basic Formless expressions and working through images from nature and human experience, without boxing Divinity into a human-like form. Despite current religious rhetoric from many different persuasions about what the Divine thinks, wills, and does, GOD did not step from the pages of the Hebrew Bible, the Qur'an, or the Buddhist texts dressed or acting like us. The fact that I can fill ten chapters of this book before discussing humanlike images for the Divine indicates that we have much work to do in widening the Divine image pool from which we fish.

If GOD cannot be limited to any one creed, and if we want to say something rather than nothing about the Divine, is there something that can be said with which most religions would agree, even though they may spell out the details in different ways? I propose Formlessness. The Deuteronomy passage at the beginning of this chapter warned Hebrew people not to make any images of That which they experienced. The Upanishads speak of Brahman's form as *"not in the field of vision: no one sees him with mortal eyes,"*[2] and Buddhahood is described as having *"no shape or color, and since Buddha has no shape or color, he comes from nowhere and there is nowhere for Him to go."*[3] With no one shape, existence, or description, Formlessness can equally be anything, the Ground of Being, the Wind beneath our wings, the Lifeblood in our veins, the Urge of the Universe, Love, Potentiality—the list goes on:

> You are the thought before I speak
> You are the urge before I sing
> You are the nudge before I act
> You are the spring before I walk
> You are the prayer before I sleep
> You are the dawn before I wake
> You are the breath before I live.[4]

Formlessness is different from apophatic theology, which avoids speaking of the Divine at all, or speaks of what It is not. Like electricity, air, or energy, something formless can be described, even if it cannot be seen, thus giving a positive characteristic to GOD. We see the trees bend even if we don't see the wind, and we see the results of electricity even if we don't put our finger on a hot wire. Formlessness also has the potential to take any shape, fill any space, operate free of limits, be imaged in a multitude of ways, and yet not limited to any one. *"Thou fillest everything and dost encompass it,"* said Rabbi Eliezer ben Judah of Worms (1176–1238), *"when everything was created, Thou was in everything; before everything was created, Thou wast everything."*[5] In Hindu tradition, the Formless Brahman takes on thousands of forms as avatars, both human and superhuman, all manifestations of the One who encounters humanity in times of need. The eternal Buddha or Buddhahood itself also has no set form *"but can manifest Himself in any form. Though we describe His attributes, yet the Eternal Buddha has no set attributes, but can manifest Himself in any and all excellent attributes."*[6] In the Hebrew Bible, the Formless One is expressed in many forms—wind, breath, sound, spirit, fire, light—and Christianity speaks of the Formless Word "becoming flesh," incarnated in the man Jesus. With Formlessness as our image of the encountered Divine, the possibilities are as broad as our imagination, and then some.

The ability of Formlessness to remain formless or take any form gives rise to contradictions in GOD-talk—known yet unknown, present yet hidden, closer than our breath yet not contained by the highest heavens, good yet wrathful, unchanging yet changing, Three-in-One yet One-in-Three, within us yet transcendent, speaking yet staying silent, and so on. The Formless "I am" can be whatever form is needed, and the Formless "I will become" is poised on the brink of millions of predicates willing to give it form. This adaptable, evolving GOD is so unlike the unchanging Greek Deity that Christianity first inherited. According to Edward Schillebeeckx, *"God is new each day. He is a constant source of new possibilities . . . God is absolute freedom. And that means that, as long as human history has not been completed, as long as the totality of history has not yet been given, we cannot know God's being—there is always something more and so there is always openness. And even the totality of history does not coincide with God's activity."*[7]

Every author, in writing a book, has a thesis in mind, some overarching concern that motivates her to go down the long path of storytelling in the first place, with her tour-guide folded umbrella held high so readers know the direction in which she is taking them while they enjoy the sights and experiences along the way. My folded umbrella, despite many diversions and sidetracks, is that we have become so saturated with Divine images of a Being separate from us with human characteristics and feelings that, for most of us, it is almost impossible to think of GOD apart from this. The Lord did this, and the Lord told me that, we say, addressing our prayers to Someone who is expected to hear, reply, and act with the promptness and courtesy we humans expect. Just listen to a few minutes of television evangelism, and you would think the preacher had just returned from a cappuccino, biscotti, and chat with GOD at the nearest coffee shop. Even if we theoretically acknowledge the Divine as formless, we still engage that Formlessness in conversational prayer as with another human being across from us or on the phone. Such personified imagery has dominated Christianity for centuries, yet this is not the only, or even predominant, Divine imagery in religious texts. This is not to say that we should never talk of the Divine in personalized images. While Formlessness is theoretically satisfactory and theologically sound, it may not be emotionally satisfying or rewarding to everyone's sensory perception—it is hard to catch in a net, address eye to eye, or hold hands with. Many of us need something more tangible or concrete to say about the Elusive One, and for others, such amorphous language is only a hair's breadth from nothingness. Rather, anthropomorphic images should not be our exclusive or dominant images to the point that we simply create a human-shaped idol that responds appropriately to our needs. In an airline magazine article, Rabbi Harold Kushner was quoted as saying:

> Intellectually, I know that God is not a person, a man who lives in the sky and has real eyes, ears, hands and sexual organs. But given the limitations of my three-dimensional mind, when I pray or when I contemplate God, I can't help thinking of God as a person even as I remind myself that references to God's hands and eyes are poetic metaphors. To me, God is the Source of the world in all its beauty, order and complexity. God is the Power that gives human beings the ability to think, to feel and to know the difference between good and bad. God is the force that gives ordinary people the otherwise inexplicable capacity to do extraordinary things, to be braver, more compassionate, more generous and forgiving than they ever thought they could be.

The first Divine encounter in Hebrew Scriptures is with the Formless *Ruach*, a "wind from God" ("mighty wind" or "spirit of God") sweeping over the face of the waters (Gen. 1:2). (*Ruach* also means breath, spirit, and life-giving element.) The King James Version translates this as "the Spirit of God," and Christian art has predominantly represented this Creating Spirit as an old man at work, a far cry from a powerful Wind coming and going at will and not seen except for its dramatic results. We have been so completely controlled by a selectivity of biblical images incorporated into our doctrines and art to the detriment or devaluation of others. John chapter 3 is a perfect example.

Christianity has long used John 3:16 to conclusively sum up the Divine dealings with humanity: "*For God so loved the world that he gave his only Son, so that everyone who believes in him may not perish but may have eternal life.*" The metaphorical Divine image here is of a single Parent, visually, biologically, and linguistically portrayed as male, offering up His only Child as a blood sacrifice in the name of love. Yet earlier in the same chapter, human transformation (salvation) is imaged in two other ways—that of emerging from the Divine womb into new life, "*being born*" or "*born anew*" (v. 3), an unarguably feminine image, and that of being "*born of the Spirit*," imaged as the Creating Wind we first met: "*The wind blows where it chooses, and you hear the sound of it, but you do not know where it comes from or where it goes. So it is with everyone who is born of the Spirit*" (John 3:8). Despite these other liberating images in John chapter 3 of a birth smelling of mother-nurture, or being overwhelmed by a strong, free wind, we constantly highlight only one metaphorical image, explaining salvation as some cosmic deal between a Father and His Son. Next time this verse is held up on a placard at a football match or paraded behind a politician being interviewed on television, think on these things.

The imagery of the Spirit-Wind giving birth to a new soul is found in the Hindu Upanishads as well: "*Where the fire of the Spirit burns, where the wind of the Spirit blows, where the Soma-wine of the Spirit overflows, there a new soul is born.*"[8] Outside my window, a howling wind is punishing the trees in my backyard. Bent thirty degrees off the vertical, a sturdy pine's bushy branches are being combed like a mane of hair. When the wind gives up for a few minutes, out of breath, the pine tree sails back into place as if nothing has happened. It is early spring in Minnesota, so other trees are still without leaves. The wind blows through their spindly branches without resistance, their trunks bending and swaying, and only if pushed beyond their flexibility are they in danger of breaking and causing havoc. As a city dweller who controls my environment with a secure shelter and who does not need a wind to drive my windmill to pump water into my faucets, or put wind in my sails to reach harbor, a falling tree is about the extent of my concern, unless the storm develops into a tornado. For people whose lives are exposed to, and dependent on the elements, however, wind is a central concern and powerful metaphor. Divine Wind (Breath) appears in many religions—the Hebrew *ruach*, Greek *pneuma*, Latin *anima*, Sanskrit *prāna*, Chinese *ch'i*, and the Polynesian *mana*. Ancient Hawaiians called their strong easterly winds *hã*, meaning the "breath of God." These winds announced the storm GOD Lono, who brought fertility, explaining the Hawaiian greeting *aloha*—"in the presence of wind, breath, or spirit." As a side note, when Captain Cook arrived on the Hawaiian Islands, he was thought to be a Divine Being arriving on Lono's breath. When they realized he wasn't, they killed him, thus white people have the name *haole*, meaning "without breath, wind, or spirit."

In the Hebrew Bible, the creating Wind blew over the formless void and velvety black in the beginning of time, transforming it into a world whose borders were defined, not in land mass or galaxies, but by the four corners from which the north, south, east, and west winds came. In Mark's Gospel, Jesus talks of gathering the elect in the last days *"from the four winds, from one end of heaven to the other"* (Matt. 24:31). While I was doing the final edit for this book, a Middle Eastern taxi driver told my friend that the earth was square because the sacred texts said so. I scratched my head for a minute trying to recall where this may have come from, then I remembered this imagery—the taxi driver had been taught to read the four corners of the earth literally. Not only did the four winds symbolize the edges of the universe, they also controlled the weather and thus survival in agricultural Palestine. The visionary in Revelation says, *"I saw four angels standing at the four corners of the earth, holding back the four winds of the earth so that no wind could blow on earth or sea or against any tree"* (Rev. 7:1). The west-northwest summer Mediterranean winds brought dew without rain at night to allow for winnowing the grain, a metaphor the psalmist borrows for his enemies, that they be *"like chaff before the wind, with the angel of the Lord driving them on"* (Ps. 35:5). The winter west winds brought essential rains and often violent storms—Jesus contrasted his disciples' ignorance at reading Divine signs with their skill at reading the seasons: *"When you see a cloud rising in the west, you immediately say 'It is going to rain'; and so it happens. And when you see the south wind blowing, you say 'There will be scorching heat'; and it happens"* (Luke 12:54–55). The east winds shattered the ships of Tarshish (Ps. 48:7), produced blighted wheat in Pharaoh's dream (Gen. 41:6), brought a locust plague to Egypt (Exod. 10:13), and blew a path through the sea for the Hebrew escape from Egypt (Exod. 14:21). When Israel later forgot their covenant, Yahweh said, "*Like the wind from the east, I will scatter them before the enemy*" (Jer. 18:17).

While we predict weather patterns scientifically today and assign anomalies to natural vagrancies of nature, ancient Hebrews believed that the wind was a manifestation of the Divine: "[*You*] *ride on the wings of the wind.* [*You*] *make the winds your messengers*" (Ps. 104:3–4). Violent windstorms also announced the presence of Yahweh, addressed Job, and transported Elijah to heaven (Job 38:1; 2 Kings 2:11). No mere human had "*power over the wind to restrain the wind*" (Eccles. 8:8), nor could they capture that mysterious, unstoppable force sweeping at will across the universe: "*Who has gathered the wind in the hollow of the hand?*" (Prov. 30:4). When Jesus stilled the storm, his followers wondered "*What sort of man is this, that even the winds and the sea obey him?*" (Matt. 8:27). Not surprisingly, given humanity's impotence in the face of such power, primal people bypassed feeble anthropomorphic metaphors for the Divine to opt instead for ones borrowed from the elements.

Despite the docile dove image for the Spirit in much Christian art, the arrival of the Divine Spirit at Pentecost was "*a sound like the rush of a violent wind, and it filled the entire house where they were sitting*" (Acts 2:2). I am holding my folded umbrella high at this point in case my tour group is looking for GOD in some European art museum. How can you draw the wind? In old navigational maps, they resorted to curly swirls coming from fat, cherub cheeks on a face reminiscent of a Greek Deity, reinforcing the idea of the wind proceeding from the Deity rather than being the Divine metaphor itself. In paintings by the Old Masters (Old Mistresses are scarce in our museums) and even in contemporary church school literature, the Divine Wind creating the universe by sweeping over the waters and speaking things into being is usually a human Creator-figure, a GOD who is like the wind or sends the wind, rather than the Divine Wind Itself of the old Gaelic song: "*I am the wind which breathes upon the sea, I am the wave of the ocean, I am the murmur of the billows.*"[9] How can we escape centuries of anthropomorphizing GOD, of making the Divine like ourselves, and thus controllable and predictable within our understandings of human character and action? Will we ever free our mind-pictures sufficiently to imagine a mighty Divine Wind, pulsing Energy, Breath of the world, life-giving Oxygen, pervasive Spirit within everything, free of our puny idolatrous forms? *"I am the supreme and fiery force who has kindled all sparks of life and breathed forth none of death,"* Hildegard of Bingen (1098–1179) said of the Divine. *"I, the fiery life of the divine substance, blaze in the beauty of the fields, shine in the waters, and burn in the sun, moon and stars. As the all-sustaining invisible force of the aerial wind, I bring all things to life . . . I am also Reason, having the wind of the sounding word by which all things were created, and I breathe in them all, so that none may die, because I am Life."*[10]

Hildegard's imagery introduces another translation of *ruach*—breath. When GOD said, *"Let us make humankind in our own image, according to our likeness"* (Gen. 1:26), a veritable field day began for humans to make all sorts of claims about themselves by virtue of being in the image of GOD (*imago Dei*). Yet we don't know what the Divine image is, so how can we know what this means—something not possessed by "lower" creatures, a Divine spark in the human soul, a Divine psychological trait? Even scholars quick to call the creation story a myth of beginnings seem loath to surrender a literal *imago Dei* claim for humanity. Shelf-loads of books argue whether this *imago Dei* was lost, corrupted, or simply overpowered in a fall, even though we are not agreed as to what it is/was. If we revisit the creation story, however, the Divine Spirit/Wind broods over the waters, a Voice speaks things into existence, and Breath enlivens the clay—not a humanlike Being in sight. What is metaphorically envisaged as a link between the Divine and human beings, however, is Divine Breath: *"Then the Lord God formed man [adam] from the dust of the ground [adamah], and breathed into his nostrils the breath of life; and the man became a living being"* (Gen. 2:7). This is not a scientific treatise on how a human being is created, *"Just as you do not know how the breath comes to the bones in the mother's womb, so you do not know the work of God, who makes everything"* (Eccles. 11:5), but a metaphorical image of something of GOD within us. Similar imagery of clay and breath was used of the Egyptian Deity Khnum: *"You have made humans on the wheel. You have formed everything on your wheel each day . . . The sweet breath of the wind goes out from him for the nostrils of Gods and humans."*[11] Ezekiel's vision was also about animating Divine Breath. After reassembling a valley of dry bones and adding flesh and skin, Yahweh tells Ezekiel to say to the breath (wind, spirit): *"'Come from the four winds, O breath, and breathe upon these slain, that they may live' . . . and the breath came into them, and they lived"* (Ezek. 37:9–10). In like manner, Yahweh would make Israel live again: *"I will put my Spirit within you, and you shall live"* (v. 14).

Stop for a moment and concentrate on your breathing . . . in and out . . . in and out . . . in and out. Our breath tells us we are alive, have life. Our moment of death is not when our body breaks down or flesh decays but when our breath stops. When Jesus died, according to Matthew's Gospel, he *"breathed his last"* or *"gave up his spirit"* (27:50). Each heartbeat and breath reminds us that the oxygen of the universe (which some call GOD) is within all of us, coming and going and shared with everything around us—humans, animals, and plants bound together in life-giving oxygen–carbon dioxide cycles. We are "feathers" on the "breath of God," Hildegard of Bingen said. Buddhists also focus on their breath to help them reach Enlightenment or the True Realization of all things. The "mindfulness of breathing" concentrates the mind on the tip of the nose where breath goes in and out, developing an awareness of life. This coming and going of breath, rather than holding onto breath, keeps us alive and helps us realize that everyone in the universe is as one organism sharing one breath. The indigenous Canadians recognized breath as a metaphor for life and connectedness with the universe. Canadian geneticist and environmentalist David Suzuki wrote:

> Every breath is a sacrament, an affirmation of our connection with all other living things, a renewal of our link with our ancestors and a contribution to generations yet to come. Our breath is part of life's breath, the ocean of air that envelopes the Earth. Unique in the solar system, air is both the creator and creation itself. [12]

"Air/breath is both the creator and creation itself"—is not this what the Hebrew myth said? Before we get too far from Hildegard of Bingen's striking imagery of Divine Wind and Breath, note something else she said of the Divine: *"I am also Reason, having the wind of the sounding word by which all things were created, and I breathe in them all."* A Divine Voice and Divine Speaking are common Hebrew images that usually tempt us to think of the Speaker, yet the source of voice and speech is breath, Hildegard's *"wind of the sounding word."* Interestingly, the English word GOD is thought to be derived from the same Indo-European root as the Irish *guth,* voice.[13] Have you ever been so short of breath that you cannot make sounds come out? The psalmist

says, "*By the word of the Lord the heavens were made, and all their host by the breath of his mouth*" (Ps. 33:6). The Divine Wind sweeping the waters "spoke" the world into being (Gen. 1:3), a stirring metaphor if you have ever heard the wind howling through the trees. If the visual image of a Creator Being walking in the garden was not so indelibly printed on our mind (even though in Genesis 3:8, the first couple "heard the *sound*" of the Lord GOD walking in the garden), we might still be able to hear this Sound and feel that Breath at work in the world.

We tell a funny story in our family about disembodied voices. When my son was in elementary school, my husband and I went away on a trip, leaving the children in my parents' care. Rules were set: bed by 9:30 p.m. and no television during the week. One night my son went off to bed but couldn't (or didn't want to) sleep. His room and the television were at the other end of the house from my parents' room, and so, just before midnight, he turned it on. As the usual warm-up clicking and spluttering noises accompanying the blank screen began to fade, the sound of his mother's voice came loudly across the airwaves into the darkened room. After a few seconds of his guilt-ridden panic, my face appeared on the screen before him. The explanation was simple. I had prerecorded devotional epilogues for use by an Australian television channel before it signed off at midnight, and my son had unknowingly selected the evening his mother was on television to defy the bedtime rules. Needless to say, he retreated with guilty haste under his bedcovers.

When we take a closer look, unembodied Sound is what we most encounter in the Bible as GOD—Speech created (Genesis 1), came through a burning bush (Exod. 3:4) and thunder (Exod. 19:19), and addressed Elijah in a cave (1 Kings 19:9). When Elijah was told to go outside because the Lord was about to pass by, what Divine form did he see? None, but he felt and heard.

> Now there was a great wind, so strong that it was splitting mountains and breaking rocks in pieces before the Lord, but the Lord was not in the wind; and after the wind an earthquake, but the Lord was not in the earthquake; and after the earthquake a fire, but the Lord was not in the fire; and after the fire a sound of sheer silence . . . Then came a voice to him that said . . . (1 Kings 19:11–13)

John's Gospel begins, not with a Being or Form, but a Divine Word, *"In the beginning was the Word, and the Word was with God, and the Word was God"* (John 1:1). We are so busy proving all sorts of things about Jesus from this paragraph that we miss what it says about GOD. Scholars think these introductory verses were originally a separate poem about creation and bringing things into being, later incorporated into John's Gospel as a prologue. Its readers would know that the Divine Voice has previously spoken through burning bushes, whirlwinds, and prophets and now was speaking through a new medium, the man Jesus. This Gospel was addressed to people no longer associated with the synagogue and decidedly more Greek-influenced, so the Greek word *Logos* ("Word" in English) was used for the Divine Voice.

Yet *Logos* had a broader meaning in Greek thought—*"The divine principle of reason that gives order to the universe and links the human mind to the mind of God"*[14]—and it would therefore take on different meanings in Christian theology with respect to Jesus than the Hebrew idea of Divine Voice speaking again, but now through the prophet Jesus (but more of that later):

> The voice of the Lord is over the waters;
> the glory of God thunders . . .
> The voice of the Lord breaks the cedars;
> the Lord breaks the cedars of Lebanon . . .
> The voice of the Lord flashes forth flames of fire.
> The voice of the lord shakes the wilderness;
> the Lord shakes the wilderness of Kadesh.
> The voice of the Lord causes the oaks to whirl,
> and strips the forest bare;
> and in his temple all say, "Glory!" (Ps. 29:3–9)

Jaroslav Pelikan's translation of the beginning of John's Gospel better reflects the original Hebrew imagery and loosens the all-too-familiar "Christian" interpretation of Jesus as the Word:

> In the beginning the (spoken) Word already was. The Word was in God's presence, and what God was, the Word was. He was with God at the beginning, and through him all things came to be; without him no created thing came into being. So the Word became flesh; he made his home among us.[15]

Breath produces voice, speech, and song, another metaphor for the Divine. Clement of Alexandria (second century CE) wrote a prayer to this "New Song," the revelation from the Word that was in the beginning and before the beginning:

> [The New Song] has made men out of stones, men out of beasts. Those, moreover, that were as dead, not being partakers of the true life, have come to life again, simply by becoming listeners to this song. It also composed the universe into melodious order, and turned the discord of the elements to harmonious arrangements, so that the whole world might become harmony . . . A beautiful breathing instrument of music the Lord made man, after His own image. And He Himself also, surely, who is the supramundane Wisdom, the celestial Word, is the all-harmonious, melodious, holy instrument of God.[16]

The most basic description of Brahman in Hinduism is also the sound said or sung whose symbol is *Om*. It begins and ends the reading of the Vedic texts and is the seed of any mantra, the sequences of sound used for meditation. For the Muslim, Allah is known only as the spoken Word revealed to Muhammad and written down in the exact Arabic in the Qur'an. Its rhythmic phrases chanted from minarets call Muslims to prayer, and the melodic reading of the Qur'an in worship incarnates Allah in their midst.

Divine revelations, whatever the religion, are never ordinary communications but usually come with a blaze of bells and whistles, whether a speaking angel for Hagar in the wilderness, earth-shaking cave reverberations for Muhammad, or a blinding light for Paul. This leads me to wonder if, rather than dwelling on the medium of Voice, Sound, and pyrotechnics, we should be describing the Divine as the prior event of "Communication." I remember being quite blown away for a period of time with the image of GOD as Communication (not Communicator, because that returns to an "idol" like us that we create). Burning bushes, dreams, thunder, and prophets are third-generation metaphors; Voice and Sound are second-generation metaphors that appear in the bushes and dreams; and the first-generation metaphor, that which drives Voice and Sound, is the act of communicating itself. This metaphor appealed to me as a writer, teacher, and artist, since my whole life is about trying to communicate something effectively. My immediate instinct when I see something beautiful or experience something mind-boggling is to communicate it by talking, drawing, or writing, since part of the enjoyment is to interpret it in some way and share it. The central belief in any revelatory religion is that communication has happened, like the excitement generated today at possible communication from other planets. The beauty of imaging the Divine as Communication Itself is that it frees us from looking behind this for a Source we cannot know or assuming that a Voice needs a Being that speaks. With computers and other technological marvels today, we know that communication can happen in ways that do not even place a communicator at center stage.

While Divine Communication is a dynamic act of GOD seeking humanity, communication is inevitably interpreted within a particular worldview, culture, and language. Every Bible story is a combination of both "revelation" and interpretation in a particular setting (although some insist their Divine revelations come to them unmediated). "*There is no pure revelation,*" Paul Tillich said. "*Wherever the Divine is manifest, it is manifest in 'flesh,' that is, in a concrete, physical, and historical reality, as in the religious receptivity of the biblical writers.*"[17] When the revelation-reception process is claimed to be all revelation, culturally limited human attempts at interpretation are unfortunately cemented in place as eternal doctrines. GOD as Communication is the most elemental faith statement across religions—no matter how much people debate the truth or falsehood of various doctrinal statements or religious claims, the central belief that makes it important enough to debate at all is the faith statement that the One has communicated with humanity, even if as briefly as "I Am." Sufi Ibn Junayd (830–910) called the whole cosmos the "Divine discourse," and in the "Hadith of the Hidden Treasure," Allah says "*I was a Hidden Treasure and I loved to be known. So I created the creatures, so that I would be known through them.*"[18]

Communication as a Divine metaphor is not exhausted by speech and song. Love, compassion, and friendship are also means of communication. *Let me know you, for you are the God who knows me,*" Saint Augustine said in his *Confessions*. "*Let me recognize you as you have recognized me.*"[19] Human communication begins with the most basic human relationship, that of mother and child even before birth. Research has shown that babies in orphanages who have not been held or hugged do not develop as well or learn to communicate as effectively as others. To be alive, in whatever form, is to communicate in some way, whether the nudge of my dog when he wants me to throw the ball again, the feeling inside that makes me want to hug someone distraught with worry, a hand slipped into another's in speechless wonder in the presence of great natural beauty, or the need to acknowledge a moment when the Divine breaks in. "*Whenever the warm living rays of the Divine Sun . . . will shine on me with unaccustomed brightness,*" sixteenth-century Italian poet Vittoria Colonna wrote, "[*I*] *take up my pen, impelled by inner love; Without quite knowing what it is I say.*"[20]

Healthy communication is two-way. The Qur'an says, "*When My servants question thee concerning Me, then surely I am nigh. I answer the prayer of the supplicant when he crieth unto Me: So let them hear My call and let them trust in Me*" (Surah 2:186). Human communication with the Divine has traditionally been labeled as prayer, but described in many ways from formal worship liturgies to the counting of beads to a shopping list of wants and needs. A recent article in a religious magazine carrying the title "Prayer works!" listed a series of incidents where the writer prayed and something happened, like narrowly avoiding an accident, just catching a train, or receiving needed money in the mail. While this may be comforting for some, it reduces prayer to a magical wand and the Sacred to a genie whose proof and worth depends on miraculous happenings and benefits received. Is asking for things what communication is all about? According to Harold Kushner, prayer is to ask GOD to be with you:

> The prayer of the terminally ill person need not be, "Please God, make me healthy." The prayer of a terminally ill person can be, "God, be with me because I am frightened. Be with me so I don't feel alone. Be with me so I don't feel rejected."[21]

In a beautiful old story, an elderly, illiterate farmhand went every day to the village church to kneel and pray before the altar. One day the priest asked him, "My child, is something bothering you?" "No," said the peasant, "Everything is fine. I just look at God and God looks at me." Some of the best communication takes place when we simply sit in silence and lose ourselves within the pulsing universe whose heart, some say, is GOD: "*Prayer is the bridge that dissolves the duality, Man and God, God and Man. When duality disappears, unity is.*"[22] This returns us to the Divine image that began this chapter, feeling the Wind on our cheeks and breathing the universal Breath:

> O worker of the universe! We would pray to thee to let the irresistible cur-
> rent of thy universal energy come like the impetuous south wind of spring,
> let it come rushing over the vast field of the life of man, let it bring the scent
> of many flowers, the murmurings of many woodlands, let it make sweet
> and vocal the lifelessness of our dried-up soul-life.[23]

Where Can I Go
from Your Spirit?

Where can I go from your spirit?
Or where can I flee from your presence?
If I ascend to heaven, you are there;
if I make my bed in Sheol, you are there.
If I take the wings of the morning
and settle at the farthest limits of the sea,
even there your hand shall lead me,
and your right hand shall hold me fast.

—*Ps. 139:7–10*

While wind and breath suggest common formless elements of the natural world that can be understood in any company, the third meaning of the Hebrew *ruach* is "spirit," an overworked and underpaid catchall term for whatever we cannot otherwise name or describe. Its companion term "spirituality" is equally elusive, something we use freely but struggle to define. Spirituality's increasing popularity today stems both from disenchantment with traditional theologies and the contemporary shift to human experience as an authentic vehicle for speaking about the Divine. Espousing a spirituality defined by one's own circumstances and experiences allows many people to continue the religious journey without jettisoning the proverbial baby with the bathwater. Religious institutions who condemn such independence should realize that, in many cases, the institution's lack of flexibility to explore more adequate Divine images has sent such seekers out on alternate paths. Rather than apostates, they are usually deeply religious people who know what is lacking and cannot be content until they find It—or at least until they are satisfied that they have properly searched. Australian commentator Caroline Jones advocates this turn to experience first and foremost:

> We Australians seem determined not to walk without question in the well-worn tracks of traditional religion but to take our own sense of spirituality as a starting point and then to see which elements of the old traditions might support it.[1]

Yet Philip Sheldrake, editor of a journal on spirituality, warns that we should differentiate carefully between what is merely good anthropology and what qualifies as spirituality, because spirituality *"can all too easily become just another word for almost every human experience."*[2] Yet is this concern a residue of the Greek dualism of body and spirit, the need to clearly identify and carefully compartmentalize the sacred and the secular rather than celebrate ourselves as whole persons?

The English word "spirit" encompasses many meanings: animating or vital Principle; Divine Beings; Divine indwelling; evil possession; supernatural messengers; the nonmaterial part of a person; disembodied soul; personal character, strength, or moral nature; vigor or lethargy; the general tone of things; and the Third Element of the Trinity. In ancient times, spirits were free-ranging supernatural powers that infiltrated every aspect of life. Ancient cultures worshiped the spirits of their dead, counting them present as long as someone could remember them and visiting their places of burial. When people gave up nomadic wanderings for city life, GODS became established in sacred places, like mountaintops and temples. GODS indicated power (with a Supreme GOD the Master planner of everything) and spirits represented formless forces. The Katha Upanishad says, *"[The Spirit] is within all, and is also outside. As the wind, though one, takes new forms in whatever it enters, the Spirit, though one, takes new forms in all things that live."*[3]

Such freedom of the Spirit allowed It to be both transcendent (beyond understanding and definition) and immanent (GOD with us). *"He came and sat by my side but I woke not,"* Bengali poet Rabindranath Tagore (1861–1914) wrote. *"Ah, why do I ever miss his sight whose breath touches my sleep?"*[4] The Qur'an also speaks of Divine immanence: *"It is We who have created man, and We know what his innermost self whispers to him: for We are closer to him than his neck-vein"* (Surah 50:16). The Immanent Spirit is not only "with" us, but also "within" us as cream hidden in milk. In fact, the whole universe can be captured in the "little space within the heart," according to the Upanishads:

> The heavens and the earth are there, and the sun, and the moon, and the stars; fire and lightning and winds are there; and all that now is and all that is not: for the whole universe is in (Brahman) and He dwells with our heart.[5]

The Indian greeting *namasti*, joining the palms with a slight bow, salutes the Divine Spirit in you from the Divine Spirit in me, reminding us of the worth of each other as Divine-bearers. The Greeks talked of *entheos* (the GOD within), that divine madness sent from the GODS, superior to human sanity and the mainspring of all worthwhile creations. "Enthusiasm" was the source of creativity. Eskimo artists, before carving an ivory piece, turn it gently and whisper, "Who are you? Who hides in you?" inviting the spirit within to come out through their carving. In mystical traditions, the Divine Spirit does not simply reside within but is so merged with us, or us with It, that there is no longer any difference. *"As rivers flowing into the ocean find their final peace and their name and form disappear,"* the *Mundaka Upanishad* says, *"even so the wise become free from name and form and enter into the radiance of the Supreme Spirit who is greater than all greatness. In truth who knows God becomes God."*[6] This annihilation of all distinctions between Divine and human was the Sufi goal in life: *"When you see me, you see him. When you see him, you see us,"* said Akhbar al-Hallaj.[7]

A local rabbi made a retreat near a once-great monastery with only an old abbot and four elderly monks left. The abbot visited the rabbi to ask for advice. The rabbi was sympathetic, "The spirit has gone out of my people as well. Almost no one comes to synagogue anymore." They wept together and read the Torah. As the abbot left, he asked again, "Is there nothing you can tell me that would save my dying order?" "I'm sorry," the rabbi responded. "All I can tell you is that the messiah is one of you." Back at the monastery the monks gathered around the abbot to hear what had happened and were puzzled over his parting words. In the following months, they pondered them during daily chores. If it were true, which of them was the messiah? Probably Father Abbot . . . but perhaps it was Brother Thomas . . . not Brother Elred because he gets crotchety, yet he is usually right . . . surely not quiet Brother Phillip but then, he is always there when you need him . . . of course the rabbi couldn't mean me . . . yet supposing he did? The monks began to treat each other with extraordinary respect in case one of them was the messiah, and on the slim chance it might be them, began to treat themselves with extraordinary respect as well. Because of the monastery's forest setting, many people wandered its paths and ventured into its chapel where they sensed this aura of extraordinary respect permeating its walls. They came back often, bringing their friends. A few young men asked to join the monks, and within a few years, the monastery was a vibrant center for spirituality once again, thanks to the rabbi's gift.

In heterogeneous biblical times, "spirit" meant many things. Pharaoh sent for all the magicians and wise men of Egypt when "his spirit" was troubled over a dream (Gen. 41:8). Yahweh sent an "evil sprit" between Abimelech and the lords of Shechem (Judg. 9:23). Saul was tormented by *"an evil spirit from the Lord"* (1 Sam. 16:14) and later, having expelled all mediums and wizards from the kingdom, asked one secretly to *"consult a spirit"* for him to make contact with the deceased Samuel, since Yahweh was not responding through the usual dreams or prophets (1 Sam. 28:6–8). Jesus gave the disciples power over the "unclean spirits" associated with possession and disease (Matt. 10:1). Angelic messengers were called *"spirits in the divine service"* (Heb. 1:14), and at a resurrection appearance, Jesus' disciples were *"startled and terrified, and thought that they were seeing a ghost [spirit]"* (Luke 24:37).

The central meaning of spirit in the Hebrew tradition, however, is the Divine Creating *Ruach* whose Breath made humans into "living beings" (Gen. 2:7): *"The spirit of God has made me,"* said Job, *"and the breath of the Almighty [Shaddai] gives me life"* (Job 33:4). Whereas in Greek thought soul (spirit) meant that rational immortal principle that distinguishes humans from the rest of creation and is separate from the lesser body or matter, in Hebrew thinking the soul (*nephesh*) meant a complete human being, body *and* spirit. The book of James borrows this fact to illustrate a point: *"For just as the body without the spirit is dead, so faith without works is also dead"* (2:26). Spirit was also used to describe the mental attitude of a person without separating it off from the whole being: *"Blessed are the poor in spirit"* (Matt. 5:3) and *"The spirit indeed is willing, but the flesh is weak"* (Matt. 26:41). As Christianity became more Greek, this holistic Hebrew "living soul" gave way to the idea of a human being divided against itself, an immortal soul forever trying to escape its encumbrance, the body.

To understand the relationship between Divine Spirit and human spirit in Hebrew thought, we need to understand that Hebrew cosmology saw human existence irrevocably interlaced with Divine existence. The Divine and human realms shared the same space, distinguished linguistically as spirit and flesh, unseen and seen, invisible and visible. When John's Gospel talks of earthly and heavenly things, it did not mean spatially separated realms of earth and heaven, as in the cosmology of Greek philosophers, but human (earthly) and Divine (heavenly) activity happening within the same space (John 3:12). While the Divine realm was not limited only to that space it shared with humans, what humans experienced of the Divine Spirit was experienced within their physical space, on their own turf. When the Israelites were agitating in the desert, Moses was told to choose seventy elders whom Yahweh would address in the tent of meeting (a place outside the camp where people received oracles from GOD): "*I will come down and talk with you there; and I will take some of the spirit that is on you and put it on them; and they shall bear the burden of the people along with you . . .*" (Num. 11:17).

Sharing space naturally meant sharing breath (spirit)—the life-giving Spirit hovering over the waters and breathing life into human beings was the same shared breath one surrendered at death. "*As long as my breath is in me and the spirit of God is in my nostrils,*" Job said, "*my lips will not speak falsehood*" (Job 27:3–4).[8] This immanent, energizing Spirit-Breath was also the transcendent, free Spirit coming and going at will, "coming upon" people to commission them for special tasks or to prophesy, "*bearing witness with our spirit*" (Rom. 8:16). King David said, "*The spirit of the Lord speaks through me, his word is upon my tongue*" (2 Sam. 23:2), and Zechariah was "*filled with the Holy Spirit*" when he prophesized about his son John the Baptist (Luke 1:67). When Daniel interpreted Nebuchadnezzar's dreams, he was said to be "*endowed with a spirit of the holy gods [a holy, divine spirit]*" (Dan. 4:18). Ezekiel said that "*a spirit entered into me and set me on my feet*" when Yahweh spoke to him (Ezek. 2:2). And when Saul was anointed king, "*the spirit of God possessed him, and he fell into a prophetic frenzy*" as proof of his commissioning (1 Sam. 10:10).[9] At Jesus' baptism, "*the Holy Spirit descended upon him in bodily form like a dove*" (Luke 3:22), and the same Spirit was passed to the disciples when Jesus breathed on them saying, "*Receive the Holy Spirit*" (John 20:22).[10]

Given the plethora of Spirit-visitations, however, we are warned to *"test the spirits to see whether they are of God; for many false prophets have gone out into the world"* (1 John 4:1). No wonder it is sometimes difficult to identify when the Bible is speaking of the Divine Spirit and when the human spirit, illustrating the shared Spirit, shared space precisely.

The creation story is also about shared space and how mortal and immortal realms came into being. The Creating Spirit made humankind, not as servants as in other ancient myths, but as friends with whom to chat in the Divine garden of immortal Beings in the cool of the evening. There is a parallel story in the *Katha Upanishad*. A student approached a sage and asked, *"Master, whence came all created beings?"* The sage replied, *"In the beginning, the Creator longed for the joy of creation. He remained in meditation, and then came Rayi, matter and Prana, life. 'These two,' thought he, 'will produce beings for me.'"*[11] In the Hebrew story, humans left this gated "immortal" community, not for a different realm, but for neighboring property outside the gates, the "mortal" realm where inhabitants eventually die. When Paul told this story, saying *"and death came through sin, and so death spread to all because all have sinned"* (Rom. 5:12), it was death (human mortality) Paul was discussing, not sin or Adam's guilt—remember, humans were sent from the garden because GOD was concerned that *"now, he might reach out his hand and take also from the tree of life, and eat, and live forever"* (Gen. 3:22). Sewing fig leaves together has been interpreted as the shame of sin, but *"the eyes of both were opened* (a Hebrew phrase for a revelation) *and they knew they were naked"*—they recognized their mortal physicality was different from the GODS who presumably did not have sexual parts (Gen. 3:7). The Hebrew Bible never used this story later as creating an unbridgeable breach or alienation between humans and GOD—the Lord is present when Eve gives birth to Cain outside the garden *"with the help of the Lord"* (Gen. 4:1), and they were never held up as a reminder whenever Israel disobeyed Yahweh. This ancient story simply explained the origins, circumstances, and locations of its protagonists, GOD and humanity, before getting into the main plot of the saga of a specific Hebrew people.

That the Adam and Eve story was about the differentiating lines between immortal Beings and mortal humans is substantiated in Genesis 6 when another crisis occurs in the shared neighborhood. Immortal "sons of God" took human wives, incurring Divine anger, not because they had sex, but because the boundary rules were again breached. While intercourse between Deities and humans regularly produced divine-human offspring in Greek mythology, immortals and mortals were separate and different by definition and from the Garden story in Hebrew tradition. The prelude to the Noah's Ark story (rarely told in church school) was the Divine reaction to such boundary crossing. GOD first limits the length of time mortals could share the Divine Breath/Spirit (that is, live)—"*My spirit shall not abide in mortals forever, for they are flesh; their days shall be one hundred twenty years*" (Gen. 6:3)—and later regrets sharing Divine breath with mortals at all and sends the flood.

With such precise definition of mortal and immortal realms, it is not surprising that there was no Hebrew belief in "human immortality"—an oxymoron. While there was passing mention of Sheol as a shadowy underworld of departed spirits, it was not an "afterlife" of such spirits. Sharing life-breath and space with the Creating Spirit happened in this life. When the Israelites were liberated from Babylon (sixth century BCE) by King Cyrus, however, they brought Zoroastrian ideas back with them, including a multileveled paradise for faithful souls and a final judgment that gave them "immortality." This idea gained ground in the second century BCE when many Hebrew youth were perishing in battle. The book of Daniel written at this time hints at a continued existence after death, not in bodily form, but shining "*like the brightness of the sky [dome]*" and "*like the stars forever and ever*" (12:3). This debate was alive and well in Jesus' time. The Sadducees rejected a resurrection, but the Pharisees accepted it (Acts 23:8), not as resuscitated bodies but as a transformed state in the Divine realm at the end of history: "*We will not all die, but we will all be changed . . . the dead will be raised imperishable, and we will be changed. For this perishable body must put on imperishability, and this mortal body must put on immortality*" (1 Cor. 15:51–53).

Drawn into this debate, Jesus took the affirmative, saying that people will be like "*angels in heaven*" as the patriarchs were alive in GOD: "*He is God not of the dead, but of the living*" (Matt. 22:32). On the cross, he told one of the thieves, "*Today you will be with me in Paradise*" (Luke 23:43). Jesus' central teaching was about the "Kingdom of God" ("Kingdom of Heaven" in Matthew). Our traditional thinking is so saturated with heaven "up there" that we miss this good news that mortals survive death in a transformed, noncorporeal state in the Divine (heavenly) realm soon to break into the human realm with which it shared space. Also caught up in this debate, Paul was accosted by a blinding Light and Voice (the usual Hebrew description for the Divine breaking into the visible realm). The voice belonged to Jesus, alive in the Divine realm as proof that a man had survived death: "*He was put to death in the flesh, but made alive in the spirit*" (1 Pet.3:18; also Acts 10:40). This was not the Greek idea of the preexistent human soul leaving the body at death to return to the heavenly realms, but a "spiritual" existence for mortals beyond death:"*Flesh and blood cannot inherit the Kingdom of God, nor does the perishable inherit the imperishable*" (1 Cor. 15:50).

Jewish people believed that their spirit/breath left the body at death but hovered around the corpse for three days before abandoning it for the shadowy Sheol. Jesus' spirit, however, had not departed after three days, as evidenced by Paul's vision (and explaining the "three days" in later Gospel "appearances," the same word as Paul's noncorporeal vision). Paul therefore called Jesus the "first fruits," both proof of human immortality and the preview of the upcoming show when GOD's kingdom would break into the human realm, bringing faithful dead with it. "*If Christ has not been raised [survived death]*," Paul said, "*your faith is futile*" (1 Cor. 15:17). This was the saving message of Jesus on which Paul staked his life—and death:

> If the Spirit of him who raised Jesus from the dead dwells in you, he who raised Christ from the dead will give life to your mortal bodies also through his Spirit that dwells in you. (Rom. 8:11)

In need of a metaphor, Paul borrowed *adam* (humankind) from the beginning myth of how immortality was lost—"*Just as one man's trespass led to condemnation for all [mortality], so one man's act of righteousness leads to justification and life for all*" (Rom. 5:18)—a metaphor that would later acquire a life of its own as a tale of sin and the fall (discussed later). I wonder if Paul would have chosen this metaphor had he foreseen its future distortions.

Hebrew shared space and Breath/Spirit cosmology changed when Christianity became defined by Greek thinking at the end of the first century. The Deities had led wild and fanciful lives in Greek epics, but in time, Greek philosophers found such antics less than satisfactory and looked for explanations beyond anthropomorphic Divine dramas. Plato described an order of Forms in the cosmos, headed up by the unchanging Form of the Good. His pupil Aristotle abandoned some of Plato's ideas, arguing for a necessary, changeless, perfect Cause behind everything to supersede less inspiring Deities. When these ideas entered Christianity, the Yahweh that shared space and Breath/Spirit with the world, breaking through the veil from time to time as visions, voice, and commissioning Spirit, gave way to an utterly transcendent First Cause, an Unknowable Good, a Divine Intelligence ruling from some far-off realm with lesser Spirits as invisible messengers roaming the world at Divine bequest.[12] The Jewish man Jesus, commissioned by the Spirit for a messianic task, would become GOD's Divine Son reminiscent of the Greek Divine Court, both ruling from outside the world. The once-free Divine Spirit, incarnated and immanent in everything and everyone, would be absorbed into a Divine Hierarchy as the third part of a Trinity, subordinated to the Father GOD and limited to messenger chores between Father and Son and their earthly ecclesial representatives. That Creating Spirit hovering over the waters, whipping up whirlwinds, and sharing Breath with creation was thus domesticated or else relegated to the margins where mystics dwelt or to other pockets of believers who rebelled against "institutionalizing" and controlling the free Spirit's movements. Since the Trinity was usually shorthanded to the Father GOD (wearing a triangular halo in Christian art), the Spirit was further banished from everyday thought and its activity only valid within ecclesial offices.

Not surprisingly, little was said about the Spirit in early Trinitarian discussions, engrossed as they were with establishing Jesus' Divine credentials in relation to the Father GOD. The Spirit was "just there" as one of the Three, no longer independent to blow where It chose (John 3:8). "*The history of doctrine,*" Elizabeth Johnson says, "*shows that the Spirit, while the first and most intimate way God is experienced, was yet the last to be named explicitly divine.*"[13] Anyone who made claims of accessing the Spirit outside church ranks was regarded as suspicious or heretical. During the fourteenth century Catherine of Sienna (later canonized and declared a Doctor of the Church) was placed under the control of a Dominican priest when she first heard Divine Voices. A century later, Joan of Arc, whose Divine Voices and military prowess helped the

French drive back the English, was burned at the stake for refusing to deny her Voices when king and church no longer wanted her input (she was also canonized later).

With the rise of Protestant traditions and their focus on the authority of the Bible, the Spirit guided believers in their reading of scripture and invigorated personal piety, but when such "in-spiration" was too far out of line with church doctrines and order, it was also suspect. Charismatic and Pentecostal persuasions claimed a special indwelling of the Spirit that led to dramatic manifestations, but these groups remained on church margins until recently. Despite its variety of genders (masculine Latin *spiritus*, feminine Hebrew *ruach*, neuter Greek *pneuma*), Johnson suggests that the "feminine resonance" in metaphors *ruach* (spirit), *shekinah* (indwelling), and *hokmah/sophia* (wisdom) may have helped the Spirit's neglect: "*Faceless, shadowy, anonymous, half-known, homeless, watered down, the poor relation, Cinderella, marginalized by being modeled on women—such is our heritage of language about the Spirit.*"[14]

But things, they are a-changing! The last twenty years has produced a rush of scholars and books within mainline theology discussing the Spirit.[15] Our postmodern world has recognized the plurality and diversity of global experiences and the need, not to unify everything into one, but to celebrate differences and the contextual nature of experiences, whether struggles against oppression, mere survival, ecological concerns, or challenges from science and technology. Rather than theology being named and shaped by a few in church or academic halls based on traditions from the past, the validity of all experiences allows us to "*take seriously the context of life in a 'groaning' world* (Romans 8:22)."[16] In this setting, talk about the free Spirit comes into its own, able to penetrate all corners of marginalization, struggle, ethnic differences, and emerging life. Jesuit Pierre Teilhard de Chardin (1881–1955) said, "*All around us, to right and left, in front and behind, above and below, we have only to go a little beyond the frontier of sensible appearances in order to see the divine welling up and showing through.*"[17]

While charismatics have long recognized this unpredictable, enabling Presence, they have also "enslaved" It for their own purposes, as did the institutional church, celebrating Its supernatural and sensational qualities while ignoring the original Pentecost where the Divine Spirit was poured out on *all* present as a commissioning for the ordinary, everyday task of telling the Divine good news (Acts 2:4). Today's theological task is to reshape our language and metaphors so that the Divine *Ruach* can blow where it will once again, taking up residence in everything. This means more than just being "in" nature but being part of nature itself, the *"unseen power who vivifies and sustains all living things, while the earth is the visible agent of the life that pulsates throughout creation."*[18] Such language moves us into even more radical territory, suggesting that our ecological disregard is, in fact, a "sin" against the Holy Spirit (Mark 3:29).

The image of the free Spirit also returns us to the fledgling church of Paul's day. Not only did Spirit-tongues of fire ignite and "in-spirit" all those at Pentecost, but each was given "spiritual gifts," not according to gender, class, or religious superiority, but for the good of the whole (1 Cor. 12:4–7). Prophesy, the Divine Spirit "coming upon" and speaking through people in the Hebrew Bible, was the prerogative of everyone and to be universally sought (1 Cor. 14:1, 24). In the early second century, however, these early egalitarian church "households" were returned to the model of Aristotelian *paterfamilias* (rule of the father) households, with free man over slave, male over female, and man over child. This model became reflected in the hierarchal church and family orders of later New Testament letters, such as Ephesians, Timothy, Titus, and Peter. The spiritual gifts given to everyone in a community, where no one but GOD could be called "father" (Matt. 23:9), were assigned exclusively to those in ecclesial offices, headed by the *Papa* (Pope) as the Father GOD's representative on earth. Order and unity, oneness in Trinity and church, became the name of the game, with the once-free Spirit employed in its service.

Releasing the Divine Spirit once again into everything raises some interesting questions. If humans share the Divine Breath/Spirit, are they not, in some sense, divine? Was the Spirit incarnated only in Jesus of Nazareth, or does the Divine Spirit "become flesh" in all of us, a question to "compost" until later in the book? And, if the Divine is within us, why do we pray to GOD "out there," signing in and out with "Dear GOD" and "in Jesus' name"? When the Wind/Breath stirs the dust so that we, for a moment, can see It, when we step out of our lethargy and protest global injustices, when we reach out to another in compassion or wonder at a sunset, are these sound-and-smell realizations of divination within us? Like husbands and wives finishing each other's sentences, do we get better at finishing the Divine sentences as we share the same Breath/Spirit? Such nontheistic, nonanthropomorphic imagery of the free Spirit unleashes our imagination and offers new visions, as it has always done, for those who will "see" and "hear." William Wordsworth, who almost became a clergyman except that life's reality rendered many church teachings shallow to him, wrote of a Presence infiltrating all he knew—*"a sense sublime of something far more deeply interfused . . . A motion, and a spirit that impels all thinking things."*[19] Wordsworth's Presence is a faith statement, as is any Divine description, something we accept or reject given the strength of the evidence or lack of it. Friedrich Nietzsche also struggled with the religion of his day, but chose a path different from Wordsworth by proclaiming GOD dead in 1882. Yet in a poem written before he went mad near the end of his life, Nietzsche pleads with his murdered GOD, with all Its torments, to return: *"The last flame of my heart— / It burns for you!"*[20]

Nature Speaks

Earth's crammed with heaven,
And every common bush afire with God.

—*Elizabeth Barrett Browning*[1]

○ ○

Therefore [God] created the verdant fields of Time and Space
and the life-giving garden of the world,
That every bough and fruit might show forth His various perfections.

—*Jami (Persian Sufi)*[2]

While many ancient people read Divine action in the powerful, natural events of wind, breath, and spirit, these were not the only metaphors borrowed from the natural world—nature in all its glory seemed to shout Divinity. "*His glory covered the heavens, and the earth was full of his praise*," the writer of the book of Habakkuk declared (3:3), and Paul also used this conclusion to argue against those who refused to acknowledge GOD:"*For what can be known about God is plain to them, because God has shown it to them. Ever since the creation of the world his eternal power and divine nature, invisible though they are, have been understood and seen through the things he has made*" (Rom. 1:19–20). Sixteen centuries later, John Calvin's famous *Institutes of the Christian Religion*, covering the scope of Christian theology in his day, began with "The Knowledge of God the Creator":

> He [God] not only sowed in men's minds that seed of religion . . . but revealed himself and daily discloses himself in the whole workmanship of the universe. As a consequence, men cannot open their eyes without being compelled to see him.[3]

Marco Pallis, in describing the traditional Tibet he knew, called it infused with the *Dharma* (the teachings of Buddha):"*It came to one with the air one breathed. Birds seemed to sing of it; mountain streams hummed its refrain as they bubbled across the stones. A holy perfume seemed to rise from every flower.*"[4] For Rabindranath Tagore, the famous Bengali poet who would sit all day in his garden as a child writing about nature, the pontifications of religious scholars were so complicated compared with "*the voice of your stars and the silence of your trees.*"[5]

The term "natural religion" has been used for centuries, but it has more than one meaning, and we need to know what is implied in different contexts and what claims are being made before we can talk about it successfully. For some, it is the moral or universal ethical principles that are somehow part of the natural order of things. Others see it as a type of religion that found its focus in the events and activities of the natural world. For others, it is a minimal set of ideas common to all religions. Still others see it as a pattern for life, a way to achieve happiness. Natural religion has also been the term for what can be deduced by reason as opposed to metaphysical or supernatural speculation. While for others, it is a position of nonbelief as opposed to special Divine revelation. It has also been used to talk anthropologically, beginning with what it is to be human rather than what it is to be GOD.

As hinted in some of these definitions, there has been hesitation in religious circles over the centuries about claiming Divine revelation through nature. If GOD is encountered through the natural world, why do we need specific revelations like those claimed through Jesus or the Qur'an, and even if GOD is revealed through nature, are human beings capable of "reading" this revelation accurately, given their original corruptness or sheer humanness? The exuberance of the likes of Hildegard of Bingen, who not only "read" nature's scriptures but also identified nature as the Divine ("*I am the rain coming from the dew that causes the grasses to laugh with joy of life*"),[6] led to much nervous shaking in ecclesiastical boots. Debate focused on what we could know by human reason and observation of nature, and what could only be known through special Divine revelation. For Christianity, with its theological arguments organized under creation, fall, and redemption, the issue was also about salvation—is this available through knowledge of GOD from creation or only through the special revelation of Jesus the Christ? The

First Vatican Council in 1870 declared the revelatory value of creation: *"If anyone shall have said that the one true God, our Creator and our Lord, cannot be known with certitude by those things which have been made, by the natural light of human reason: let him be anathema."*[7] However, the Divine mysteries revealed through Christ and the church were necessary for full salvation.

While the Enlightenment squelched a lot of speculation about what could be known about GOD, the burgeoning scientific advances of the nineteenth century threw further wrenches into the works—what of nature is orchestrated by the Divine and thus revelatory, and what is simply the product of natural laws? Florence Nightingale, a theologian in her own right, bridged this divide by arguing that the Divine was revealed daily through the natural laws of the universe, if only we were attuned to observation: *"God himself is teaching us every day by His Laws, what he is. His ways only show the way imperfectly. Both natural and moral Philosophy teach us every day His character . . . In other words, not only touching the heart but teaching the intelligence."*[8] Karl Barth's booming Protestant voice during two World Wars would declare all natural theology faulty because it suggested we could know the Divine Creator apart from the Divine Redeemer revealed through Jesus. Sally McFague, a present-day proponent of nature spirituality, says of her earlier days, *"As a Protestant and erstwhile Barthian, I was myself for many years such a resister. Only 'the Word' that reached my ears conveyed the presence of God, never the sights before my eyes."*[9] What Barth seemed to forget at times was that revelation, even biblical stories about Jesus, is not unmediated, but reinterpreted many times throughout history and influenced by prevailing philosophies of the day. Fortunately, Barth's total rejection of nature as a bearer of the Sacred was later challenged using the same scriptures from which he made his claims—one does not have to read far to know that Hebrew people certainly encountered Yahweh through nature: *"Those who live at earth's farthest bounds are awed by your signs; you make the gateways of the morning and the evening shout for joy"* (Ps. 65:8).

If nature is the revealer or container of the Divine, what metaphors from the natural world other than wind, breath, and spirit have found their way into GOD-talk? Since ancient people believed the world was made up of four elements—earth, air, fire, and water—these featured early and have had a resurgence in recent times as people, disenchanted with traditional religious ideas, look for religious roots in ancient texts and rituals. Mother Earth is one of the oldest, if not the oldest, Divine image. To indigenous people in many lands, She is a sacred living Being and should be treated as such. Early missionaries in Bolivia were stunned when the locals poured a little of the eucharistic wine, the sacred blood of Christ, onto the ground for *Pachamama*, the Earth Mother, before they drank their own. For others, Western agriculture has violated Her and continues to do so. "*You ask me to plow the ground,*" a Native American said. "*Shall I take a knife and tear my mother's bosom? You ask me to dig for stone. Shall I dig under her skin for bones? You ask me to cut grass and make hay and sell it, and be rich like white men. But how dare I cut off my mother's hair?*"[10] Reverence for the earth is also central for Aboriginal Australians. The shapes of its mountains and rivers were formed by sacred ancestors, like the Rainbow Serpent (All-Mother) emerging from the earth and bursting to expel all living creatures that now inhabit it. The Aboriginal poet Oodgeroo (also known as Kath Walker) once asked her father, "How did we get on without God before these white people came into our country?" "Very well," her father replied, "because we had the Earth Mother to protect us. She was always there." When Oodgeroo asked why She was not called God, her father answered, "Because there are no Gods. God is in the mind. Can you see God?" Oodgeroo replied in the negative. "Can you see the Earth Mother?" her father asked. When Oodgeroo nodded, her father replied, "Question answered."[11]

The Earth Mother is both giver of life and taker of all, representing the cycles of birth and death. She is the Sumerian Inanna, the Egyptian Isis, the Greek Persephone and Gaia, the Babylonian Ishtar, the Hindu Kali, the Native American Shawnee and Spider Woman, and the African Yoruba Yemaja, to name a few. She is also simply the GODDESS to thousands who have rediscovered her underneath centuries of patriarchal smothering by male GOD images. Biblical scholars have recovered traces of her as *Sophia-Wisdom* and *Shekinah*. *El Shaddai*, the Divine title usually translated "all sufficient" or "almighty Lord," comes from *shad* meaning "breast," Yahweh the nourishing Breasted One. Florence Nightingale made a note of this in her Bible against "God Almighty" in Genesis 17:1: "*Shaddai derived from Mamma—the Breast, and signifies that we are dependent on God for every blessing as the infant on its mother's breast and its mother's care. Jehovah assures Abraham that he is able to perform his covenant by styling himself El Shaddai, the All Sufficient God."*[12]

While an Earth Mother giving birth alone to all that existed is found in some ancient cultures, other cultures paired the Earth Mother with what early anthropologists called a male Sky GOD. The two were complimentary and both necessary, but in time, these delicately balanced scales would lean to one side. The lone creating, genderless "Wind" in Genesis would take form, not as birthing Earth Mother but as a Sky Father. Interestingly Enlil, "Lord Wind," the chief GOD of the Babylonian pantheon (by virtue of being the city GOD of Nippur) at the time of Abraham's departure from the Mesopotamian area, was the Creator GOD said to have separated heaven and earth and also sent a flood to destroy humanity. Enlil had a wife, however, Mother Goddess Ninlil, who was originally a grain GODDESS, but on marrying Enlil, became "Lady Wind."[13] This raises fascinating questions as to whether Lady Wind was "blown away" en route to the promised land, leaving only a Hebrew version of Enhil as the "Lord Wind" of Genesis. Much has been written in recent times about the loss of a nurturing Earth Mother image in traditional theology, but She is making her return, not only in GODDESS movements, but also in ecological theology where the universe is again being described as a nurturing Divine Body. *"The earth is alive and generous and wants to nourish us and that's why we're alive,"* Australian environmentalist John Seed says, *"because she's nourished us all the way along, without a moment's pause. We only have to stop breathing for three minutes and we're dead. I don't even have to remember to breathe. I can breathe when I'm asleep. So she's pushing that air in, she's breathing me all the time and I'm too arrogant to notice it."*[14]

Fire is the second of the four classical elements, the Divine *Agni* of Vedic tradition that mediated between humans and GODS and laid waste whole regions of the earth, but was also heat, light, hearth fire, ritual fire, and the funeral pyre. For Rabindranath Tagore, *Agni* is the fearful Freedom that releases the body in death by burning it to ashes: *"My body will be one with you, my heart will be caught in the whirls of your frenzy, and the burning heat that was my life will flash up and mingle itself in your flame."*[15] For Japanese people, Fuji, the GODDESS of the Hearth who gave her name to sacred Mount Fuji, was responsible for warmth and cooking heat. In Hebrew stories, Yahweh was also manifested as fire—a Voice in a burning bush that was not consumed (Exod. 3:2), a pillar of fire to lead escaping Hebrew slaves (Exod. 13:21), and hidden in a smoking mountain (Exod. 19:18). Once the temple was built in Jerusalem (tenth century BCE), the itinerant Cloud and Voice gave way to the Divine Presence in the temple, symbolized by light from the eternal Flames on ten golden lamp stands (1 Kings 7:49). On the flip side, Yahweh was "*a devouring fire, a jealous God*" (Deut. 4:24), and a refining fire testing and maturing the faithful: "*I will put this third into the fire, refine them as one refines silver, and test them as gold is tested*" (Zech. 13:9). In the New Testament, the Divine Spirit came as tongues of fire at Pentecost (Acts 2:3), and this imagery would continue in Christianity, both as an external charismatic sign and a metaphor for experiencing the Divine Presence within. John Wesley described his conversion experience as his heart "strangely warmed," and Quaker founder George Fox (1624–1691) encountered the Divine "like a fire within."

Air, the third element, has already been discussed as wind and breath, leaving us the fourth element, water. In ancient Mesopotamian stories, water was the original element from which all life emerged. *Enuma Elish*, the ancient creation story from the city of Babylon, begins with Tiamat as the female Watery Void existing before heaven, earth, or Divine Beings. She mates with Apsu, the freshwaters, creating the first generation of GODS. Their son Ea kills Apsu and assumes power, producing a son Marduk (Merodach). Tiamat, encouraged to fight this takeover, is slain by grandson Marduk, and her watery body is divided to form the heavenly waters and the ocean. Marduk becomes exalted over other GODS for slaying Tiamat, the original Watery Mother. This story becomes more relevant when we realize that this "takeover" and exultation of Babylon's GOD Marduk originated in the city of Babylon's rise to power and conquest of other city-states. In time, Marduk became the chief GOD of Babylonia, the area into which many city-states were absorbed, and eventually the universal GOD. Since the southern Mesopotamian city of Ur was one city conquered by Babylon around the calculated era of Abraham, this adds significance to Abraham's departure, taking his city GOD Yahweh with him. Just as the Creating "Lord Wind" Enlil separated the heavens from the earth, and Marduk (originally a storm Deity) divided Tiamat's watery body to form heavenly waters and the ocean, the Creating "Wind" of Genesis swept the *"face of the waters"* to separate *"the waters that were under the dome from the waters that were above the dome"* (1:7).

Given the dependence on water in ancient Palestine, both as rain and fresh springs, water symbolized the refreshing, life-giving presence of Yahweh. Water is a multivalent metaphor that can mean thirst-quencher—*"I seek you, my soul thirsts for you; my flesh faints for you, as in a dry and weary land where there is no water"* (Ps. 63:1); rain, ice, and snow for the crops—*"By the breath of GOD ice is given . . . He loads the thick cloud with moisture"* (Job 37:10–11); rivers, oceans, and floods— *"You visit the earth and water it, you greatly enrich it; the river of GOD is full of water"* (Ps. 65:9); purifier and cleansing agent— *"Wash me thoroughly from my iniquity, and cleanse me from my sin"* (Ps. 51:2); waters of ritual—*"I [John the Baptist] baptize you with water for repentance"* (Matt. 3:11); and life-giving fountain—*"They have forsaken me, the fountain of living water"* (Jer. 2:13). Each year at the Festival of Tabernacles, Jewish priests brought water from the pool of Siloam to pour on the temple altar as a libation for sins—living or running water in contrast to stagnant water. The passage from Zechariah 13:1, *"On that day a fountain shall be opened for the house of David and the inhabitants of Jerusalem,"* was read, reminding people of a time when they would be at peace, and living water would flow out from the temple and Jerusalem. No wonder his hearers were blown away when Jesus claimed at the same festival to be this "living water":*"Let anyone who is thirsty come to me, and let the one who believes in me drink. As the scripture has said, 'Out of the believer's heart shall flow rivers of living water'"* (John 7:37–38).

Water as a Divine image is not restricted to Judaic and Christian traditions. The flowing stream is a central metaphor in Daoism (Taoism)—one "flows with" the *Dao*, the life-principle of the universe, and to be "with," not "against," the *Dao* is to be fulfilled. The *Dharma* (teaching) in Buddhism has been called a great living river: *"The fish and turtles of other teachings swim about in its depths and push against its current, but in vain. Buddha's Dharma flows on, pure and undisturbed."*[16] The Upanishads describe final liberation as our little self lost in the greater Self, like a drop of water lost in the sea, something St. Teresa of Avila (1515–1582) also used for the mystical union of the human soul with the Divine—*"when a little stream enters the sea so that henceforth there shall be no means of separation.*"[17] Water is also the Divine purifying agent in most religions. Every Islamic mosque has an outside area for ritualized ablutions prior to entering, and every Hindu temple has a bathing pool in its courtyard. The river Ganges, streaming from the head of the GOD Shiva, is the most sacred of waters for purification rituals. The September 2005 *Times of India* reported that a company was collecting Ganges water from Gangotri and packaging it to sell further down where the river became more polluted, so that people could have pure water for their puja ritual. While many agreed this bottled Ganges water would be far safer, others worried, "How will I know it is really Ganges water?" In Hebrew tradition, priests performed washing rites before offering sacrifices, and people could not enter the temple without washing first. Ritual immersion (baptism) began as a purification ritual but later incorporated repentance (Mark 1:4), and since the followers of Jesus were no longer part of the synagogue and many were non-Jews, baptism replaced circumcision as an initiation rite. The Ethiopian eunuch, reading Isaiah on his way home, was approached by the apostle Philip and told the "good news." As they passed some water along the road, the Ethiopian cried, "*Look, here is water! What is to prevent me from being baptized?*" (Acts 8:26–38). While this baptism had little to do with correct place, dress, technique, and words, baptism would evolve into a central Christian sacrament, with divisive arguments as to its proper method and meaning. Despite the stated aim to return to the original terms, translators of the King James Version of the Bible retained "baptism" rather than the original "washing," since baptism had become such a major Christian ritual and quite different from its mundane beginnings.

As for metaphors beyond the classical four, the sun as source of light, heat, and the passage of days captured the religious imagination from the beginning of recorded time, and still does. There is the family joke told on the artist in me. Whenever I made the last turn into our road in the Australian countryside after picking up the children from school, the sun was beginning to drop below the wide skyline, creating a sequence of unbelievable colors. Each time I would say, out of sheer joy at its magnificence, "If you tried to paint the colors of that sunset, you could never make it look real." After a while, the children learnt to parrot my comment long before the last turn, but at least they remember it, and the beauty, to this day. The sun was the Divine ancestor of the Incas, and *Nihon* (Japan) is a derivative of *ni*, "sun," hence the Japanese slogan, "The Land of the Rising Sun." Roman emperors were considered Sun GODS, and when emperor Constantine prepared for his final battle for sole supremacy of the Roman Empire, he had a vision of the cross superimposed over his symbol, the sun, hence his later tolerance of Christianity. Hebrew people were certainly conscious of sun worship in the religions around them—in King Josiah's reform, any priests who had made offerings *"to Baal, to the sun, the moon, the constellations, and all the host of the heavens"* were deposed, and their sun chariots burned (2 Kings 23:5, 11). However, despite being instructed not to make any Divine images, including sun, moon, and stars (Deut. 4:19), this did not stop the Hebrews from using the sun as a Divine metaphor: *"For the Lord God is a sun and shield: he bestows favor and honor"* (Ps. 84:11).

There is a greater light than the sun in religious experience, the illuminating Light beyond all metaphors: *"All things shine with the shining of this [Brahman's] light, this whole universe reflects his radiance."*[18] The Qur'an calls Allah *An-Nur*, the Light of the heavens and the earth, Light upon Light (Surah 34:35), and the book of Isaiah waxes eloquent about a time when Yahweh's Light will be all that is necessary in Jerusalem: *"The sun shall no longer be your light by day, nor for brightness shall the moon give light to you by night; but the Lord will be your everlasting light"* (60:19). The goal of Buddhism is to reach "enlightenment," described as "the lights coming on." *"Following the Noble Path is like entering a dark room with a light in the hand,"* the Buddha said, *"the darkness will all be cleared away and the room will be filled with light."*[19] According to 1 John, *"God is light and in him there is no darkness at all"* (1:5), and Jesus claimed this Divine Light within himself and also in his followers: *"You are the light of the world . . . Let your light shine before others, so that they may see your good works and give glory to your Father in heaven"* (Matt. 5:14, 16). No wonder early Christians called their baptism an "illumination." It is hard for us with immediate and continual access to electricity to fully comprehend the promise of an everlasting light that did not depend on the times of the sun, the phases of the moon, or a reliable supply of candles. In medieval Europe, since the church was the center of a walled town, the whole town became church space—a physical and spiritual fortress. The church spire reached up to the Divine, and when Gothic architecture came into vogue, the soaring spire brought the Light down to shine through its stained glass windows, the transcendent Light made immanent. It was this metaphorical Divine Light within and around him that finally brought Leo Tolstoy to GOD and saved him from suicide. *"Man is a weak and miserable creature when God's light is not burning in his soul,"* he wrote. *"But when it burns (and it only burns in souls enlightened by religion), man becomes the most powerful creature in the world. And it cannot be otherwise, for what then works in him is not his own strength, but the strength of God."* [20]

We can't leave Divine Light without mentioning "glory," that difficult to describe biblical word we say all the time in the Lord's Prayer:*"For the kingdom and the power and the glory are yours forever"* (Matt. 6:13).[21] In its original meaning, glory was the radiance of Divine Light and Fire, often accompanied by a Voice, as a visible, earthly manifestation:

> The glory of the God of Israel was coming from the east; the sound was like the sound of mighty waters; and the earth shone with his glory . . . As the glory of the Lord entered the temple by the gate facing east, the spirit lifted me up, and brought me into the inner court; and the glory of the Lord filled the temple. (Ezek. 43:2, 4–5)

On Mount Sinai, Moses asked of Yahweh, *"Show me your glory, I pray"* (Exod. 33:18), but was firmly informed that, while Yahweh would show graciousness and mercy, the Divine Face would not be on view (v. 20). When Moses came down from Sinai with the tablets of the covenant, the skin of his face "shone" because he had been talking to GOD (Exod. 34:29). In the New Testament, Jesus was "transformed" before three disciples in an encounter with Yahweh, so that his face *"shone like the sun, and his clothes became dazzling white"* (Matt. 17:2). John's Gospel talks of Jesus exhibiting the Divine Glory (John 1:14), and the letter to the Hebrews calls him the *"reflection of God's glory"* (Heb. 1:3). Note, however, that this Divine Glory is not something exclusive but is also reflected in us—it *"has shone in our hearts"* (2 Cor. 4:6).

"O send out your light and your truth; let them lead me," the psalmist said, *"let them bring me to your holy hill and to your dwelling"* (Ps. 43:3). If Light personifies the Divine, something about mountains also sparks the religious imagination. Show me a mountain, and I can

almost guarantee there is a sacred story somewhere associated with it. I remember sitting on the verandah of a chalet in Schladming, Austria, with a wall of towering, craggy Alpine slopes dominating the skyline across the valley. Sometimes clouds hovered over the high peaks as if hiding some Sacred secret, only to roll away, revealing again these unchanging marvels. If I turned away for a moment, a year or a century, the walls of rock would still be there when I looked again. In the valley below, twin spires of the Catholic and Lutheran churches proclaimed the eternal glory of the Lord, but they were like frail toothpicks compared with these mountains. There was a time when those spires did not exist, and there will be a time when they disappear, yet those mountains will still watch over that space as they watched primal tribes in the past and will watch technology-satiated tribes of the future. How arrogant of humans to imagine the Divine in human images, I thought, when these mighty mountains are metaphorical possibilities. The first time I saw the Grand Canyon and watched its rocky escarpments change from light gray blues to deep blues to purple, pink, red, and finally black, my eyes filled with tears as the psalmist's words flooded into my mind: "*I lift up my eyes to the hills—from where will my help come? My help comes from the Lord, who made heaven and earth*" (Ps. 121:1–2).

Since they reach up to the heavens, the traditional abode of the GODS, mountains and hills are sacred locations. Down a side street in Vienna, Austria, full of Western sculpture and architecture, a sushi bar opens onto the sidewalk with a bench and a few stools, a miniscule refuge for Japanese tourists weary of brats and sauerkraut and westerners addicted to raw fish. A disproportionately large picture of Mount Fuji, the Japanese symbol of peace, power, sacredness, and eternity, dominates this tiny eating place. Fuji's symmetrical snow-covered sides slope up to a flat summit that looks as if a passing sushi knife has sheered it off horizontally. Divine both in Itself and as the abode of Divine Beings (*kami*), Mount Fuji is as beloved as Mount Sinai is to the Hebrews and Uluru to Australian Aborigines. When Buddhism became established in Japan, climbing Mount Fuji became an exercise in devotion and asceticism, although many climbers today are more likely tourists than religious devotees, just as they are at Uluru. Sacred mountains also feature prominently in Chinese landscape paintings. The Chou emperors (1122–221 BCE) sacrificed to four sacred mountains as the abodes of the GODS, the number rising to five during the Han period (206 BCE–220 CE), with others added later. Mount Meru is the Hindu cosmic mountain that reaches between heaven and earth, represented by the highly ornate gate towers, covered with a plethora of Divine avatars, that loom over entrances to Hindu temples. In Hebrew tradition, sacred mountains were associated with Yahweh, whether Mount Sinai or Mount Zion, and Jesus' conversation with the Samaritan woman focused on the Jewish-Samaritan debate over the correct place to worship, whether the Samaritan's sacred mountain of Gerizim or Jerusalem's Mount Zion (John 4).

Mountains are also sacred places to go, literally and figuratively. Many significant moments for Jesus took place on mountains: his temptation (Matt. 4:8), the sermon on the mountain (Matt. 5:1), his transfiguration (Mark 9:2), his private devotions (Matt. 14: 23), his betrayal (Matt. 26:30), and his ascension (Acts 1:9–12).[22] Mountain pilgrimages feature in stories of the saints, and the spiritual journey is described in many religions as climbing a mountain:

> Until we have reached the top of the mountain we cannot see in full glory the view that lies beyond; but glimpses of light illumine out path to the mountain. These glimpses of light give us faith, because then we know, not with the external knowledge of reading books, but with that certainty of faith that comes from moments of inner life.[23]

And what of the view from the top? Do we meet the Divine there? Not necessarily, says George O'Brien, because when we view the whole world from such a perspective, we see where Divinity really is, "*already down there, in every nook and precinct with the churchgoers and the commuters equally, but we lack the perspective to see how this is so.*"[24]

On a smaller scale, rocks symbolized the Divine in the Hebrew Bible as a multimeaning metaphor of security, refuge, and deliverance, "*The Lord is my rock, my fortress, and my deliverer, my God, my rock, in whom I take refuge*" (2 Sam. 22:2–3); a sure foundation, "*See, I am laying in Zion a foundation stone . . . a sure foundation*" (Isa. 28:16); salvation, "*Blessed be my rock, and exalted be my God, the rock of my salvation*" (2 Sam. 22:47); and hiding place, "*You are a hiding place for me; you preserve me from trouble*" (Ps. 32:7). When rocks are piled one on the other, fortresses and towers became metaphors for Divine protection:"*For you, O God, are my fortress*" (Ps. 59:9) . . . *a strong tower against the enemy*" (Ps. 61:3). In the absence of electronic security systems and stealth missiles, Hebrew people respected any means of protection and defense available to desert wanderers and tribal city dwellers—no wonder the Divine was also imaged as weapons: *"the shield of your help, and the sword of your triumph!"* (Deut. 33:29).

In contrast to such warlike imagery, the Divine is also the protective wings of the mother bird, the preservation of life, not extinction. *"[God] will cover you with his pinions, and under his wings you will find refuge"* (Ps. 91:4) was part of the liturgy for entering and exiting the Temple. Worshippers would see cherubim's wings hovering protectively over the Ark of the Covenant, reminding them of an eagle's wings hovering over her young: *"You will not fear the terror of the night, or the arrow that flies by day, or the pestilence that stalks in darkness, or the destruction that wastes at noonday"* (Ps. 91:5–6). They would remember their stories of how Yahweh rescued them from slavery: *"You have seen what I did to the Egyptians, and I bore you on eagles' wings and brought you to myself"* (Exod. 19:4). When park rangers were surveying the aftereffects of the Mount Saint Helens volcanic eruption in Washington State, they found the body of a charred adult bird sitting bolt upright under a tree. As they wondered why she had not flown away from the flames and heat, a small chick struggled out from under her black, lifeless wings: *"As an eagle stirs up its nest, and hovers over its young; as it spreads its wings . . ."* (Deut. 32: 11). Mothering Wings are still needed for our protection today, although the danger list has changed—terrorism, nuclear war, inner city violence, HIV/AIDS, and global warming.

Not only did Divine eagle wings protect their young by sheltering them or bearing them off at appropriate moments, they also attacked their enemies: *"Look, he shall swoop down like an eagle, and spread his wings against Moab"* (Jer. 48:40). Anyone who has seen the deadly accuracy of an eagle diving after its prey can almost feel the sharp beak on the back of the neck. Swooping down also reminds us that an eagle builds its nest on the highest peak, always higher than its prey, which was probably in the psalmist's mind: *"Lead me to the rock that is higher than I; . . . Let me abide in your tent forever, find refuge under the shelter of your wings"* (Ps. 61:2, 4). Understanding the context before making claims about the Divine from a metaphor is helpful. The Hebrew *nesher,* translated as "eagle" in English, was used for a number of birds with different characteristics and propensities. "*Wheresoever the carcase [carcass] is, there will the eagles be gathered together*" (Matt. 24:28, KJV) is more accurately rendered as vultures, birds hard to distinguish when flying high but known for where they hang out. When the wise man in Proverbs says that acquired wealth suddenly "*takes wings to itself, flying like an eagle toward heaven*" (Prov. 23:5), this is thought to be the imperial eagle (*Aquila heliaca*), the bird said to be able to see into the sun. When Yahweh's "*horses are swifter than eagles*" (Jer. 4:13), the eagle in mind was probably the golden eagle (*Aquila chrysaetos*), known for its speed.[25] This ornithological sidetrack reminds us that metaphors can enlighten, confuse, or deceive, depending on whether we catch the analogy intended by the writer—a Divine Vulture is hardly the *nesher* with which the faithful would wish to be compared in "*those who wait for the Lord shall renew their strength, they shall mount up with wings like eagles*" (Isa. 40:31).

In contrast to the eagle, the dove as the metaphorical Spirit image that descended on Jesus at his baptism (Matt. 3:16) has a very different biblical history. The dove (pigeon, turtledove) was gentle, docile, and tender—"*Be wise as serpents and innocent as doves*" (Matt. 10:16); naïve and silly—"*Ephraim has become like a dove, silly and without sense*" (Hosea 7:11); and weak and powerless—"*Do not deliver the soul of your dove to the wild animals; do not forget the life of your poor forever*" (Ps. 74:19). A pair of doves or pigeons, the only birds permitted for sacrifice in the temple, could be offered by poor families like Mary and Joseph to purify a woman after giving birth (Luke 2:24), an indication of their lowly status, since a dove and a sheep were required of the rich (Lev. 12:6–8). Add to this lowly, gentle image the fact that "dove" was an erotic endearment for a woman—"*Open to me, my sister, my love, my dove, my perfect one*" (Song of Sol. 5:2); was associated with GODDESSES Astarte, Ishtar, and Inanna from prebiblical traditions and the sacred Peleiades (priestesses) and Venus; its eggs had aphrodisiac powers; white doves suggested purity; and we have a Divine image decidedly tipping the scales in the direction of the feminine. How did the dove become the symbol of the Holy Spirit? The easy answer is the Spirit's descent like a dove at Jesus' baptism, but this same Spirit came as a roaring wind, fire in a burning bush, and tongues of flame at Pentecost.[26] Given the Spirit is linguistically feminine in Hebrew and the dove's association with GODDESS cultures, I can't help but wonder whether this imagery is a remnant of all this, especially as the Spirit later became subordinated to the Father GOD.

Since Victorian England's armchair anthropologists analyzed the religions of their colonized world according to their own religious categories, Australian Aborigines were classified as without religion because their complex beliefs in ancestral Beings often in animal form did not look enough like Victorian Divinities—a "proper" religion, according to English tastes, worshipped spiritual Beings and preferably a high GOD. Yet Aboriginal people have an impressive story in *Alcheringa* (inadequately translated as "Dreaming"), *"that powerful spiritual reality active in creation time in the beginning,"* and continuing *"as a reality that gives spiritual life to our present reality."*[27] Their Creator Spirit, often portrayed as a Rainbow Serpent, emerged from the earth long before the missionaries, traveled the landscape leaving trails of life, and returned to the land through caves, waterholes, and sacred sites. Known by many names, this Serpent gave life and laws to the ancestors, all creatures, and the landscape itself. Many missionaries condemned this Serpent image (which was also sacred and associated with GODDESSES in prebiblical religions), especially since the snake was linked in Christianity with sin and fall—they forgot that Hebrew people found it a life-saving symbol when held up by Moses in the desert (Num. 21:6–9). Today, Aboriginal Christians are reclaiming this image along with other images, sifting for themselves which Hebrew-Christian metaphors are useful and which are alien. While Aboriginal people were taught about the Good Shepherd, the introduction of sheep deprived them of their land, and Australian "shepherds" killed their ancestors. Aboriginal people are individually responsible for special "countries" determined by a complex grid based on place of conception and birth and also kinship lines through parents, yet they lost their "scriptures," the sacred stories inscribed in the landscape and read and preserved through ceremony, receiving a "foreign" scripture instead. As one Aboriginal elder said, *"While European missionaries were pointing our eyes to heaven above, their European brothers were stealing the land from under our feet below . . . before we said Amen, our land was gone."*[28]

Yet Aboriginal Law finds genuine comparisons with ancient Hebrew stories. Aboriginal land was also formless and void at the beginning, waiting for the Creator Spirit, just as the Hebrew story says. The Creator Spirit/Breath of Genesis shared space with the human realm, just as Aboriginal Sacred Beings did, unlike the missionary's GOD who dwelt in some far off, splendid heaven. *"The land is a living place made up of sky, clouds, rivers, trees, the wind, the sand,"* Aboriginal elder Patrick Dodson says, *"and the Spirit has planted my own spirit there, in my country. It is something—and yet it is not a thing—it is a living entity. It belongs to me, I belong to it. I rest in it. I come from there."*[29] The Creating Rainbow Spirit caused plants, animals, fish, and birds to emerge from the land and its waters, as the Genesis account also described: *"Let the earth bring forth living creatures of every kind: cattle and creeping things and wild animals of the earth of every kind"* (Gen. 1:24). Human beings were created from the earth in Aboriginal stories and return to the land at death, each person's spirit belonging to the Creator Spirit, all reminiscent of the Divine Spirit breathing life into clay in Genesis. The Aboriginal concept of different "countries" assigned by kinship lines and the people as stewards is affirmed in Yahweh's covenant with Abraham: *"From one ancestor he made all nations to inhabit the whole earth, and he allotted the times of their existence and the boundaries of the places where they would live"* (Acts 17:26). Perhaps the most refreshing parallel is the Aboriginal version of John 1:1, exchanging the Greek *Logos* with all its philosophical and linguistic baggage for their own Divine metaphor:

> In the beginning was the Rainbow Spirit, deep in the land. And the Rainbow Spirit was with God, the Creator Spirit, and the Rainbow Spirit was God. The Rainbow Spirit was in the beginning with God. The Rainbow Spirit emerged from the land, transformed the land and brought all things into being on the land. With the Rainbow Spirit came life, and the life is the light of all people. [30]

To discuss all the Divine images borrowed from nature—tree, stars, food, wine, tent, shrine, lion, bear, lamb, rainbow, and vine—would take several volumes, but you get the picture. In order to speak of a Presence experienced in their midst as they sat around their fires, our ancestors borrowed images for their stories that would most impact the hearers and evoke wise nods of agreement from above their skin blankets. Such metaphors painted the scene in vivid brushstrokes and colors, pictures that lose immediacy and sensual power in our culture unless, of course, we have camped in the vicinity of wild beasts or need somewhere to hide from a host of arrows coming our way. Who can say which images are closer or closest to the mark, or if any have even an element of truth—we can only speak of the Formless in forms with which we are familiar. "*Let God be God*," theologian Matthew Fox said, "*and show her face in whatever new ways it shows . . . God is in every being, so every being is, in some way, a book about God . . . Whether you're talking tiger or elephant or galaxy or star or you or me, we're all in the image of God. Yet also, God is none of these things.*"[31]

Divine Attributes:
GOD Is Like . . .

> The incomprehensibility of God makes it entirely appropriate,
> at times even preferable, to speak about God in nonpersonal or
> suprapersonal terms. Symbols such as the ground of being
> (Paul Tillich), matrix surrounding and sustaining all life (Rosemary
> Ruether), power of the future (Wolfhart Pannenberg), holy mystery
> (Karl Rahner), all point to divine reality that cannot be captured in
> concepts or images. At the same time, God is not less than
> personal, and many of the most prized characteristics of God's
> relationship to the world, such as fidelity, compassion, and liberating
> love, belong to the human rather than the nonhuman world. Thus it
> is also appropriate, at times even preferable, to speak about God
> in personal symbols.
>
> —Elizabeth Johnson[1]

While the Divine-in-Itself seemed eternally enveloped in mystery, it made sense to ancient peoples that the Divine character might be detectible—not everything about It, but at least some traits of Divinity that might be useful in describing that Something. In Islam, there are some three thousand names for Allah, each expressing a Divine attribute: one thousand known only to the angels, one thousand known only by prophets, three hundred in the Torah, three hundred in the Psalms of David, three hundred in the New Testament, and ninety-nine in the Qur'an.[2] The ninety-nine beautiful names from the Qur'an are recited in Muslim devotion:

The Beneficent, The Merciful, The Sovereign Lord, The Holy, The Source of Peace, The Guardian of Faith, The Protector, The Mighty, The Compeller, The Majestic, The Creator, The Evolver, The Fashioner, The Forgiver, The Subduer, The Bestower, The Provider, The Opener, The All-Knowing, The Constrictor, The Expander, The Abaser, The Exalter, The Honorer, The Dishonorer, The All-Hearing, The All-Seeing, The Judge, The Just, The Subtle One, The Aware, The Forbearing One, The Great One, The All-Forgiving, The Appreciative, The Most High, The Most Great, The Preserver, The Maintainer, The Reckoner (of what people do), The Sublime One, The Generous One, The Watchful, The Responsive, The All-Embracing, The Wise, The Loving, The Most Glorious One, The Resurrector, The Witness, The Truth, The Trustee, The Most Strong, The Firm One, The Protecting Friend, The Praiseworthy, The Reckoner (the number of all things), The Originator, The Restorer, The Giver of Life, The Creator of Death, The Alive, The Self-Subsisting, The Finder, The Noble, The Unique, The One, The Eternal, The Able, The Powerful, The Expediter, The Delayer, The First, The Last, The Manifest, The Hidden, The Governor, The Most Exalted, The Source of All Goodness, The Acceptor of Repentance, The Avenger, The Pardoner, The Compassionate, The Eternal Owner of Sovereignty, The Lord of Majesty and Bounty, The Equitable, The Gatherer, The Self-Sufficient, The Enricher, The Preventer, The Distresser, The Propitious, The Light, The Guide, The Incomparable, The Everlasting, The Supreme Inheritor, The Guide to the Right Path, The Patient.[3]

None, not even all of these together, define the total reality of the One—if that were possible, we would then have to ask what is beyond GOD. Instead, these descriptions are mere pointers to the Mystery, human characteristics that might in some way reflect the Divine. This list also demonstrates how universal and broad are the Divine characteristics across religions, since we look for what we most honor or need in ourselves. We are swamped today with theologians, television evangelists, gurus, and mullahs, telling us exactly what GOD is like, what the Divine thinks, and what we should or should not do, yet such modern self-confidence was anathema in the beginning of religious history. While the ancients might assume a Divine Mind, it was a closed Mind unless that Divine chose some sort of self-revelation.

In order to talk about Something that seriously impacts us (something without impact, like a rock or disinterested energy, needs no special explanation), we need to be able to say why we care about It, and thus we make claims about Its character or attributes with regard to us. It is impossible in a chapter or two to investigate all the characteristics pegged on the Sacred in religious history, nor even all those assigned by Hebrew and Christian stories—even to examine the ninety-nine beautiful Names for Allah would take volumes. Instead, I will highlight in this chapter a few "mega-characteristics" most associated with Divinity in order to show how humanly and culturally shaped they are.

Benjamin Jowett believed that everyone, whether Moses, Maimonides, Buddha, or Gandhi, was searching for Something greater and better than themselves that could be summed up as "the Idea of Good."[4] This is not surprising since Jowett was the Victorian expert on Plato, who is credited with this phrase. Bypassing the eccentric Greek Deities of his day, Plato argued for universal Forms. Everything we see and experience (transient images) has permanent, eternal Forms (realities) that allow these temporal things to exist. A "considered life," therefore, will move from the transient good, true, and beautiful things to the eternal realities behind them, the Forms of the Good, Truth, and Beauty, of which the Good is the highest:

> One who contemplates absolute beauty and is in constant union with it will be able to bring forth not mere reflected images of goodness but true goodness, because one will be in contact not with a reflection but with the truth.[5]

Plato's ideas influenced Augustine, the first comprehensive architect of Christian theology, such that Augustine talked of GOD as *"not only good but Goodness itself."*[6] Despite the repeated Creation chant *"and God saw that it was good"* (Gen. 1), Augustine also had to say something about how evil came to be in the world. Rejecting the dualism of two eternal principles at war, he described evil, not as a created thing, but anything "other than" the good.

This idea of an eternal and "good" Real behind the temporal unreal was not unique to Plato or Greek philosophy. The *Brhadaranyaka Upanishad* says, *"From the unreal (asat) lead me to the real (sat)! From darkness lead me to light! From death lead me to immortality!"*[7] Buddhist Enlightenment was considered a state surpassing human thought that *"can not be made clear by words; it can only be hinted at in parables."*[8] The Sufis also spoke of two worlds coexisting:

There is the outer world which appears to exist, and seems solid and permanent, but in truth is an illusion. And there is the inner world which many people deny, and is invisible to the senses, and yet it is real and eternal . . . The outer form passes away, but the world of meaning remains forever.[9]

Scholars have identified an interesting global development between 800 and 200 BCE in the quest for human meaning. A series of great religious leaders arose across the globe during that time to guide human thought in a positive direction. Prior to this Axial (pivotal) Age, religious life was mostly about propitiating unpredictable and autocratic GODS (who may or may not have a moral code) however one could. In this new era, the concept of a universal, indescribable, benevolent Force, whether GOD or something that energized the human spirit, emerged in Hinduism, Buddhism, Jainism, Daoism, Zoroastrianism, Confucianism, and the Hebrew prophets. Along with this idea of some universal Concern for humanity came new ideas about how to live, including moral fortitude, good works, and an understanding of human unity.

"God is good" is the Christian mantra for everything, whether the mealtime grace "*God is great. God is good. Let us thank Him for our food*" or those void-filling words in situations when the opposite seems more apparent. The phrase rolls off our lips as if the Bible is saturated with this claim, and there is no need for explanation or qualification. Yet this is not so. In fact, when I went online to find all the biblical references to "God is good," I was considerably surprised. Unless I missed a few pages, GOD is not called good in the Hebrew Bible until after the exile. In six hundred verses containing the word "good" in association with GOD, the Creator created a good world, gave good land and gifts to people, told good news, expected humans to be good, knew the difference between good and evil; but not until a liturgical chant after the exile, "*For he [the Lord] is good, for his steadfast love endures forever toward Israel*" (Ezra 3:11), is GOD called good, and the constant repetition of this one phrase accounts for all post-exilic references to what we assume is the fundamental description of GOD.[10] Even then, the phrase makes no attempt to describe the Divine as Ultimate Goodness or Goodness-Itself, as Plato did, nor does it specify what was meant by good—moral, successful, or beautiful? The majority of references linking GOD and goodness, therefore, are about Divine action, such as creating, enduring love, faithfulness, mighty deeds, and deliverance, and how these appeared "good" to the recipients.

"God is good" is surprisingly rare in the New Testament as well. United States president Thomas Jefferson (1743–1862), writing to the president of Yale University about "crazy theologists" speculating amongst themselves and creating schisms, said:

> [Jesus] has told us only that God is good and perfect, but has not defined him. I am, therefore, of his theology, believing that we have neither words nor ideas adequate to that definition. And if we could all, after this example, leave the subject as undefinable, we should all be of one sect, doers of good, and eschewers of evil.[11]

Jefferson was referring to the Gospel story where the rich man asks Jesus, "*Teacher, what good deed must I do to inherit eternal life?*" Jesus answered, "*Why do you ask me about what is good? There is only one who is good*" (Matt. 19:16–17). Mark and Luke put a slightly different answer on Jesus' lips, "*Why do you call me good? No one is good but God alone*" (Mark 10:18). Apart from this one story, the only other comment in the New Testament is a reference back to the Hebrew liturgical chant while urging the faithful to long for spiritual milk, "*if indeed you have tasted that the Lord is good*" (1 Pet. 2:3). As for the popular image of the Good Shepherd, there is one New Testament reference to Jesus as the "good" Shepherd (John 10:11, 14). This imagery mirrored the Hebrew Bible images of GOD as Shepherd to Israel (Ps. 80:1; Isa. 40:11), which did not include the adjective "good" and also raises questions as to what "good" might mean in such imagery—faithful, clever against wild beasts, or morally superior. Given such paucity of biblical references to GOD as "good," we need to ask whether what is assumed to be a central biblical claim originated more from Plato, through the pen of Augustine, who was always so concerned about moral good and evil. This is not to deny Divine Goodness in any way; it is simply a wake-up call as to the origins and interpretations of claims we make about the Divine.

And what of the opposite possibility? In the novel *Angela's Ashes*, Angela is confiding her frustrations to friend Bridey about her unemployed alcoholic husband and never-ending pregnancies producing both dead and living babies. Bridey scolds her by saying, "*God is good.*"

Angela replies that God may be good for someone somewhere, *"but He hadn't been seen lately in the lanes of Limerick."* When Bridey tells Angela she will go to hell for saying such things, Angela replies, *"Aren't I there already?"*[12] The problem with assuming the Divine metaphor of Good, whether Plato's Form or one gleaned from scripture passages, is that contradictions inevitably present themselves that have to be defused with theological gymnastics. How can you defend an all-good, all-powerful GOD when evil exists in the world? Either the All-Powerful One can prevent evil and won't, or wants to prevent evil but can't. In the former, GOD is not merciful or good; in the latter, GOD is not omnipotent. Many attempts have been made down the years to solve this "theodicy" dilemma (discussed later), including limiting or redefining Divine power, reinterpreting free will in all sorts of ways, or even suggesting GOD created both good and evil. *"Not even on the most distorted and contracted theory of good which ever was framed by religious or philosophical fanaticism,"* John Stuart Mill wrote in Victorian times, *"can the government of nature be made to resemble the work of a being at once good and omnipotent..."*[13] Such is the problem when we cement in place a Divine attribute that invites other awkward questions.

What does it mean to say that GOD is good anyway? Is good a moral, aesthetic, or physical category? It would be silly to limit the Divine satisfaction at creation *"and God saw that it was good"* to "moral" good, yet early in Christian history, good became irrevocably linked with evil as the church obsessed over morals. Yet "good" can also mean harmonious, beautiful, and lovely. Some Australian Aboriginal Christians use *Marrkapmirr*, meaning "altogether lovely and worthy of affection" as a term of endearment for GOD. What a difference if children first encountered Divine Loveliness rather than the moralistic Sky GOD judging every move. What a difference if countries ceased labeling each other morally good or evil, according to their own agendas, and sought instead the recovery of harmonious relationships. The parable of the prodigal son is usually preached as the father forgiving his son's moral weaknesses, but this was not why the son returned— he wanted to restore relationships even if it meant settling for something less than that of a parent and child (Luke 15:11–32). "Good" as an aesthetic category strives for a peaceful, relational world while always acknowledging that people can refuse to love each other, and that the Divine can never force anyone to be "good" or to form empowering relationships. It is worth putting this book down for a moment to reflect on how it would be if we spoke of the Divine, the world, and ourselves as "good" in aesthetic rather than moral terms. So caught up in good versus evil debates, we have lost that sensual Love and Beauty that Rabindranath Tagore described:

> Thou ever pourest for me the fresh draught of thy wine of various colors and fragrance, filling this earthen vessel to the brim. My world will light its hundred different lamps with thy flame and place them before the altar of thy temple. No, I will never shut the doors of my senses. The delights of sight and hearing and touch will bear thy delight.[14]

Assigning Divine goodness to the aesthetic box is not something I pulled out of my hat—it is no stranger to religion. Thomas Aquinas called the Divine the most beautiful thing in the universe; philosopher Alfred North Whitehead (1861–1947) described GOD as *"the poet of the world, with tender patience leading it by his vision of truth, beauty and goodness"*;[15] Dag Hammarskjöld said that *"all things have meaning and beauty in that space beyond time where Thou [the Divine] art"*;[16] and Turkish poet Fazil (1904–1983) wrote, *"Beauty, wherever it is seen, whether in humanity or in the vegetable or mineral world, is God's revelation of Himself; He is the all-beautiful."*[17] I remember one day racing from place to place with hectic little jobs. As I swung into a parking lot to pick up some theater tickets, all around the theater entrance had been excavated and a narrow wooden plank placed temporarily to escort patrons across the chaotic building site. Recent rain had added a layer of black, sticky mud to the debris, broken tiles, steel construction beams, and machinery. However, on the stump of an old tree sacrificed in the name of progress, someone had placed a gold-painted Grecian urn overflowing with yellow and orange plastic flowers, no doubt an old theater prop. Although totally fake and a tad tacky, it stood as an intimation of beauty and color in the chaos. I stopped for a minute, smiled, connected with the construction site artist and my place in the world, and then stepped on with a lighter, calmer step.

Stunned at the dearth of "God is good" biblical references, I nervously typed "love" into the online Bible, thinking I might also blow this traditional assumption. Rest assured. The Hebrew Bible is full of GOD as Love, especially Yahweh's steadfast love and covenantal faithfulness: *"I have loved you with an everlasting love; therefore I have continued my faithfulness to you*" (Jer. 31:3). This Divine love was not dependent on what the Israelites did to earn that love, although Yahweh did get angry when they disobeyed and even regretted making humans at one point. Instead, it was a relational mothering love of compassion and perseverance: "*Can a woman forget her nursing child, or show no compassion for the child of her womb? Even these may forget, yet I will not forget you*" (Isa. 49:15). While disobedience required repentance and restoration, the covenant never ceased because of the steadfast love of Yahweh. When Jesus was asked to nominate the most important commandment, he did not select from the famous Ten but combined two from the plethora of Hebrew laws that included things like not using a chisel on a stone altar (Exod. 20:25), how long a male slave could be kept (Exod. 21:2), and the number of sheep to be paid for slaughtering another person's animal (Exod. 22:1). The following passages—"*You shall love the Lord your God with all your heart, and with all your soul, and with all your migh*t" (Deut. 6:5) and "*The alien who resides with you shall be to you as the citizen among you; you shall love the alien as yourself, for you were aliens in the land of Egypt*" (Lev. 19:34)—became, on Jesus' lips, "*You shall love the Lord your God with all your heart and with all your soul, and with all your strength, and with all your mind; and your neighbor as yourself*" (Luke 10:27). Rather than moral commandments about adultery, theft, and falsehood, these described an aesthetic, relational response—harmony, not "oughts," and loving and being loved, not good and evil. Loving GOD and others for a moral reward (heaven), or out of fear (hell) is hardly true love, and loving the unlovable just because we should is hardly compassion. If only those who demand the Big Ten be posted in every public place in America to return us to moral values would settle instead for the commandments Jesus chose.

Very few of the forty-four references to love in the Gospels are about GOD as love, however. Apart from a passing comment in Luke (11:42), all such verses are in John's Gospel (and 1 John, probably from the same community). It is interesting to ponder that, had John's Gospel not been included in the New Testament canon (and it was in doubt), there would be hardly any Gospel references to GOD as love. This dominant emphasis in John's Gospel has an explanation. Recently excluded from the synagogue, John's community needed assurance that Yahweh's steadfast covenantal love was still theirs outside Judaism: "*They who have my commandments and keep them are those who love me; and those who love me will be loved by my Father"* (John 14:21). The covenant is now no longer about keeping the moral laws but about loving GOD and each other:

> Beloved let us love one another, because love is from God; everyone who loves is born of God and knows God. Whoever does not love does not know God for God is love . . . God is love, and those who abide in love abide in God, and God abides in them. (1 John 4:7–8, 16)

Divine Love appears in many religions, expressed in their own unique metaphors. One of the most beautiful creation imageries comes from the Hindu *Rig-Veda*—you can almost feel and see the events unfolding in Technicolor:

> There was not then what is nor what is not. There was no sky, no heaven beyond the sky. What power was there? Where? Who was that power? Was there an abyss of fathomless waters? There was neither death nor immortality then. No signs were there of night or day. The One was breathing by its own power, in infinite peace. Only the One was: there was nothing beyond. Darkness was hidden in darkness. The all was fluid and formless. Therein, in the void, by the fire of fervor arose the One. And in the One arose love: Love the first seed of the soul. [18]

The creation of Love is also found in Greek stories. In the beginning, formless Chaos was brooded over by unbroken darkness. Two children were born to Chaos, Black-winged Night (darkness) and Erebus (the unfathomable depth where death dwells), and these two gave birth to Love, *"the longed-for, shining, with wings of gold."*[19] The Hebrew creation story is also about Love and relationship. The Creator created humans for conversation in the garden in the cool of the evening and then made skin coats for them against the cold, beautiful, and practical images of friendship and love in the Palestinian environment. Upanishad translator Juan Mascaró reiterates this imagery in Hinduism: *"God has need of us, even as we have need of God. Why should God need us, unless it were to give us His love?"* [20] Hindu avatars are incarnations of this Divine Love and their male/female unions, Krishna and Radha, Shiva and Shakti, model the Divine-human union, a union not dependent on what humans do, but on a relationship. *"If I call not thee in my prayers,"* the poet Tagore said, *"if I keep not thee in my heart, thy love for me still waits for my love."*[21]

Divine Love is not something theoretical or vague but also suggests a Divine Lover. Our Hebrew ancestors had an earthy and healthy respect for love and marriage in all its physicality and did not hesitate to use erotic, sexual love as a metaphor for Divine encounters. The most striking example is the Song of Solomon, which began life as a love song of ancient Mesopotamia, perhaps sung at a wedding to describe the physical delights a young couple would find in each other. The lovers express sexual delight in each other in a mutually satisfying relationship free of moral or gendered hierarchies: *"Upon my bed at night I sought him whom my soul loves"* (3:1); *"O that his left hand were under my head, and that his right hand embraced me!"* (2:6); *"Let him kiss me with the kisses of his mouth!"* (1:2); *"My beloved is mine and I am his"* (2:16). Both desire, feel, and speak boldly to the other with sexual energy and personal power, taking turns to lead and lingering in uninhibited expressions of delight over the other's body, stroking with hands and words: *"As a lily among brambles, so is my love among maidens. As an apple tree among the trees of the wood, so is my beloved among young men* (Song of Sol. 2:2–3). In a more subdued medieval way, Maimonides would also mirror this enthusiasm of his ancestors in answer to the question "What is the love of God?"

> It is to love the Eternal with a great and exceeding love, so strong that one's soul shall be knit up with the love of God, and one should be continually enraptured by it, like a love-sick individual, whose mind is at no time free from his passion for a particular woman: the thought of her fills his heart at all times, whether eating or drinking.[22]

Celibate Christian theologians spiritualized the overt sexual imagery of the Song of Solomon into the celibate Christ's love for the church. By the fourth century, anything to do with sex had been effectively rooted out from the "courts of the Father" as sin—the Divine King/Father should evoke awe and fear, not a sexual response. We are still suffering from the fall-out of such theology. In contrast to the wedding in Song of Solomon, Christian marriages, until recently, only hinted at lovemaking and then only in connection with reproducing the species. In classes where I explore all sorts of Divine imagery, including that of Lover, I ask students to comment on which images work for them. Even among youngish, progressive women in healthy relationships whose experiences of love are no doubt associated with erotic, physical expression, there is always a distinct hesitancy to follow the Hebrew lead and take seriously any Divine image that suggests anything sexual. A classical exception to this, however, was a woman student struggling to describe an intense mystical experience when another older woman, totally absorbed in her classmate's story, blurted out to affirm her—"like having an orgasm." Everyone went silent, the woman who had said the words more stunned than anyone, and then the whole class broke into delighted laughter, realizing the silliness of not being free to speak of one of the most powerful everyday love metaphors from human experience. The poet Tagore had no such qualms:

> He [God] it is, the innermost one, who awakens my being with his deep hidden touches. He it is who puts his enchantment upon these eyes and joyfully plays on the cords of my heart in varied cadences of pleasure and pain. He it is who . . . lets peep out through the folds his feet, at whose touch I forget myself.[23]

Nor did the mystics occupying the margins of the institutional church have such qualms—they reveled in erotic language and simply fell in love with the Divine, running with all the sexual imagery of the Song of Solomon to describe their union with their Lover. For Mechtild of Magdeburg, her Divine Lover desired her from before the world began as she also desired Divine Love: "*And where the desires of two come together there love is perfected.*"[24] Hadewijch of Antwerp, a thirteenth-century Beguine, was overpowered by her Lover, the strong one against her weakness: "*She does with me what she wishes; / Nothing of myself remains to me.*"[25] Rabi'a, orphaned, made homeless, and sold into slavery in eighth-century Basra (Iraq), was finally released by her master when he saw a light illumine her while she prayed. After becoming a hermit, Rabi'a wrote, "*Kings have locked their doors and each lover is alone with his love. Here, I am alone with You.*"[26] In a class on Valentine's Day, a single red rose lay on each desk as my students arrived, placed there by another student who had struggled for years with ambivalent messages about GOD, sexuality, male power and abuse, and had found liberation and new Divine images during the course. Explaining the roses, she said, "Through this class, I have found my Valentine." The metaphor of Lover does introduce the distraction of anthropomorphism, however, if we focus on lovers rather than what passes between them—Love. Because we are steeped in a Divine Being with whom we relate, we constantly stray into language about the love of a GOD, rather than imaging Love itself as the manifested Sacred in the world, free of any "idol" form.

What exactly *is* Love? "*Love is one of those big words that live on the right side of human worth*," George O'Brien said. "*But, like physics and ice hockey, it has to be carried on with inadequate equipment . . . Those who preach love as the world's solution often have an exaggerated notion about our abilities in the field.*"[27] I find it helpful to imagine Love as a unifying, reconciling Force within this universe, operative in different degrees in different people, including Jesus, Dorothy Day, and Martin Luther King. Love is invisible, but I see manifestations or incarnations of what I imagine It to be in the lives and actions of those around me. At the memorial service of a dear friend who left some twenty grandchildren ranging in age from twenty-one to newborns, three of the older grandchildren presented a combined eulogy to their grandmother, supporting each other through tears and tissues as they read what they had composed. As one broke down, arms encircled her as another kept reading over her shoulder until the first one recovered sufficiently to continue. Their message was about the love and encouragement they had experienced from their grandmother and how they would miss both this and her. Looking directly at two cousins still babies in arms, one of them said, "*You will never know, as we do, what Grandma's love was like, and so we take responsibility to tell you about her and try and give you a taste of her love.*" My friend had achieved "immortality" through the Love that possessed her and which she had passed on to her grandchildren. The dying Morrie in *Tuesdays with Morrie* also speaks about this immortality:

> As long as we can love each other, and remember the feeling of love we had, we can die without every really going away. All the love you created is still there. All the memories are still there. You live on—in the hearts of everyone you have touched and nurtured while you were here . . . death ends a life, not a relationship.[28]

Divine Love encompasses other attributes—the center of any true religion is said to be compassion, "suffering with." Compassionate Bodhisattvas forfeited Nirvana in order to remain in the world until all were saved: "*As long as beings who are still reappearing suffer, may I become their medicine, their doctor and their nurse, until everyone is healed.*"[29] Yahweh was called El Rachum, the Compassionate or Merciful One: "*Because the Lord your God is a merciful God, he will neither abandon you nor destroy you*" (Deut. 4:31). The Qur'an calls Allah "*the Cherisher and Sustainer of the worlds*" (Surah 1:), what Rev. Zebedee Masereka of Uganda described as making sure that "*what He has created, He will hold onto. He makes sure He sticks on you.*"[30] Love and Mercy includes protection and refuge in whatever form that takes—rock, fortress, stronghold, deliverer, or everlasting arms. The word *Islam*, generally translated as "surrender," comes from the same root "s-l-m" as its Hebrew cognate "sh-l-m" (shalom), peace and safely.[31] And GOD as "savior" or "liberator" also comes from a practical, this-worldly desire for refuge and deliverance. "*In the Caribbean,*" Rev. Everson T. Sieunarine says, "*we speak of a Liberating God who always frees, whether it's women from psychological or physical bondage, people from abuse, youth to think and imagine their future, people not to be enslaved by politicians.*"[32]

A saving, liberating, protecting GOD produces hope. According to Auschwitz survivor Primo Levi, if the prisoners had been told at the end of a long winter that they would spend another winter in camp, they would have just grabbed the electric fence, yet even when they did face the next winter, they did not end it all because of a "*last senseless crazy residue of unavoidable hope.*"[33] What is hope? The Hebrew word suggests waiting, trust, expectation, and confidence: "*For you, O Lord, are my hope*" (Ps. 71:5), the conviction that Yahweh would fulfill the Divine promises as long as they were faithful. When both Israel and Judah were destroyed, hope seemed to be a third victim, yet as we trace Hebrew history through its postexilic years, hope returned, bolstered with new scenarios. In the New Testament, hope was the badge of the true believer—but what of those for whom GOD does not seem good, loving, faithful, or sustaining? What of those who have no hope or see no reason for hope within the world? What of those who have placed themselves within Divine love and protection, believing the promise that "*no evil shall befall you, no scourge come near your tent*" (Ps. 91:10), yet have not experienced things that way? Is hope real, or is it—hopeless?

Goodness, love, protection, and source of hope as Divine characteristics still force us to cross our fingers behind our backs at times, hoping that someone will not challenge us with evidence of One that is not loving, not protective, not always good. Let's face it, we still grasp in the dark for sturdy enough pegs on which to hang our Divine images, and many opt for Leo Tolstoy's conclusion: *"I did believe in something, without being able to say what it was. I believed in God, or rather I did not deny God, but what kind of God I could not have said."*[34] What is GOD like? If we are truthful, the attributes we assign to the Divine come from our experience (or lack of it) of the Something (or nothing), and they will be our faith statement, our decision as to how we will view the world: *"To acknowledge that which we cannot see, to give definition to that which we do not know, to create divine order out of chaos, is the religious dance."*[35]

The Power
of the One

What if there are ways of conceiving a just and loving God
    other than on the model of omnipotence?
What if there are ways of imagining divine power
    that do not make a mockery of human freedom?
What if the divine power can achieve its purpose in the world
    only if we join with it in the project
    of co-creating a more loving and just world?

                   —*Carol P. Christ*[1]

According to author Jack Miles, "*Much that the Bible says about* [God] *is rarely preached from the pulpit because, examined too closely, it becomes a scandal.*"[2] While talk about Divine love, refuge, mercy, and goodness is decidedly comforting and secure, we do not have to read far into any religious tradition to find that people have also identified a wild, angry, and fearful Divine as well. The consequences of disobedience to Yahweh spelled out clearly in the Law were far from warm and fuzzy. While steadfast love was promised to those who kept the covenant, the opposite was true for the defiant: "*I the Lord your God am a jealous God, punishing children for the iniquity of parents, to the third and the fourth generation of those who reject me*" (Exod. 20:5). Thunder and lightning crashed around the terrified desert wanderers as they pleaded with Moses to protect them from Divine judgment, to which Moses replied in less than comforting words: "*Do not be afraid; for God has come only to test you and to put the fear of him upon you so that you do not sin*" (Exod. 20:20). Anna Leonowens of *Anna and the King of Siam* fame, while teaching English to one of the King's many children, read aloud the passage, *"For whom the Lord loveth he correcteth; even as a father the son in whom he delighteth"* (Prov. 3:12, KJV). The little girl looked up at Leonowens and asked anxiously, *"Does thy God do that? Ah! Lady, are all the Gods angry and cruel? Has he no pity, even for those who love him? He must be like my father, he loves us, so he has to be rye [cruel], that we may fear evil and avoid it."*[3]

Juxtapositioned here is what Rudolph Otto called the *mysterium tremendum et fascinans*, a mix of paralyzing terror producing inward shuddering, and an irresistible fascination or desire to draw closer.[4] This is why holy places have usually been separated from everyday life. While Aboriginal people of northwestern Australia did not know Otto's Latin phrase, they felt the same awe, respect, and inadequacy as they approached their sacred Wandjina figure paintings on the rock walls of caves, first announcing their presence and intentions and then asking permission to enter. Holy places in Hebrew society, whether the initial Tent of Meeting or later the Holy of Holies in the temple, were kept distinct from daily life so that Yahweh could not be approached casually, but with a deep awareness of creaturely inadequacy. When Isaiah was confronted by Yahweh in the temple, he cried: *"Woe is me! I am lost, for I am a man of unclean lips, and live among a people of unclean lips; yet my eyes have seen the King, the Lord of Hosts"* (Isa. 6:5). Respect and fear are two sides of the one coin—only contemporary thinking has converted GOD into a best buddy who never scares us or acts contrary to our will. Richard Rodriguez experienced this ambivalence growing up. In his American Catholic school, he was a sinner before the all-powerful Divine Judge, Christ the Sacrifice, and the Virgin Mother, who squashed the serpent of sin under her foot. By third grade, he had learned to distinguish between venial and mortal sins, sins of commission and omission, perfect and imperfect contrition, limbo and purgatory, heaven and hell. In his Mexican immigrant home, however, he and his family were suppliants rather than sinners—*"We prayed for favors and at desperate times,"* Rodriguez remembers. GOD was the One with the power, not to judge and punish, but to empower their vulnerable lives, and his mother's Mexican and South American saints interceded for them, especially the Mexican Virgin Nuestra Senora de Guadalupe. *"She could have appeared to anyone in the whole world, but she appeared to a Mexican . . . dark, just like me,"* his mother would say.[5]

While Divine Love was expressed as fidelity and loyalty, looking out for the chosen people, Divine Anger was the response to disloyalty or disobedience: *"We are consumed by your anger; by your wrath we are overwhelmed."* (Ps. 90:7). In a culture where disasters were Divinely orchestrated and natural laws waived by Divine will, Yahweh's wrath was often demonstrated through the powers of nature—blight, pestilence, famine, and flood. Since Divine Anger is mentioned over five hundred times in the Hebrew Bible, the message was simple: *"No harm happens to the righteous, but the wicked are filled with trouble"* (Prov. 12:21). In the New Testament, Paul begins his letter to the Romans with the warning: *"The wrath of God is revealed from heaven against all ungodliness and wickedness of those who by their wickedness suppress the truth"* (1:18). Most of us today (but not all) have severed that direct connection between natural events and Divine power, since we understand the workings of nature better and know its vagaries are not Divinely orchestrated, yet this attitude is relatively recent. One hundred and fifty years ago, Florence Nightingale challenged such prayers for deliverance in the Book of Common Prayer that began *"Although we for our iniquities have worthily deserved a plague of rain and water . . ."* or *"We do now most justly suffer for our iniquity . . ."* *"What is faith?"* she asked. *"Is it belief that God will break his own laws, that he will vary from the nature whence they spring?"*[6]

The question at stake is omnipotence, GOD as all-powerful, another taken-for-granted belief about the Divine, like goodness and love. What does it mean? Some say it means GOD can do anything and everything, but if we are honest, this raises problems. Can the Divine do things that are logically contradictory, like draw a square triangle, or only what is possible to be done? As for free will, if we have this, can GOD manipulate us to do the Divine will, and if so, did we have free will in the first place if our actions and will are determined by GOD or can be overridden? *"It is impossible that our act should be both free and yet a logical consequence of a divine action which 'infallibly' produces its effect,"* philosopher Charles Hartshorne (1897–2000) argued. *"Power to cause someone to perform by his own choice an act precisely defined by the cause is meaningless."*[7] The London *Daily Telegraph* of July 3, 2004, reported a novel excuse from the Indian Railway Minister for the dreadful safety record of India's rail network, the largest in the world and averaging some three hundred accidents a year on sixty-seven thousand miles of track used by thirteen million passengers daily. "Indian railways are the responsibility of Lord Vishwakarma [the Hindu God of Machines]," said the Railway Minister, "so is the safety of passengers. It is his duty [to ensure safety], not mine." In his seventeenth-century epic *Paradise Lost*, John Milton espoused the same sort of passive submission: *"Prayer against his absolute decree no more prevails than breath against the wind."*[8]

And what about evil? If GOD is both all-powerful and all-good, why does evil exist and why does a loving GOD permit suffering (the "theodicy" question mentioned earlier)? In Albert Camus' novel *The Plague*, a little town in France infected with the plague is cordoned off from the rest of the world for months. Father Paneloux, the local priest, believed the plague was sent as Divine punishment and thus could not be questioned. *"We must accept the dilemma and choose either to hate God or to love God,"* he said, *"and who would dare to choose to hate Him?"*[9] This dilemma has been around at least as long as the Greeks and comes from trying to hold three "truths" together—GOD is all-good, GOD is all-powerful, and evil exists. As Greek philosopher Epicurus (341–270) said, *"God either wishes to take away evils, and is unable: or He is able, and is unwilling; or He is neither able nor willing: or He is both willing and able."*[10] Thus we dive into the muddy discussion of whether GOD wants to do certain things and chooses not to do them, or whether GOD cannot do everything and is thus impotent in some situations. When Rabbi Harold Kushner's son was dying from a terrible illness suffered since birth, the books Kushner turned to for comfort *"were more concerned with defending God's honor, with logical proof that bad is really good and that evil is necessary to make this a good world, than they were with curing the bewilderment and the anguish of the parent of a dying child. They had answers to all their own questions, but no answer for mine."*[11] Arguments aplenty have been launched in the Divine defense. Some say GOD self-limits the Divine self; others talk about GOD causing all things, even the bad; some talk of a greater purpose not seen in seemingly contradictory events of life, a sure way to silence questions; and still others simply call it a mystery and continue to claim contradictory Divine attributes. Some prior questions, however, which may help us move beyond our dilemma include: What does omnipotence mean? How did it come to be assigned to the Divine? Why is an all-powerful GOD so essential for some people, and what type of power is being claimed?

Power joined the list of Divine attributes very early in religious history as humans sought Something to protect them against their seemingly impossible foes, human and cosmic. Israel was no exception. Although ancient Palestine later reaped considerable exposure from Christianity's appropriation of its history, it was actually an area only 250 miles long and averaging 50 miles wide.[12] During biblical times, its population is estimated as around 150,000, with the biggest cities only some 3,000 strong. In King Solomon's time, Jerusalem would have been like a tiny country village today, with about 2,000 people. Palestine was extremely vulnerable politically, squashed as it was between the powerful civilizations of Egypt and Mesopotamia. Constantly overrun by enemy tribes, ruled by a succession of political powers, short on natural resources with its scraggy hills, poor soil, and scarcity of water, it was a marginal society and economy in so many respects. The majority of its inhabitants were poor, subsistence farmers scratching out a living, if they owned land at all, giving credence to the prophets' relentless calls for justice for the "poor of the land." Palestine's political history was scarcely better—"*nasty, brutish, and short, characterized by dissension, treachery, corruption, frequent bloody assassinations, and ultimately the failure to create a viable state*," according to archeologist William Dever. The good life for which they dreamed was not on the scale of affluent Western expectations, but simply a time when tribal wars would cease and they could enjoy, without threat, the fruits of productive farms and vineyards. "*It may be unsettling to some readers,*" Dever says, "*but the fact is that ancient Israel was an obscure cultural and historical backwater of the ancient Near East. It would have been long forgotten except for its one memorable contribution to civilization: the Hebrew Bible, and the memory of Israel's faith and vision of human destiny that it enshrines.*"[13]

Affirmations of Yahweh's power litter the Hebrew Bible—the Lord strong and mighty, mighty in battle (Ps. 24:8); the awesome Lord most High (Ps. 47:2); the Deliverer (Ps. 3:8); Wonderful Counselor, Mighty GOD (Isa. 9:6); the One who made the earth by Divine power (Jer. 10:12). When Christianity adopted this Jewish story and added splashes of Greek philosophy, the concept of Divine power became cemented in the creeds, "I believe in God, the Father Almighty." Ever since, the traditional understanding of Divine power has been that of might, ultimate control, and benevolent domination. GOD created the world, governs it, has divine purposes for it, and is in control of its future. The "omni" in omnipotent indicates that Divine power is not like ours but is unrestricted and unsurpassed. Although medieval theologians enjoyed asking hypothetical questions about what omnipotence actually meant, John Calvin refused to limit it in any way, saying that omnipotence was the Divine ability to do whatever the Divine willed, remembering, of course, that the Divine moral character would not countenance anything arbitrary or capricious. The Geneva Catechism's definition of "almighty" says that GOD *"has all things under his power and hand; so that he governs all the world by his providence, constitutes all things by his will and rules all creatures as seems to him good."*[14] Calvin imaged this Divine power metaphorically in the roles of Lord and King (sovereign governance) and as Father (providential care), and by making unlimited Divine power central to his theology, he had no choice but to also admit Divine responsibility for evil, qualifying this confession by saying that GOD uses evil to bring about good and that the guilt for evil is on humans, not GOD. While Calvin argued his way out thus, it is difficult to hold such conflicting "truths" in our world without being twisted in contradictory knots.

This image of Divine omnipotence is shared with Islam, the cousin of Judaism and Christianity. The word *Islam* means both submission to Allah's will and the peace gained by submission. Allah is all-powerful and all-predestining, and everything happens within the will of Allah: *"You shall not will except as Allah wills"* (Surah 81:29). In the Qur'an, Allah tells Muhammad, *"Would you, perhaps, torment yourself to death [with grief] because they would not believe? If We will, We can send down to them from the skies a sign before which their necks will remain bent in submission"* (Surah 26:1–4). Given all this, how can one argue for free will? Rumi made an attempt:

> When God assigns a particular lot to a person, this does not preclude consent, desire and freedom. God sends suffering to all of us from time to time. Some react by fleeing from God; others react by moving closer to him . . . each person freely decides how to respond.[15]

Muslim Canadian journalist Irshad Manji is not convinced. Such "out-sized reliance" on the Divine simply minimizes the human role and leads to passivity, she says:

> "Inshallah," we instinctively sigh. "If God wills." No. We must will. We've got to be God's partners in the journey to justice. "But who are we?" some of you might ask. After all, it's drilled into us that God is great! "Allahu Akbar!" Only when I educated myself did I learn the actual meaning of this phrase—God is greater. Greater than His creatures, yes, but that's not a statement of our inconsequence.[16]

Are there different ways to understand Divine power? After all, there are many descriptions and images of how power works within our world. Why did we select this particular one of ultimate "power over" for the Divine? I hate to point the finger at the Greeks again, but an unchanging, independent, all-powerful Perfection comes more from Greek philosophy than from the dust of Palestine where Yahweh strug-gled, had changes of mind, repented of having created humanity, and lived out Hebrew history step by evolving step. The Greeks said that a changing GOD could not be perfect because change led to something better or worse, thus admitting an imperfection prior to or after the change. GOD also had to be totally independent and separate from the world, unaffected by it, had to know everything (omniscient), and had to be all-powerful. In the twentieth century, Charles Hartshorne and others have challenged these notions, suggesting that such a Divine Being was a tyrant over its subjects, something we no longer respect in real life. If Something is all-powerful, it means that everything else has no power; if Something is totally independent of us, it cannot love because love means being moved and affected by the suffering and joy of others. *"Divine sovereignty sounds to some of us like a confession,"* Hartshorne says, *"an admission that it is sheer power, not unstinted love that one most admires . . . No worse falsehood was ever perpe-trated than the traditional concept of omnipotence. It is a piece of unconscious blasphemy."*[17]

Using the ideas of his predecessor Alfred North Whitehead, Hartshorne turned the Greek tables on the all-good, all-powerful tran-scendent GOD, saying instead that *"God is involved in world process in such a way as to influence, lure, persuade, empower it, but not to control, coerce, or manipulate it . . . God may be thought of as the universal Eros that draws all things to godself.*"[18] This immanent persuasive Power that lures us and the world toward harmony and richness, toward the good and the beautiful, is the maximal capacity to influence and be influenced, a Power not of domination or "power over" but of empowerment, "power with." In contrast to an omnipotent GOD, persuasive Power does not impose from without a cradle-to-grave predetermined plan on the world and its individuals, censoring those who go astray. Rather, It offers the best possibilities for transformation in each moment, persuading us to accept them but then working within our choices, good or bad, toward transformation in the next moment, an ever-evolving process (these ideas are called process theology, discussed later in the book). Such Power does not conflict with human free will because the lured person has the responsibility to accept the lure or not.

Nor does it raise the theodicy question "Why do bad things happen to good people?" because, since humans and the world are free to reject such persuasion, Divine Power does not control all the events of the world, even though seeing the best possibilities. Such Power can therefore be impotent in situations where we and the world choose lesser options or simply repeat past behavior, and the future also remains open depending on the sequence of choices made in our world. Since this Empowering Power is the very "life-blood" within everything and involved in every interconnected moment, It is also affected, suffering when human choices cause suffering and pain for themselves, others, the world—and GOD. This is the GOD of Harold Kushner who, faced with the contradictions of an all-powerful, all-good GOD at his son's death, refused, like Job, the religious platitudes:

> I would rather affirm God's goodness while compromising his power. I would rather believe in a God who sees things happening that he does not want to happen but cannot stop them. I think goodness is of more religious value than power. [19]

Rather than an all-powerful GOD choosing to help some and not others, bad things happen to good people because the laws of nature do not differentiate between good and bad people, and because people, individually or corporately, refuse the persuasive Power's invitation toward mending creation and its creatures. Kushner could thus interpret the

Holocaust as a psychological rather than a theological question. *"How could people have done such things to each other?"* he asks. *"How could human beings have so totally misused the freedom that God gave us? At the very outset, God said he would give us that freedom so we could choose good over evil, and he would not take it away, no matter how dangerous we were to his creatures."*[20]

The possibility of Divine impotence, even though it offers an answer for the theodicy question, is not so comforting to those who want GOD to be a transcendent, all-powerful "Fix-it" Creator. Even those who live happily every day with persuasive Power cry out in times of crisis to a GOD who might just once break the natural laws. In one of Susan Howatch's novels, a conversation between two Anglican priests highlights these different Powers. Refuting an external all-powerful GOD, priest Aysgarth says:

> If you make the mistake of seeing God as utterly transcendent, a remote force which shoots off the occasional impossibility whenever it chooses to do so, then of course you'll wind up by deciding He's above the laws of science and you'll be seeing miracles everywhere. But the Modernists prefer to think of God as immanent in the world, working through the laws of science and nature. They believe that if only one can dispose of this archaic and unhelpful model of the transcendent God, one can form a theology which is far more pertinent to the mid-twentieth century.

The second priest, Mellors, defends the traditional image of an all-powerful GOD somewhere beyond the world and acting on it:

> What utter rubbish! If we've got to be alive in the middle of this abominable century, the last thing we need is an immanent God who's wallowing around in this disgusting pig-sty with us—we want a God up above the mess, who can lean down and haul us out of it! It's your model of God which is unhelpful and archaic! . . . The road to redemption is decked with blood, sweat and tears, not in moonlight, red roses and a bunch of angels twanging harps.[21]

Such imaging of Divine Power working within the world crosses religions. In Maori traditions, *mana* as power and identity is the sacred essence within a person, the loss of which can cause a breakdown, and the Dakota Indian word for GOD means "something powerful" and is used for anything deemed powerful. When the missionaries first heard the Dakotans using this GOD-word for many different things, they thought they had many GODS, but they were simply recognizing that mysterious internal Power that all things possess to varying degrees. A rather beautiful metaphor of the nurturing life-giving Power in which we live, and without which we cannot live, comes from the Sikhs: *"You are the ocean, embracing all, knowing and seeing all. How can I, a fish in the ocean, ever perceive the limit of what you are? Wherever I look, there you are. If I leave you, I gasp and die."*[22] The doctrine of GOD as separate from the world and creating *ex nihilo* (out of nothing) is actually not in the Hebrew Bible, but was a later theological development to argue that the Almighty was the ultimate Source of all that is—that there was nothing before and nothing equal to the Omnipotent One. In the Genesis story, however, the Creator creates within the formless void and darkness, an already existing primordial chaos from which the Creator brought forth order and design. This Creating Power *within* the world then and now invites and needs our cooperation as co-creators to continue to mend creation, or in another metaphorical image, since this immanent persuasive Power is the center of the Universe, we are "in" GOD's Body.

While the omnipotent GOD was traditionally dressed in the robes of King, Father, Warrior, and Lord, male "power-over" images in a male-led society, the image of persuasive Power working within the world as GOD's body is a more feminine image—nurturing life in the womb, nourishing life from breasts and body, ongoing feeding and encouraging into maturity. Before the link was made between intercourse and conception, ancient women were considered "powerful" because they could create and bring forth life from their bodies unaided, or with the help of the GODS, a different type of power from monarchical power. Yet we must be careful not to fall into the same trap of assuming persuasive power as exclusively feminine, just as dominating power has been labeled masculine. Some ancient GODDESSES were powerful rulers and warriors, and many children, even in middle age, find it almost impossible to escape a dominating mother, especially when this maternal "power over" is claimed as nurturing concern. A student once protested vehemently in class when another student wished her husband would "babysit" their children more often. Why is it "babysitting" when the father nurtures and not when the mother is in charge, she asked? She had just come from the courts, where her son, the primary caregiver for his child, had come close to losing child custody to his ex-wife simply because she was the mother, even though she showed little interest in her child.

There are plenty of folk who will put up with unbelievable horrors and grinding oppression believing that somehow this is the predestining, all-powerful Divine Will and forgetting, or perhaps are unaware, of biblical images of persuasive Power within us. In Psalm 139, this empowering Spirit knows us, even in our mother's womb (v. 13), hems us in behind and before (v. 5), is ever present (v. 7), and directs us toward change and transformation: "*Search me, O God, and know my heart; test me and know my thoughts. See if there is any wicked way in me, and lead me in the way everlasting*" (v. 23–24). The constant theme of the Gospels is empowering by the Divine Spirit, whether of individuals or communities. Jesus invites his followers to abide in the Father as he abides in the Father—us in Divinity and Divinity in us (John 14:17, 20). Luke says the Kingdom of GOD is among or within you (Luke 17: 21), as does the Gospel of Thomas, which did not make it into the canon: "*If you bring forth what is within you, what you bring forth will save you. If you do not bring forth what is within you, what you do not bring forth will destroy you*" (Gospel of Thomas, 70). "*The seed of God is in us*," Meister Eckhart said. "*If the seed had a good, wise and industrious cultivator, it would thrive and grow up into God. Now the seed of a pear tree grows into a pear tree . . . the seed of God into God.*"[23]

In the metaphorical imaging of persuasive Power, evil is not another powerful Being in a cosmic battle with the All-Powerful, but the result of less than good responses to the Divine Nudge. This "cause and effect" is obvious in some instances, such as driving too fast and ending up in hospital, but not so obvious in situations like cancer and natural disasters. Some cancers are genetic malfunctions from pollution, some floods and droughts result from poor land management, hunger happens with unequal distribution of wealth, and so on, but there are also many "bad" things whose connections we cannot know from our limited view of the world. The future, therefore, depends in large part on our making good choices, influenced by, and open to, this persuasive Power. Suffering, whether ours, others, or GOD's, results when egotistical, life-denying choices are made rather than transforming ones. GOD does not create suffering, but as part of this interconnected world, suffers with us, endlessly putting up with our failures and what we do to each other and ourselves, without overruling our actions. This suffering One is not foreign to Hebrew people—didn't Yahweh say, *"I have observed the misery of my people who are in Egypt; I have heard their cry on account of their taskmasters. Indeed, I know their sufferings"* (Exod. 3:7)?

When William Sloan Coffin (1924–2006) faced his Riverside Church congregation after his young son died in a self-inflicted car accident, he did not talk about Divine will or about why it happened. Instead, he told them that he was consoled knowing that, as waves closed over his son's car, GOD's heart was the first of all their hearts to break. The image of Persuasive Power, rather than an all-powerful GOD who could have but did not prevent this tragedy, allowed Coffin to deal with his grief, just as that same vulnerable Power also endured the pain of Jesus' cruel death, brought about by those who refused to listen to his message. In a letter to *Christian Century* magazine, a reader described how the accidental death of his fourteen-year-old son brought with it the "death" of his GOD who "sovereignly controlled" everything. After the funeral, he hung a crucifix over his son's empty chair at the dinner table:

> Displaying a crucifix is a no-no for us Reformed types, but every evening when I had to stare at Rob's empty chair in front of me, I could lift my eyes to the crucifix and remember God had suffered a grief such as mine . . . Though I question how much of life God's sovereignty controls, I find it easier to love the God who suffers than I did the one who controls. Twelve years later I still look to that crucifix and find solace and hope.[24]

Again, the struggle is how we describe Divine Power, given our own "powerlessness" in the world and the claims we make for GOD as loving and good. Buddhism does not have this problem because the reality of being alive and being human is, according to the first Noble Truth, that "all is suffering":

> Birth is suffering, old age is suffering, sickness and death are sufferings. To meet a man whom one hates is suffering, to be separated from a loved one is suffering, to be vainly struggling to satisfy one's needs is suffering. In fact, life that is not free from desire and passion is always involved with distress. This is called the Truth of Suffering.[25]

Given that inescapable fact of being human, the goal is not to wonder "Why me?" but to do something about it. The following Noble Truths deal with freeing oneself from things that cause suffering by following the eightfold path of right living to Enlightenment, that state of compassion or "suffering with." This is not so different from persuasive Power. It is certainly true that life is full of suffering, as the Buddha described, and the goal is to move toward transformation, wholeness (salvation) for ourselves and our world. Buddhists cultivate "power" within themselves through meditation and lifestyle to make this move; others call that "power within" GOD.

After September 11, religious leaders swamped television screens with explanations about why it happened and whether it was the Divine will or the force of evil, and the perpetrators also made claims of acting within the Divine will. Such explanations on both sides come from theologies of Divine Omnipotence. In a poem I wrote on that terrible day, I cried instead to that all-compassionate, ever-persuasive Power continually trying to mend our world and creation, even in the face of the worst creaturely resistance and rebellion:

As the dust settled
    and the number of missing rose,
I shouted at God
    with all the sounds I could muster.
Then I looked, and saw that One
    sitting, sorely disheveled,
    in the midst of the rubble.
Cradled in the Divine lap
    was not one, but thousands
    of broken, bleeding children.
God was shouting too
    as giant tears trekked relentlessly
    into the divine Mouth.
God's heart, the collective heart
    of the world was broken.
I stumbled through twisted steel
    to sit by the Suffering One's side.
I gathered a few dying souls
    into my own small lap.
A Divine arm tightened around me
and we wept together.

Imago Dei

God created us in his own image.
To describe God is to describe perfect humanity.

—Rumi[1]

One small, ambiguous phrase in the Hebrew story of creation has given license to all sorts of speculation. We are happy to fast forward over the instructions in the same chapter to eat the earth's vegetation without parallel permission to eat the animals, to ignore the repetitive chant *"and God saw that it was good"* in favor of seeing the world and its inhabitants as flawed, yet we gleefully stop to scoop up this other little phrase, like finding the perfect shell on a beach, putting it at the top of our theological list of treasures, and arguing all sorts of things from it. Why? Because we like it. We benefit immensely from the line *"Then God said, 'Let us make humankind in our own image, according to our likeness'"* (Gen. 1:26). The funniest part about our theological obsession with this idea (*imago Dei*) is that the majority of biblical experts and their commentaries have always begun by saying its exact meaning is problematic. The 1871 *Cyclopaedia of Biblical, Theological and Ecclesiastical Literature* says, *"No one doubts that the phrase 'image of God' denotes in general a likeness of God; but the opinions of theologians have always been different respecting the particular points of resemblance."*[2] Despite this, theologians still call it a fundamental concept of Christian theology. Who made it so, and who benefits from the comparison?

Over theological centuries, some have argued a physical likeness, others an intellectual likeness above the "lower" animals, others a spiritual or moral likeness, some a likeness lost in the fall that may or may not be regained, others a likeness in the soul, and still others a divinity in everyone. Despite the generic "humankind," some have argued that only men were made in the Divine image, and some have even questioned whether the woman possessed a soul at all. The Greek philosopher Aristotle (384–322) famously argued that the male fetus was "animated" (received its soul) forty days after conception, but the female not until ninety days, and he also declared that men were three quarters spirit/mind and one quarter matter and women three quarters matter and one quarter spirit/mind, making the medieval argument that the *imago Dei* was the soul's rationality decidedly favor men. It takes little extra brainpower to realize that such a theory also supported the assumption that GOD was male, since the Divine could not possess an inferior mind. Naturally, feminist theologians have taken a closer look at such readings and done some reworking. *"If women are created in the image of God, without qualification,"* Elizabeth Johnson says, *"then their human reality offers suitable, even excellent metaphor for speaking about divine mystery, who remains always ever greater."*[3] As I said in an earlier chapter, the only hint within the creation story of what the *imago Dei* might be is the Divine breath breathed into clay at creation, but with so much wallowing in human sinfulness, we ignore this image of the Divine in us. Again, this is metaphorical, just as the *imago Dei* idea itself is metaphorical, but at least these are read from the same story, honoring cohesiveness rather than extracting the *imago Dei* claim from its context to argue all sorts of other things.

The *imago Dei* has also been recruited over the centuries to argue the superiority of human beings as the pinnacle of creation. *"The whole universe (and even in some sense the angels, Hebrews 1:14) was only created for man, which is the reason why he was not created till all other things were ready for him,"* the same nineteenth-century theological encyclopedia cited earlier explains. *"The faculties which other creatures present only in a limited, disconnected manner, were in him united into a harmonious whole; moreover, in him alone, of all creatures, was the personal spiritual life of God mirrored; and by direct inspiration of the divine breath of life, the spirit was infused, by which he became a spiritual, self-conscious, free and individual soul.*"[4] "Man" here is the generic English term for humankind, but interestingly, in answer to those who argued both the inferiority of women and a progressive creation from lowest to highest, sixteenth-century commentator Henricus Cornelius Agrippa published his *Declamation on the Nobility and Preeminence of the Female Sex*, made immediately available in French, English, Italian, and German. Agrippa argued that women's inferiority was based on cultural assumptions and that the opposite could also be argued from canon law, Hebrew texts, and Greek philosophy:

> For when the Creator came to the creation of women, He rested himself in this creation, thinking that he had nothing more honorable to create, in her was completed and consummated all the wisdom and power of the Creator; after her no creation could be found or imagined . . . woman is the ultimate end of creation, the most perfect accomplishment of all the works of God and the perfection of the universe itself.[5]

Galileo's severe ecclesiastical censure was also about traditional theological claims of human superiority made from creation. By supporting fellow scientist Copernicus' theory that the earth was only one planet revolving around the sun, he put an end to centuries of human confidence that this world was both the center of the universe and of Divine concern. John Calvin, who died the year Galileo was born (1564), had also praised Divine Love for not creating Adam until *"all manner of good things,"* such as light, stars, and food, had been lavished upon the universe for the benefit of human beings, *"the noblest and most remarkable example of his [God's] Justice, wisdom and goodness . . . when his image is placed in man a tacit antithesis is introduced which raises man above all other creatures and, as it were, separates him from the common mass."*[6] Calvin vehemently condemned all idolatry, whether Persians worshipping the sun, *"stupid pagans"* fashioning stars into GODS, or Egyptians making Divine representations in animal forms, yet he did say that *"the Greeks seem to be wise above the rest, because they worshipped God in human form."*[7] Calvin did not see that his own descriptions of how the Divine acted in the world were also "idols," as is any theological system that tries to make the Divine fit into the parameters of our definitions; and some years later, theologian Jerome Bolsec publicly criticized Calvin's double predestination as exactly that: *"Those who posit an eternal decree in God by which he has ordained some to life and the rest to death make of him a Tyrant, and in fact an idol, as the pagans made of Jupiter.*"[8] Bolsec was subsequently arrested.

Until quite recently, belief in the superiority of human beings based on the *imago Dei* argument has hardly been challenged, and a similar hierarchy exists in Islam: "*Human beings sit on a high throne; other creatures are on the steps leading up to the throne.*"[9] I remember reading a book on theological anthropology by a famous theologian as part of a doctoral seminar. Huge chunks of his argument were based on the unquestioned assumption that humans were superior to animals. With nothing more than my extremely savvy English Pointer dog as evidence, I challenged this in class, arguing that we cannot know what animals think or process nor can we assume that their actions are merely reactive while ours are consciously considered. My "naïve" comments were dismissed, as they did not fit the famous author's arguments, yet current work on chimpanzees supports my challenge. There is only a 5 percent difference between the genomes of the chimp and those of humans—can 5 percent account for all the superiority we assign to ourselves? We have long assumed that language differentiates us, since we can talk and therefore think independently and reflectively, but we now know that chimps can play tricks on humans and think their way through many situations. While their different pharynx structure does not allow them to talk as we do, once taught to use sign language they can communicate, and they even continue to sign when humans are not present. Have we made ourselves superior to chimps and other living creatures simply by being the ones that name the criteria?

Traditional Christianity will no doubt continue to argue the *imago Dei* so as not to destabilize the doctrines and also to retain its advantages for human self-esteem and superiority, but how can we claim this in any useful way when we don't even know what the Divine image is? It also chastens us to realize that, in Charles Darwin's day, this *imago Dei* argument that humans were created separately and with mental and moral categories superior to the animals, did not necessarily include people from what were then called "black" (African and Aboriginal) or "dusky" (Asian) races. Victorian anthropologists and theologians pondered as to whether such "primitiveness" was due to deterioration in unfavorable circumstances, or whether they were "not human" in the first place. If they were not human, they did not have a soul and therefore did not need to be evangelized.[10] Darwin's realization that the "savages" of Patagonia had minds just like his, together with the successful adaptation of "natives" brought to England, shed a different light on this arrogance, yet Bishop Samuel Wilberforce (1805–1873) would have no part in the Darwinian application of natural selection to his kind, calling it *"the degrading notion of the brute origin of him who was created in the image of God"* and accusing Darwin of "making guesses." Darwin's response to this *"arrogance which made our forefathers declare that they were descended from demi-gods"* was a prediction that a time would come when people would be amazed that anyone ever believed humans were a separate creation.[11]

If human beings are said to be in the Divine image, it is a small step to say that the Divine is therefore "like" humans. Did GOD make humans in the Divine image, or did humans make GOD in human images? *"Men say that the Gods have a king,"* Aristotle said in his *Politics*, *"because they themselves either are or were in ancient times under the rule of a king. For they imagine, not only the forms of the Gods, but their ways of life to be like their own."*[12] I have intentionally arrived at this chapter without as yet imaging the Divine in a human form (except for "Lover" in relation to Love). I sincerely hope this demonstrates how truncated and limited our traditional Divine imaging has been, totally overrun as we are by the sole images of GOD as a Father, King, or Lord, writ large over against us and assigned the human traits we honor. It is not that we should never image the Divine in this way. Rather, we must not let human images become the dominant or only ones, at risk of their being seen as literally true, and a host of other "human" characteristics attached to the Divine because of them. Even though we may acknowledge that the Divine is not a being like us, we often act as if the opposite was true. Having sounded this warning note repeatedly for the last ten chapters, we can now talk of how people have described the Divine in anthropomorphic metaphors, realizing always that such talk is metaphorical and that such images are only some among many.

In a class, I asked people to describe their image of GOD, and without hesitation, one woman said, "Nana Stricker's soft arm." Her earliest memory of love was the arm of her grandmother as she snuggled against it for comfort, an image paralleled in the Hebrew Bible by lambs being gathered into the Divine protective arms (Isa. 40:11) and the assurance: *"The eternal God is your dwelling place, and underneath are the everlasting arms"* (Deut. 33:27, RSV).[13] A similar imagery appears in Buddhist thought: *"Faith makes us feel that we are in the presence of Buddha and it brings us to where Buddha's arm supports us."*[14] In Michelangelo's famous Sistine Chapel painting of the creation of Adam, the Creator reaches a finger out from heaven that doesn't quite touch that of the reclining Adam, but in the less popularized section of the painting, a rather anxious-looking Eve sits beside GOD in heaven, encircled protectively in the other Divine arm. Early Christian artists were hesitant to portray GOD in such bodily graphics, representing Presence and Communication instead by a hand protruding from a cloud and with a rolled scroll if a message was being delivered. There is a story told of Johnnie Dixon, the child of a struggling New Zealand farming family. His first-grade teacher, determined that school would be a good experience for him, met his bus and took his hand to introduce him to his class. At lunchtime, she took his hand to show him around the school, and after school, she took him to the bus. With each new experience, she took his hand to help him through it. At Christmas, when the class was asked to draw things for which they were thankful, Johnny drew his teacher's hand. The story does not end there. When the teacher died, the hand drawing was still on her bedroom wall, and a jet-lagged John Dixon, head of a large New York company, flew nonstop to New Zealand to say his last thank you at her funeral.

While GOD could not be seen, Divine Eyes could see—didn't we sing at church school "GOD sees the little sparrow fall?" In its biblical setting, this image speaks, not of magically reviving a fallen sparrow, but of compassionate Eyes that do not miss the natural end of the lowliest bird. Yet these compassionate Eyes have more often been portrayed as spying Eyes—GOD sees everything we do. If we pinched our sister as a child, it was recorded for posterity even if our mother missed it, like some Divine Santa Claus grading children naughty or nice, only the consequences were much worse than no gifts at Christmas. I worried about those spying Eyes. While it was flattering to think that the great Creator was interested in the minutest details of my rather mundane life and was prepared, if properly approached, to grind the whole machinery of the world to a halt for my benefit, I could not see how the Divine One could keep a scorecard on every person in the world or see everything that happened, even from that lofty panoramic view. Whether GOD could do it was, however, less of a concern than why GOD would spend so many Divine hours as a cosmic accountant with an overload of clients when there were so many other interesting things to do. And anyway, what was the point of human life simply being a trial-run for merit in the next world? In Christian art, the Divine was often depicted as an eye, sometimes encased in a triangle to indicate that it was GOD's eye. The symbol was both good and bad news—good because the Divine Eye is watching over us, but bad because It missed nothing. A huge triangular eye stares down from Neamt Monastery's tower in northern Romania into the enclosed courtyard where the monks spend most of their time—not even the darkest corner is immune from Its gaze. Similarly, in an old hunting lodge in Krasna Hnora in Slovakia, I noticed a makeshift painting of the Divine Eye over the exit from the kitchen, reminding kitchen servants that GOD was watching if they left early. Given the thin line of separation between the master of the house and GOD in those days, the eye of either would give cause for pause.

While arms, eyes, and hands are body parts used metaphorically for Divine action, the Israelites also described Yahweh in roles from daily life: vineyard owner (Jer. 2:21; John 15:1), archer (Lam. 3:13), potter (Isa. 64:8), and cook (Ps. 23:5), to name a few. Yet never did they imagine Yahweh was out planting grapes in the vineyard or shooting literal arrows into someone's vitals. Biblical scholar Marcus Borg has described two general groupings of Divine metaphors in the Hebrew Bible: monarchical or dominant anthropomorphic images such as King, Father, Warrior, and Lord, where GOD is a transcendent ruling Being in judgment or dominion over human beings; and the Spirit metaphors already discussed of Wind, Breath, Wisdom, and Compassion, where the Divine works in, with, and around us rather than "other than" us.[15] The monarchical metaphors were used almost exclusively after the fourth century CE when Christianity became part of the Roman Empire and have thus remained until recent challenges highlighted this discrepancy. British hymn writer Brian Wren has analyzed Divine images from three sources: the *Methodist and Ecumenical Hymnbook, Songs of Praise* on British television, and ancient prayers, liturgy, and creeds still used in churches. Of the two hundred and ninety images, 73 percent were KINGAFAP metaphors (King, Almighty-Father, and Protector), with the Divine portrayed as a dominant male ruler giving commands. Of pronouns used for the Trinity, 1,422 were masculine, one neuter, and none were feminine, even though the Spirit (*Ruach*) in Hebrew is feminine. Of the 76 percent male images in the Hymnbook, 81 percent indicated power over others. Such selective usage makes ordinary people in the pews assume these are the major biblical Divine images.[16]

Given Hebrew predilection for war, Yahweh was imaged early as the mighty Warrior, Leader in battle, and Lord of Hosts. Moses also called Yahweh his Banner or Standard, lifted up in battle so all could keep eyes on the leader (Exod. 17:15). The warrior Yahweh did not shrink from violence and destruction. Although some of Israel's enemies may have brought this on themselves through wickedness or disobedience, some were simply in the wrong land at the wrong time and were destroyed *"by the edge of the sword all in the city, both men and women, young and old, oxen, sheep and donkeys"* (Josh. 6:21). Such Divine action justified the violence of the Crusades of the Middle Ages when the feudal Christian Deity again headed up the army to reclaim Jerusalem from the infidel. En route, the crusaders also destroyed Jewish settlements and, on arrival, slaughtered all Jews and Muslims within the city in a horrific mass murder. With hands still wet with blood, they no doubt sang the old battle-stained Psalm, *"O sing to the Lord a new song, for he has done marvelous things. His right hand and holy arm have gotten him victory"* (98:1).[17]

This language of Divine militarism is still with us, justified on both sides by the Divine Warrior in the lead. But how can this be when the Christian Commander-in-Chief, the GOD of Abraham, is also the Divine Warrior of the Muslims; and Israel's Lord of Hosts, the GOD of Abraham, is also the Military Chief of the Palestinians? Why are soldiers on one side heroes and the opposition insurgents; why is aggression on one side a just war and that of its opponents "evil"; how can opposing leaders both have a mandate from the Divine? *"We are living in a time when the power of religious language and religious sentiment has once again been affirmed in the most alarming and dreadful of ways,"* religion scholar Mona Siddiqui says. *"Our current conflicts are political in nature but have assumed a different character as they are reflected and discussed increasingly through religious language."*[18] While a Divine Warrior may have comforted people in a desert tribal culture, is it still valid in a world where military action, such as in Vietnam and Iraq, does not necessarily solve the issues, and where disagreements could be negotiated in more peaceful ways? Images of a

Divine Warrior create a culture of violence in the name of GOD, especially when warring nations claim that their version of the Divine needs defending against "other" GODS so "truth" can prevail. A little girl, writing about September 11th in a school class, explained why this war was different from all other wars: *"This is the war that I saw."*[19] Again, our images matter. A culture where institutional violence is sanctioned by an appeal to a Divine Being who approves such behavior and even advocates it to believers will produce people who accept violence as part of the societal norm. *"Wrong does not cease to be wrong because the majority share in it,"* Leo Tolstoy said.[20]

In the book of Judges, there is a story of a mighty warrior Jephthah who made a vow to Yahweh, *"If you will give the Ammonites into my hand, then whoever comes out of the doors of my house to meet me, when I return victorious from the Ammonites, shall be the Lord's, to be offered up by me as a burnt offering"* (11:30–31). Yahweh does not seem to protest this human sacrifice—the text simply says *"The Lord gave them into his hand"* (v. 32). Jephthah no doubt assumed within his culture that a lowly, disposable servant would meet him—if so, the story would never have been told. Furthermore, since welcoming the warrior was traditionally the women's role, he must have thought women servants would be first to arrive. But no, his only child, an unnamed daughter, appeared with timbrels and dancing. The daughter comforted her cowboy father (whose moral fiber was so great he could not break his vow) by accepting death at his hand as fitting payback for what the warrior Yahweh has done, *"given you vengeance against your enemies, the Ammonites"* (v. 36). Yet the Ammonites were not, strictly speaking, Jephthah's enemies. He had been thrown out of his home and town because he was illegitimate, and Israel's elders had later hired him as a paid mercenary, agreeing to make him their leader should he win, hence his bribe for victory. Jephthah *"did with her according to the vow he had made"* (v. 39), the Bible's description of a father burning his young daughter on an altar as a trussed sacrifice. There is no mention of Jephthah's wife or her feelings about her only child's murder—she was also a possession to be traded by male warriors, human and Divine. What story, whether fact or myth, could be more corrupt from start to finish and with the Divine Warrior as a central player?

Our images of GOD determine the culture we create around such images. German theologian Dorothee Soelle (1929–2003) never lost her shame over her homeland generating two world wars. In the high school in which she taught in the 1950s, few students knew any Nazi history—some thought they were good because they had built the autobahns. When Soelle introduced Holocaust studies, despite opposition from both school authorities and parents, she made the students count off in threes in order to emphasize that every third Jew went to the gas chamber.[21] What GOD-images were in place in Germany to both spawn and justify this culture of violence and anti-Semitism and also lull so many Christians into complicity? During the civil rights conflict in the United States, Martin Luther King Jr. said, *"What is so disturbing is not the appalling actions of the 'bad' people but the appalling silence of the 'good' people."*[22] One of my students, troubled by glib Christian arguments contrasting a violent Hebrew Bible GOD with a New Testament GOD of love, wrote in a paper:

> I can, off the top of my head, recall three divine killings in the book of Acts. Maybe a better distinction between the Old and New Testament is that in the Old Testament God is a mass murderer, whereas, in the New Testament, God is a sniper. In both, God kills. The Old Testament is using the nation of Israel as a tool to demonstrate God's plans and purposes, so the violence is on a large international scale. In the New Testament, individual relationship with God is the main overall theme, so the wrath of God is poured out on individuals.

The Divine warrior is not unique to Jewish and Christian traditions. The Hindu *Mahabharata* epic (begun fifth century BCE) is a mammoth tale of battles between two families. The famous *Bhagavad Gita,* part of this epic, recounts Lord Krishna's advice to the warrior Arjuna who does not want to fight against family and friends: *"What is this crime I am planning, O Krishna? Murder most hateful, murder of brothers! Am I indeed so greedy for greatness?"*[23] Lord Krishna calls Arjuna's hesitancy mere *"scruples and fancies, weakness and cowardice"*:

> Death is certain for the born. Rebirth is certain for the dead. You should not grieve for what is unavoidable . . . He who dwells within all living bodies remains forever indestructible. Therefore, you should never mourn for anyone.[24]

War and a culture of violence are again justified, but this time through belief in reincarnation and reward. How many fine young men and women have died across the globe and down the centuries because of promised favors from the Deities? Even today, young Muslim extremists are prepared to die in suicide bombings because Allah the Warrior promises them heavenly delights for their sacrifice: "*Whoso fighteth in the way of Allah, be he slain or be he victorious, on him We shall bestow a vast reward*" (Surah 4:74).

There was also a Hebrew dream of a day when this violent culture led by the mighty Warrior would come to an end. "*In days to come,*" the book of Micah says, "*many nations shall come and say: 'Come, let us go up to the mountain of the Lord . . . that he may teach us his ways and that we may walk in his paths' . . . They shall beat their swords into plowshares, and their spears into pruning hooks; nation shall not lift up sword against nation, neither shall they learn war any more*" (4:1–3). The prophets continually railed against violence and injustice in any form, and Jesus pushed the command against killing even further—do not even be angry with one another (Matt. 5:22). As for an eye for an eye, turn the other cheek and pray for your enemies because it is the peacemakers who are blessed (Matt. 5:9). Prior to Roman emperor Constantine (280–337), many church fathers were pacifists, taking seriously the command not to take up swords and even refusing to serve in the Roman army. Tertullian (155–230) said an unreserved "no" to war, and Origen (185–254) said "no but . . ." admitting to some righteous causes. However, once the warrior Constantine defeated his final opponent and declared Christianity tolerable within his empire, the church fathers spelled out a "just war" theory, marginalizing pacifism in an imperially connected church. Pro-war arguments included a superior Divine knowledge of events; prevention of more disastrous occurrences; the Divine right of the ruler, based on kingly, warrior Divine metaphors; and the inability of death to kill the soul, hence the glory of martyrdom. Later, the necessity of force and violence was argued when the Divine Will demanded a particular end, as in the Crusades, yet the dilemma of contradictory images remains—the Warrior GOD of Abraham is also the "*Prince of Peace*" (Isa. 9:6).

The Hebrew *shalom* (peace) means comprehensive well-being, wholeness, completeness, or as a longer version whose origin I have lost says, "*may you have all that is necessary for your material well-being and may you have harmonious relationships with yourself, within yourself, with others, with God.*" Interestingly, peace is not necessarily the absence of war or strife, which is how we usually use it. In John's Gospel, Jesus said, "*I have said this to you so that in me you may have peace. In the world you face persecution. But take courage; I have conquered the world!*" (16:33). Such peace does not depend on external circumstances but is a confidence that, whatever is happening, we still abide in the Divine Presence. A once-upon-a-time story tells of a king offering a prize for the best painting on "peace." One finalist painted a calm lake with a perfect sky. The other finalist painted a rugged mountain, an angry sky, lightning, and a wild waterfall, looking nothing like peace until the king looked closer. Behind the waterfall in a tiny bush growing out of a crack in a bare rock, a bird had built a nest and was sitting on it. The king chose this painting.

What visual images come to your mind when you hear the word "peace"? I think of paintings of the lamb lying down with the lion, originating from a much more explicit biblical scenario:

> The wolf shall live with the lamb, the leopard shall lie down with the kid, the calf and the lion and the fatling together, and a little child shall lead them. The cow and the bear shall graze, their young shall lie down together, and the lion shall eat straw like the ox. The nursing child shall play over the hole of the asp, and the weaned child shall put its hand on the adder's den. They will not hurt or destroy on all my holy mountain. (Isa. 11:6–9)

The artist in me calls for paint tubes and brushes. For ancient souls squeezing out an existence in a semibarren land where humans and animals compete for scarce food sources down the food chain, this image of peace is an impossibility, but is this not what hope is—recognizing the impossible yet not giving up the dream? And, by extension, if the lion lies down with the lamb, will the gerbil not eat its young and the cat not maul the sparrow? Will trout fishermen who make a religion of throwing the line and an art of preparing the perfect fly lay down their rods? Will the hunter embrace the deer and the butcher release the steer? Will an Israeli soldier embrace a Palestinian freedom fighter and a fundamentalist accept another's truth claim? Will the most powerful nations in the world lay down their nuclear arms as they command others to do? "*It may be that Allah will ordain love between you and those of them with whom ye are at enmity,*" the Qur'an says. "*Allah is Mighty, and Allah is Forgiving, Merciful"* (Surah 60:7). The Divine Peacemaker might be forgiving, but unfortunately, people are not so merciful. As a young soldier in the Crimean War in the 1850s, Tolstoy later wrote:

> ... The negation of the doctrine of non-resistance and the failure to comprehend it are always in proportion to the degree of power and wealth of civilized people ... All those whose life is directly funded on violence ... will always adopt a negative attitude towards the idea that it is possible to apply to life the doctrine of non-violent resistance to evil.[25]

Despite faithful efforts of many peacemakers, nations for the most part have avoided taking seriously the Arbiter of Peace who urges people to break swords into ploughs or nuclear weapons into recycled metal (Mic. 4:3), assigning this scenario to some unknown eschatological future or other-worldly existence. In the meantime, it is military business as usual.

Once Israel settled down in the promised land, the charismatic leadership of Moses and Joshua gave way to clan chieftains or judges, a term for military, administrative, and legal functions. Later, when greater unity was deemed necessary, Israel insisted on a king *"so that we also may be like other nations, and that our king may govern us and go out before us and fight our battles"* (1 Sam. 8:20). Yahweh pointed the Divine finger at Saul, who became the first king or "anointed one" around 1000 BCE, but not without considerable heart-searching—would a king usurp the Divine rule of Yahweh? Ruler and King then became obvious Divine metaphors: *"a great King above all Gods"* (Ps. 95:3), *"the king of Israel, the Lord"* (Zeph. 3:15), *"the King of Glory"* (Ps. 24:7). David, who succeeded Saul, was considered the model king, despite some appalling incidents, including arranging Uriah's murder in order to claim his wife Bathsheba. David and Bathsheba's son Solomon also adorned the office, but then the monarchy declined. Israel dreamed of a time when the kingdom would be restored again with another king like David under the Divine King who would judge the world (not just Israel) with righteousness and establish a reign of peace, justice, and mercy to which *"all the nations shall stream"* (Isa. 2:2). The author of Revelation developed this imagery to exalted heights of visionary grandeur with a transformed Jerusalem and Divine King on the throne, not somewhere else but in the midst of the people: *"See, the home of God is among mortals. He will dwell with them as their God"* (21:3).

The role of a leader, whether clan chieftain or king, included judging and administering justice; thus Yahweh was also the Divine Judge whose task included judging all the earth, not some time later but in the present: "*I know that the Lord maintains the cause of the needy, and executes justice for the poor*" (Ps. 140:12). Such Divine judgment included those who disobeyed as well as those who were righteous, and so Hebrew people, as GOD's covenant people, could take comfort when their circumstances were not going according to plan—their time of justice would come. The Qur'an also declared GOD's justice saying, "*Allah wrongeth not even of the weight of an ant; and if there is a good deed, He will double it and will give (the doer) from His Presence an immense reward*" (Surah 4:40). But is this what the righteous Job found? The book of Job is one of the most discussed and disturbing biblical books because it depicts a saintly man with whom the Divine toyed in a serious way. We fly to Yahweh's defense with all sorts of arguments, but let's face it, the story is about undeserved suffering in the face of Divine inactivity or worse, Divine permission. When his friends blame him, Job does not succumb to guilt but argues his case before the Divine Judge. Even at the end, we are not sure of the logic or the outcome, as if invited to draw our own conclusions about Divine justice. When Hebrew people around Jesus' time began to embrace the idea of a reward after death, the day of judgment was moved to an end-time judgment for all the earth that, with visions borrowed from Revelation, swelled by the Middle Ages into an otherworldly reality far more important than life itself. Since constant war and ravaging black plague had reduced life expectancy to around thirty-five, paintings depicting saints going to blissful delights in heaven and sinners torn apart by horrific monsters in hell created a very receptive audience at Mass.

A just Divine Judge image remains decidedly comforting today for people whose everyday experience is of injustice and oppression—violence is not limited to physical battles, twentieth-century Russian author Aleksander Solzhenitsyn said in his Nobel Prize acceptance speech, "*Violence, less and less embarrassed by the limits imposed by centuries of lawfulness, is brazenly and victoriously striding across the whole world.*"[26] Liberation theology emerged among the poor and oppressed of South America when they were encouraged to take seriously the biblical Just One who refused to be defined by the ruling elite and instead, showed a predilection for those living in inhumane conditions, contrary to the Divine Will. Violence of any form is inevitably linked with power: who has it, how it is used, and for what reasons. Institutional violence results when such power is used by churches, governments, or races to construct systems that, by their very structure, do violence to a particular subset of people. A Divine Judge demands that we act justly by challenging such structures and addressing the gross inequities in society. While everyone is not born with equal opportunities, a culture of justice and a Just GOD requires us to share each other's load and care for those who are deprived of justice. A rotary group expecting a visit from their district governor had to negotiate around a disheveled, homeless man slumped on the stairs to their club. Some actually walked over him. When the meeting was about to begin, the homeless man got up, walked into the hall, and took off his tatty clothes. He was the district governor. Some members applauded while some were embarrassed and others downright angry. It was one thing to talk about serving the poor and the homeless but another thing to act out of their comfort zones. The district governor, who had done this in other clubs as well, then told stories of the busy waitress who had come out to tell him to stay around until after the meal, when she would get him a blanket for the night, and of the couple who literally picked him up and took him inside for a meal.

A Divine Judge can also be threatening. Many people believe in the GOD of love out of fear of not believing in the GOD who " *with his hand he will hurl them* [*the wicked*] *down to the earth*" (Isa. 28:2). In a class, I asked people to recall how they felt in their childhood about GOD. One woman immediately said "terrified." Her children's Bible came complete with detailed pictures, all in red, of the Rapture. Cemeteries were broken open with fully clothed, smiling people going straight to heaven while others were left behind in the open graves with horrified looks on their faces. Unless she was good, she was told, she may be the only one in her family left behind. Another person was scared whenever her grandparents visited because, behind her parents' backs, they told her she needed to be saved if she wanted to go to heaven, yet she didn't know how one got saved. In a more light-hearted memory from another couple, if any of their children left their shoes where they were not supposed to be, the parents would say to each other in the child's presence, "It looks like the Rapture must have happened . . . (naming the child) has been taken right out of her shoes."

Fear of the Divine Judge has not abated. The best-selling *Left Behind* series of novels are just that, the terror and trials of those left behind at the Rapture. I have just flicked past a Christian television program on how to approach strangers to give them a gospel tract. The sole content of the "gospel" (good news) to offer verbally with the tract was bad news—confess your sins and repent right now or you will go to hell. A friend of mine grew up during the era of Communist paranoia in the United States and was told that, should a Communist come to her door, she must admit to being a Christian, even though they might do dreadful things to her. Terrified of being caught between the GODless Communists and her Judging GOD, she had secretly devised a plan to commit suicide should this happen. Rabbi Harold Kushner says, "*I worry about preachers and smugly devout people who picture a God who can hardly wait to catch us in a mistake and send us to hell. I could not learn from a teacher if I thought that teacher enjoyed flunking people more than teaching them . . . And I cannot worship a God who set His role as being our judge rather than our teacher.*"[27]

Since warriors, kings, and judges were almost exclusively male in ancient societies, constant use of these images for GOD today, while claiming the Divine has no sex, also reinforces Divine "maleness"—to depict GOD as a queen would bring immediate protests. The Anglican Articles of Religion declared GOD to be "*without body, parts or passions,*" yet "He" was used for GOD rather than "It"—but without body parts or passion, do we have a person? Since It denotes something inanimate or, if animate, less than a human being, we don't like to use It for GOD, thus the rules of the English language have "created" a GOD with gender and personhood, an idol. This is not just an aberration of language, however. Until recently in our culture (and still alive and well in some parts of it), maleness has been defined as superior to, and over against, femaleness, with males still carefully avoiding "female" traits—it is still more acceptable for a girl to be a "tomboy" than for a boy to be "effeminate." With these attitudes built into our psyche, it is ridiculous to say that referring to GOD as He is an insignificant language convention. So long as the political and business climate celebrates toughness, bullishness, and individual competition, GOD will be epitomized by masculinity, as defined by that culture, in order to earn universal respect and worship. It is no coincidence that as contemporary theologians challenge exclusively male-dominant images for the Divine, men's groups like the Promise Keepers have emerged, gathering men together in football fields, that symbol of male prowess and bonding, to command them to take back their headship of the family as ordained by GOD.

Part of our contemporary problem is that in sacred texts from patriarchal societies very few female images appear in the public sphere. While Deborah may have been a judge (Judg. 4:4), she is only briefly mentioned, and while Judith and Esther may have had books named after them for heroically saving the Hebrew people, they both did it, not from positions of political or public power, but by playing on the sexual Achilles' heel of powerful men. So long as biblical metaphors and stories are considered the only appropriate way of talking about the Divine, only male human images will be honored and appropriated, prostituting the Divine to ancient cultural rules of patriarchy. According to Elizabeth Johnson, this *"absolutizes a single set of metaphors and obscures the height and depth and length and breadth of divine mystery. Thus it does damage to the very truth of God that theology is supposed to cherish and promote."*[28] Since female anthropomorphic images other than domestic mothering images are rare in the Bible, we need to appropriate them from women's contemporary experiences if we are going to use anthropomorphic images in a balanced way. This is not to diminish the Divine mothering images discussed in the next chapter, but rather to honor all women's experiences. *"Until a strong measure of undervalued female symbolism is introduced and used with ease,"* Johnson says, *"equivalent imaging of God male and female, which I myself have advocated and still hold to be a goal, remains an abstraction, expressive of an ideal but unrealizable in actual life."*[29]

With the absence of a nongendered singular pronoun in English, people complain about the awkwardness of repeating "GOD" instead of "He" and "humankind" instead of "mankind," but we have unlearned other words no longer considered acceptable, and reluctance to do the same for GOD suggests a lurking suspicion that we are not quite sure that GOD is not male. Exclusively masculine images now reduce the Divine for me, not because I want to call GOD "She," but because forcing myself to adjust my language to move beyond gendering the Divine has exposed me to a larger, more nuanced Divine vision of Limitless and Formlessness. When explaining why I thought it important to avoid talking about GOD only in male terms, the man to whom I was speaking said it made him feel "castrated," indicating that there was something psychologically important for him about GOD being imaged as male. If that is so, what have women felt for centuries about a Divine spoken of only as "He"? Men do not realize that they have lived as the norm for centuries, never experiencing what it is to be the "lesser other" of the species, to have their bodies and abilities named negatively. A fifty-something woman told me once that she always felt like the little match-girl when she read the Bible. She wondered why she did not feel warmed by it until she realized that she was not "inside" the circle being addressed, but "outside" in the cold, trying to keep warm with tiny matches. Bernadette Cozart builds gardens in run-down American cities to create something of beauty. She tried every branch of Christianity and then what she calls "the big four" (Buddhism, Islam, Hinduism, Judaism), looking for the Divine *"but always that face was missing. Wherever I turned, I felt that void."* When she turned to GOD-DESS spirituality with its feminine Divine images, she said, *"For the first time, I looked into the face of the One Most High and saw my own face reflected there."*[30]

In the Family Way

God rejoices that he is our Father;
And God rejoices that he is our Mother;
And God rejoices that he is our true Spouse,
And that our soul is his beloved wife.
And Christ rejoices that he is our brother.

—Julian of Norwich[1]

While the Bible is full of warriors, kings, prophets, and enemies, the family was the basic unit in biblical society. The nuclear unit, with the male as the head, consisted of parents, unmarried children, and nonkin such as slaves and permanent visitors. More than one nuclear unit from a common ancestor formed the extended family, living together or in adjoining houses and often sharing work or a trade. If the common male ancestor was no longer living, authority was decided between the male heads of nuclear families. A group of extended families formed the clan, and the ultimate clan was the nation. The Hebrew Bible laws provided a basis on how all levels of society should live together: "*You shall not covet your neighbor's house [household]; you shall not covet your neighbor's wife, or male or female slave, or ox, or donkey, or anything that belongs to your neighbor*" (Exod. 20:17). Not surprisingly, Yahweh's activities were also described in metaphors drawn from various family and clan roles, and it is in this domestic scene that we encounter feminine Divine images.

The old joke says, "My husband and I argue over religious differences. He thinks he is GOD and I don't." GOD was imaged as husband to Israel in the Hebrew Bible, and Jesus was called the bridegroom of the church in the New Testament. While a Divine Husband image may seem romantic, especially in the Song of Solomon, there are major problems, since the Divine Husband is usually portrayed as the good and faithful one, given the power structures of the family, and the wife (Israel or church) the unfaithful one, or at least likely to teeter toward that possibility. An Israelite husband as the head of the household had legal control over children and wife, or wives. Marriages were contracted early by fathers, with the husband's family "purchasing" the bride from her father. Inheritance passed from father to son or, in the absence of sons, to a daughter who then had to marry into her father's tribe. Ensuring that a man's children were really his "seed" led to all sorts of scrutiny and suspicion as to a woman's "purity." It might come as a surprise to some that the term "adultery" in the Hebrew Bible was specifically about a married or betrothed woman having intercourse with someone not her husband—the concern was the paternity of any offspring. Punishment for adultery depended on who "owned" the woman and where she was having sex (or being raped). If she was married or engaged, both parties were put to death, since the woman did not cry out for help; if she was raped in the country where no one would hear her, only the man died if it could be proved he did it (not for "adultery" but for defiling another's property); if the woman was not yet engaged, the man paid a fine to her father and married the woman, never to divorce her (Deut. 22:22–29).[2] Men could have many wives (but a woman only one husband) and if she did not "please" him, he could write a certificate of divorce and send her away (Deut. 24:1). Why so much detail? Because with such a male-favoring climate with an obsession as to whether a woman had been defiled or had committed adultery, we need to be cautious about transferring Divine Husband metaphors centering on faithful men and unfaithful wives, or about male "headship" or ownership, into our culture as if they also apply to twenty-first-century situations.

In the book of Hosea, faithful Hosea is married to Gomer, a *"wife of whoredom"* (1:2), a relationship used as a metaphor for GOD's faithfulness to unfaithful Israel, who has prostituted herself to other GODS. Yahweh, like Hosea, longs to take unfaithful Israel back as "wife." In Ezekiel 16, Jerusalem as the "bad wife" does not fare so well. Although abandoned at birth and rescued by Yahweh, who raises her, marries her, and showers good things on her, Jerusalem plays the whore, sacrificing even her own children. As her deserved punishment, the Divine Husband offers her to previous lovers for gang rape, followed by torture and a stoning death. Only then does the Divine Husband, acting with loving kindness, forgive her. In the book of Isaiah, Yahweh's relationship with Israel is described as a husband who divorces his wife quickly in anger, quite acceptable in this culture, but then takes her back: "*In overflowing wrath for a moment I hid my face from you, but with everlasting love I will have compassion on you, says the Lord, your Redeemer*" (Isa. 54:8). Yahweh is praised for His "love" but not condemned for His moodiness in the first place. The Divine Husband metaphor in the Hebrew Bible, therefore, sanctions domination, possession, violence, and murder, calling it love and faithfulness—we convict husbands today for such domestic violence and murder. As biblical scholar Athalya Brenner says:

> I regard the violent description of YHWH as a professional soldier and dissatisfied husband who tortures his "wife" as unacceptable, on general humanistic-ethical as well as theological and social-gendered grounds. I regard the relevant passages as pornographic and beyond salvation not only for feminists but also for any objector to violence, be that violence divine or religious or otherwise.[3]

Yet the Divine Husband image is still very much in use. The New Testament substituted "church" for "Israel," with Christ the faultless, loving bridegroom to whom the bride comes and by whom the bride is "redeemed." Again, the problematic one in the partnership is the bride as compared to the perfect bridegroom. Theologians have run with this metaphor for centuries, speaking of the church as "her," Christ's wayward bride, and from this metaphor have argued for a literally male priesthood. An essay C. S. Lewis wrote in 1948 on women priests says:

> Only one wearing the masculine uniform can (provisionally and till the Parousia) represent the Lord to the Church; for we are all, corporately and individually, feminine to Him. We men may often make very bad priests. That is because we are insufficiently masculine. It is no cure to call in those who are not masculine at all. A given man may make a very bad husband; you cannot mend matters by trying to reverse the roles.[4]

Here, the metaphor has become biological reality. If Christ is the bride-groom to the female church, then Christ's representatives as "husbands" to the bride (even though they are called fathers) must be male because women can't be husbands. Although the church was metaphorically designated "female" in the first place in a male-ruled society, in what way is it *physically* "female" in that it requires a physically male part-ner? With such reasoning, we should also argue that the Israelites were literally whores in relation to their faithful husband Yahweh.

This husband-wife metaphor in Ephesians 5, legitimated by a metaphorical "marriage" between Christ and the church, is still used today to physically define women. Although the parallel instruction in the same chapter that slaves obey their masters has been dismissed as culturally outdated and punishable by law, that wives obey their hus-band's headship is somehow eternally validated by the metaphor of Christ as head of the church. Again we ask, "Who benefits from such selective reading?" The contentious passage reads in full:

> Be subject to one another out of reverence for Christ. Wives, be subject to your husbands as you are to the Lord. For the husband is the head of the wife just as Christ is the head of the church, the body of which he is the Savior. Just as the church is subject to Christ, so also wives ought to be, in everything, to their husbands. Husbands, love your wives, just as Christ loved the church and gave himself up for her, in order to make her holy by cleansing her with the washing of water by the word, so as to present the church to himself in splendor, without a spot or wrinkle or anything of the kind—yes, so that she may be holy and without blemish. In the same way, husbands should love their wives as they do their own bodies. He who loves his wife loves himself. For no one ever hates his own body, but he nourishes and tenderly cares for it, just as Christ does for the church because we are members of his body. "For this reason a man will leave his father and mother and be joined to his wife, and the two will become one flesh." This is a great mystery, and I am applying it to Christ and the church. Each of you, however, should love his wife as himself, and a wife should respect her husband. (Eph. 5:21–33)

Because a male Christ was metaphorically described as the patriarchal husband of the "female" church, any husband, regardless of capabili-ties or disposition, has automatic authority over any wife, who must be "subject" to him in everything. Borrowing similar biblical metaphors, should we also argue that any ruler today, for example, the president of the United States, has absolute authority to do whatever he/she wishes to the nation because GOD as the Ruler of the world has such absolute authority?

This Ephesians passage, not written by Paul but at the end of the first century CE, reflects more than Jewish ideas about men and women. While Paul's "good news" collapsed social hierarchies—"*There is no longer Jew or Greek, there is no longer slave or free, there is no longer male and female; for all of you are one in Christ Jesus*" (Gal. 3:28)—later Greek-influenced Christianity returned Aristotle's Household Codes almost word for word in Ephesians, Colossians, 1 Peter, and the Pastoral Epistles as the "Christian" rule for families. Aristotle had said in his *Politics*, "*The male is by nature better fitted to command than the female . . . It is true that in most cases of republican government the ruler and ruled interchange in turn . . . but the male stands in this relationship to the female continuously.*"[5] Judaism had also promoted a hierarchal ordering, with Jewish men praying every day, "*Thank God for not making me a Gentile; thank God for not making me a woman; thank God for not making me a slave,*" the categories Paul systematically reversed in Galatians 3:28 above. Jewish historian Josephus wrote in that era, "*The woman, says the Law, is in all things inferior to the man. Let her accordingly by submissive, not for her humiliation, but that she may be directed, for the authority has been given by God to the man.*"[6] This ancient cultural subordination of women, rejected by Jesus and Paul, had been "divinized" once again as the evolving church slid back into the prevailing culture, perpetuating its biases down to us today.

With the husband biblically legitimated again as head of the wife, gendered cultural accessories were also applied to women in the church—keeping silent, full submission, no authority over men, modest dressing, head covering, and salvation through childbearing.[7] While the Ephesians passage began with the egalitarian ring "*Be subject to one another,*" the mood changed. Although husbands must love their wives, wives are subject "*in everything*" to husbands (v. 24) as the bride-church to the bridegroom-Christ. Another parallel, without being fully spelled out, emerged—as the husband-Christ makes the wife-church holy "*by cleansing her with the washing of water . . . to present her without spot and blemish*" (v. 26–27), the husband as head "keeps pure," by inference, a blemished or potentially wayward wife. This "biblical" male headship, with all its ramifications from a society where women were possessions and under constant "purity" surveillance, led America's Southern Baptists to amend their belief statements in the last decade to include: "*A wife is to submit graciously to the servant leadership of her husband, even as the church willingly submits to the headship of Christ . . . The wife has the God-given responsibility to respect her husband and to serve as his 'helper' in managing their household and nurturing the next generation.*"[8] As we speak, the Sydney Diocese, at odds with Australia's Anglican Communion, refuses to ordain women or allow women to teach adolescent boys, argued on male headship as a literal mirror of Christ's headship over the church. Realizing their argument would be laughable in the Australian public sphere where women are successful lawyers, politicians, and business leaders, the Sydney Diocese claims that the biblical injunction still holds in church and home. They have bolstered this "headship" argument with an interpretation of the Trinity where Christ, although fully divine, is eternally subordinated to the Father in role and function: "*Christ is the head of every man, and the husband is the head of his wife, and God is the head of Christ*" (1 Cor. 11:3). While this argument was labeled heresy by the fourth-century creeds, a twenty-first-century church in a major capital city of the world with a culture totally different from desert tribal patriarchy is fiercely promoting it.[9] Once again, biblical texts can argue anything if those constructing the arguments want something badly enough, but does this justify something that seriously limits and damages women today, especially when five verses further on in the same Ephesians chapter and the same discussion on family order, the slave is instructed to obey his master—something we have outlawed today as illegal?

While having a husband is not a universal experience, having a father is. Whether absent or present, known or unknown, kind or cruel, everyone has some emotional response to "father" depending on interactions with their own father. If human fathers are all-powerful, arbitrary, or abusive, a Divine Father can be expected to punish without reason or warning. An international news report in 2002 read: "*An Iranian cut off his seven-year-old daughter's head after suspecting she had been raped by her uncle. The post-mortem examination showed she was a virgin. 'The motive behind the killing was to defend my honor, fame and dignity,' the father said.*" On the other hand, if fathers are strong and loving, that love can mirror a Divine Father. In another news report, an Ethiopian man watched 100,000 people in his country die from famine. His family survived because he sold his two oxen, but without the oxen he could no longer plow his field and plant crops, and so his food source was gone. "*When my children cry because they are hungry,*" he sobbed, "*it is very hard to be a father.*" Early in life, children internalize the answers to two questions—is this world safe and trustworthy, and am I loveable? Their answers are shaped by, and will affect, their attitudes to the world and GOD. A student, having a hard time in class with a discussion of the Divine Father image, wrote:

> When I take classes that deal with my faith, I always try to detach myself and become nothing more than an observer. What I've learned is that there is a huge difference between what I know to be true in my heart and what I know to be true in my mind . . . If I think about it all too much, I lose my faith. God isn't logical, so I'm not even going to try to make him something I can grasp with my mind; that belittles God.

Her next sentence illuminated the deeper struggle—her Divine Father must not fail her like her real father had: "*What is God to me? God has been my father since mine left. God is someone who loves me more than I could ever love anyone else. He is my hope and without him I have no future.*"

Although "Father" has dominated Christian Divine images, GOD as Father occurs only fifteen times in the Hebrew Bible, signifying a male progenitor, the head of a family or clan (including nonbiological members), or a title of leadership or honor. GOD, the creating and preserving One, "fathered" or "fashioned" Israel: "*O Lord, you are our Father; we are the clay, and you are our potter; we are all the work of your hand*" (Isa. 64:8). As Mary Mills points out, this is hardly a biological metaphor:

> God is presented as an adult male figure, but one lacking divine parents, siblings or children. The surface level of the Hebrew text reveals a solitary figure, lacking even a partner or consort. This leaves a vacuum, a lack of family which is balanced by human beings who can be described as "sons of God."[10]

The hands-on parenting role in Hebrew times was more adequately described in "mothering" metaphors: "*As a mother comforts her child, so I will comfort you*" (Isa. 66:13). Father is also not the central Divine image in the New Testament. Of two hundred and forty-five references, almost half are crowded into John's Gospel, where the author draws a giant family metaphor to assure this community that they are still children of GOD. Jesus occasionally used the Aramaic *abba*, an intimate family term for father (Mark 14:36), and invited his followers to do the same in the Lord's Prayer (recorded only in Matthew and Luke), yet Jesus also talked much of the "Lord God," the "Kingdom," and the "living God." Paul also used the Father metaphor on occasions to stress a change of status for believers: "*For you did not receive a spirit of slavery to fall back into fear, but you have received a spirit of adoption. When we cry 'Abba! Father!' it is that very Spirit bearing witness with our spirit that we are children of God*" (Rom. 8:15–16). Yet this is by no means Paul's normal verbiage for GOD. As we will see later, although Father is not the dominant Divine metaphor of scripture, Father became the exclusive term for Divinity once the Trinitarian metaphor was established in the fourth century, with His earthly representatives called *Papa* (Pope) and "Father."

While for many people a father metaphor does justice as a Divine image, for many others it does not. Sexually and psychologically abused daughters find ambivalent comfort in a Divine Father, and current priest scandals have rendered the "ecclesiastical father" image horrific for many altar boys. Such ambiguity applies with any metaphor, including GOD as Mother, which is why one metaphor should never be used exclusively for the Divine or be suggested in any way as reality. A male student in a course on feminist theology described his struggles with family metaphors in his final essay:

> My journey has been one of much pain, and now I am sitting here writing this paper, a thirty-two-year-old survivor of childhood sexual assault from my father and extensive physical, verbal, and emotional abuse at the hands of both my mother and my father. With this in mind it is easy to see how traditional images of the Godhead are not helpful to me . . . It carries too much baggage. To relate to God as father requires either a denial or, at best, some kind of sleight of hand which does away with the utter pain and suffering that I associate with a father figure.

A maternal image was no better for him, nor any family metaphor, as his siblings constantly colluded to sacrifice him as the family scapegoat.

Fortunately, rather than walking away altogether, he was able in time to jettison human metaphors, even though his church tut-tutted in disapproval. A cosmic beyond human Love became his salvation. He concluded his paper:

> I would simply like to state that writing this paper has been an incredibly invigorating leg of my own personal journey. Many may label me as way out of line with the images of God I have presented. They, however, have not walked a mile in my shoes, or experienced a day with the intensity of my broken and shattered innocence, or had to come to terms with my lost childhood, indeed my lost family.

In a long past life, I was a research microbiologist. The gram stain test (a dye placed on bacteria that turned them red or blue, thus giving information about the organism) was the central classification tool, even when other tests became available. The professor I worked with thought this a false hierarchy, since gram stain reactions might not even be an important differentiation between organisms, just the first one used. As his lowly assistant, I performed a barrage of tests on hordes of bacteria and then we classified them, with the help of newly available computer technology, according to their greatest number of similarities and giving the gram stain no special value. Over the years, as I diverted from microbiology to theology, I applied my professor's concerns to "classifying" GOD. Early church theologians zeroed in on certain biblical images that suited their context and arguments without analysis as to whether these were the most frequently used in the scriptures or even the most important. Divine Wisdom (Hebrew *Hokmah*; Greek *Sophia*), preexistent and aligned with the Creator, was a common Divine metaphor in the Hebrew Bible:

> The Lord created me at the beginning of his work, the first of his acts of long ago. When he established the heavens I was there, when he drew a circle on the face of the deep . . . when he marked out the foundations of the earth, then I was beside him, like a master worker; and I was daily His delight, rejoicing before Him always, rejoicing in His inhabited world and delighting in the human race (Prov. 8:22, 27–31)

Sophia-Wisdom paralleled the Logos-Word of John's Gospel: "*In the beginning, the Logos-Word already was. The Word was in God's presence, and what God was, the Word was. He was with God at the*

*beginning, and through him all things came to be; without him no cre-
ated thing came into being"* (John 1:1–3).[11] Yet *Sophia*-Wisdom took an
early demise in the Christian tradition (perhaps because It was a feminine image), while *Logos*-Word became applied to the second person of
the Trinity.[12]

Even if father is a biblical metaphor, can we transfer its Middle
Eastern tribal chief meaning to a hotdog-eating, ballgame-loving, SUV-
driving father today? Fatherhood, and the characteristics applied to GOD
through this metaphor, is defined differently in different contexts. In a
Confucian-influenced Chinese setting, the family and its continuity comes
before its transient members. The father as head has absolute authority
and traditionally acts differently from the mother. Confucius said:

> Here now is the affection of a father for his sons: He loves the worthy
> among men, and places on a lower level those who do not show ability. But
> that of a mother for them is such, that while she loves the worthy, she pities
> those who so not show ability. The mother deals with them through her
> affections, and is not concerned with showing them honor. The father is
> intent on showing them honor, and is not concerned with his affections.[13]

In such a culture, a Divine Father would focus on family honor,
demanding that children act in ways that preserved honor regardless of
their abilities or how this affected them. A loving GOD would look
more like the mother, dealing "through her affections," yet this would
be a subordinate image and thus not suitable for GOD. Our Divine
images matter because they drag along cultural baggage. When missionaries first went to China, there was no Chinese word for a lone GOD.
In Chinese cosmogony, heaven is male and earth is female and a GOD
without a female counterpart was not productive of harmony. Rather
than adapting their metaphorical Divine images to include both masculine and feminine elements, the missionaries retained their lone masculine GOD image, using *tianzu* (Master of Heaven) and *shangi* (Supreme
Ruler), simply ignoring the Chinese Divine feminine, even though the
Creator GOD in Genesis is referred to as "Us" (Gen. 1:26) and there are
feminine Divine images in the Bible.[14]

A recent Australian survey found that mothers played the biggest
role in childhood faith development and were more likely to be the positive influence in this process. Yet the historical church has systematically portrayed women as subordinate to men, even laying on them the

blame for sin through Eve. Aristotle argued that only male seed con-
tributed to the fetus and produced male babies. If the womb as flower-
pot for the seed failed in its task, a defect "not of nature's intention"
resulted, a "misbegotten male" (female). Aristotle's biology was
adopted in the Middle Ages by Thomas Aquinas, who turned it into theology by arguing that this female inferiority and defectiveness through
the Divine afterthought, Eve, brought sin into the world and thus
deserved subjection to a male head. In fact, Aquinas, secluded from age
five in an all-male monastery, saw little use for women: "*It was necessary for woman to be made, as the Scripture says, as a helper to man
not, indeed, as a helpmate in other works, as some say, since man can
be more efficiently helped by another man in other works; but as a
helper in the work of generation.*"[15] Aquinas' biblical exegesis was as
faulty as his biology in this instance—*ezer*, long interpreted here as
helper or inferior assistant, is the same word used for Yahweh: "*My help
comes from the Lord, who made heaven and earth*" (Ps. 121:2). The
problem with patriarchy is not just that the male is head, but that this
male-led model becomes the assumed rule for all governance, whether
home, church, or nation, making it impossible to seriously consider feminine images for the Divine, even though they are in the Bible.[16]

Despite Aquinas' assessment of the female role in pregnancy and
childbirth as merely "*helping*" men "*in the work of generation,*" creation and nurture have long been associated with female power. In an
interview on Lakota Indian lore, Russell Means described his tribe's
awe of childbirth through an ancient story of how men watched
women grow with child and then give birth. "*Then they looked at one
another,*" the story ended. "*How can God be a male entity?*" Means
asked. "*I find that insulting.*"[17] Middle Eastern traditions also have
Earth Mothers bringing forth life—Tiamat the Watery Void from
which all things came and Woman Wisdom at work before creation.
Were these female Divine images once part of a Creating Pair absorbed
into one Hebrew Creating GOD? The Canaanite Mother GODDESS
Asherah, consort of principle Deity El and mother of the GODS, was
associated with green trees and forest sanctuaries, life-giving icons in a
barren land. According to William Dever, the term *asherah* occurs over
forty times in the Hebrew Bible and is linked with cutting down green
trees, poles (*asherim*), or groves of trees, hints of hunting out still-exis-
tent Asherah worship (2 Kings 17:10; Isa. 57:5). Archeological digs in

Palestine have found hundreds of small terracotta figures with accentuated hips, breasts, and pubic triangle, which Dever believes are Asherah figures once worshipped in private by Israelite women. Just as Hannah made a vow to Yahweh for a child, village women did the same to Asherah, away from priestly prying eyes. Dever also believes that references to *Hokmah* present with GOD from the beginning and to *Shekinah* are also references to Asherah, half of the Divine couple present from the beginning:

> It "fleshes out" that concept of God, brings the Divine mystery closer to the heart of human experience, and yes, to the mystery of human sexual love. We humans are engendered; if we are to think about God at all, it must be in a way that combines all that is best in males and all that is best in females . . . If God has indeed created us—male and females—"in his own image" (Genesis 1:27), then it must be in his and her images (remember the Hebrew text has "God" in the plural).[18]

Just as male images for the Divine include fighting battles and "fathering" nations, female Divine images include carrying a child in the womb, giving birth, and breastfeeding. Yahweh says to Jeremiah, *"Before I formed you in the womb I knew you, and before you were born I consecrated you"* (Jer. 1:5), and Isaiah speaks of the Lord *"who formed you in the womb"* (Isa. 44:24). By naming GOD male, such creating images have been visualized in art and the mind as an external Creator putting something into a womb from outside, like modeling with clay, but that totally distorts these images—a human being slowly taking shape within the Divine Mother, feeding through an umbilical cord from Her body, soaking up Her antibodies against disease, and being totally dependent on Her as both Creator and Sustainer. When the time comes, the Divine Creator says, *"I will cry out like a woman in labor, I will gasp and pant"* (Isa. 42:14). The image does not stop there. We are nurtured by *El Shaddai*, which, as we have seen, can be translated as the Breasted One, and gradually weaned—*"I have calmed and quieted my soul,"* the psalmist said, *"like a weaned child with its mother"* (131:2). If you feel put off by all these "female body fluid" images for GOD, this is hardly surprising, since women were once banned from worship while menstruating, needed "purification" or "churching" after childbirth, and, until a decade or so ago, were discouraged from breast-feeding in public, all derived from the "impurity"

and "shame" of the female body, disqualifying it from seriously representing the Divine. Yet a child's biological dependence on its mother is
a central human experience and should be as available in its fullness as
images of toiling in the vineyard or ruling a nation.

Nurturing does not stop with weaning—"*It was I who taught
Ephraim to walk, I took them up in my arms*" (Hosea 11:3), and when
Israel fell and skinned its knees, "*As a mother comforts her child, so will
I comfort you*" (Isa. 66:13). The Buddha also lighted on this imagery,
"*Just as a mother always loves her child, He does not forget that spirit
even for a single moment, for it is the nature of Buddhahood to be compassionate.*"[19] I wrote the following poem when my friends and I were
watching our children struggle through the vicissitudes of teenage years
and into the precipitous world of young adulthood:

> The pain of labor is nothing
>> compared with the ongoing pain
>> of watching ones once birthed
>> struggling to find themselves
>> and going down for the first . . .
>> second . . . even third time.
> Sometimes I feel there is so much
>> of my soul on loan to them
>> that there is none left within myself.

At a monastery retreat, a woman described her mother's constant sacrifices for the family such that she grew up assuming this was a woman's
destiny. On the farm, her mother would catch, kill, pluck, and cook the
chicken for the evening meal. At the table, the chicken was first passed
to her father, who always took breast meat, then to her brothers, who
took wings and legs, then to her to take what was left. Her mother took
the remaining piece, the chicken back almost devoid of meat. The
woman always assumed her mother liked the chicken back best, until
she reflected on it in adulthood. Her mother had died at fifty-four, and
the daughter still wondered whether from malnutrition. In symbolic
memory of her mother, she now eats only breast meat. As she told this
story, nods of recognition went around the table as other women
recalled similar situations. Yet even the Virgin Mother is celebrated for
her self-negating qualities—passive acceptance of an unsought pregnancy to a Father GOD; selfless nurture of a male child, only to watch

his career and murder from afar; and her sudden promotion, not for herself but as a motherlike go-between for humanity to access her males—Divine Husband and Son.

So long as women are seen only in self-negating, disposable roles, males in particular cannot image GOD as Mother, even though they have benefited from such mothering all their lives. Women are more than soft touches, which is probably why the Religious Right are so frightened of single mothers raising children alone and thus disproving their argument that women need a strong man to rule them. In the prodigal son parable (Luke 15:11–32), the Divine Father welcomes home his son and prepares a feast in his honor—there is no mention of how the mother who raised him felt on his return. When Rembrandt painted *Return of the Prodigal Son*, however, the Father's hands embracing the kneeling son are different—one is a woman's hand and the other a male hand, the Divine parent. *"The mystery, indeed, is that God in her infinite compassion has linked herself for eternity with the life of her children,"* author-priest Henri Nouwen (1932–1996) wrote about the painting. *"She has freely chosen to become dependent on her creatures, whom she has gifted with freedom. This choice causes her grief when they leave; this choice brings her gladness when they return. But her joy will not be complete until all who have received life from her have returned home and gather together around the table prepared for them."*[20] Strong Divine mothering images correct my farcical memories of Mother's Day as a child of the fifties. We made buttonholes of white chrysanthemums and fern anchored with a pin and handed them to the mothers as they arrived for worship. The sermon oozed with syrupy sweetness about self-sacrificing, self-abasing mothers, and special hymns were dusted off for this one day. After the smiling mothers left to cook the required Sunday roast for their families, the male-led church ignored them for another year, returning to important male business. As I wrote this, a few lines from one of those Mother's Day hymns popped into my mind, confirming my worst memories:

> The glory of mother,
> The gift of God's love,
> Inspires us to worship
> The Father above . . .

Need I say more—the glory of mother leads us to worship the "Father" above. *"Why,"* Dorothee Soelle asked, *"do people venerate a God whose most important quality is power, whose interest is subjection, whose fear is equality?"*[21]

The use of only domestic metaphors for female images of the Divine, however, diminishes women. *"Nurturing and tenderness simply do not exhaust the capabilities of women,"* Elizabeth Johnson says, *"nor do bodiliness and instinct define women's nature; nor is intelligence and creative transformatory agency beyond the scope of women's power; nor can the feminine be equated exclusively with mothering, affectivity, darkness, virginity, the Virgin Mary, or the positive feminine archetype without suffocating women's potential."*[22] There are plenty of powerful, public women and passive, private men. Both women and men went to death in Roman times for being Christian—Perpetua left a husband and child when thrown to the wild beasts, and Blandina was tortured on a cross. Similar stories of brave women in public roles continue today. If we make a claim that humanity is made "in God's image," all female Divine images are as appropriate as male ones; and if there are not enough feminine images preserved in our patriarchal Bible (and a variety at that), we need to find them from within our contemporary context and use them. A recent American survey showed that, while most liberal congregations accepted women pastors, 94 percent in one such congregation surveyed could not accept female GOD images—they could think of GOD abstractly in feminine images but could not think it "concretely or physically," yet they had no problem thinking concretely about GOD in male images.

One common, nongendered family image for Yahweh in the Hebrew Bible is hospitality, crucial in a desert society. Abraham and Sarah prepared a meal to accommodate three Divine visitors who came to bring them good news (Gen. 18:1–15). In the following chapter, Lot extends hospitality to two "angels," later to defend these house guests against a male gang rape, but the hospitality goes badly wrong when Lot offers his young daughters *"who have not known a man"* for the drunken mob's pleasure instead: *"Let me bring them out to you, and do to them as you please; only do nothing to these men, for they have come under the shelter of my roof"* (Gen. 19:8). The psalmist praises Yahweh's hospitality—*"You prepare a table before me in the presence of my enemies . . . my cup overflows"* (Ps. 23:5)—and Jesus recommended hospitality as a way of life—*"Whoever welcomes you welcomes me and whoever welcomes me welcomes the one who sent me*" (Matt. 10:40). The Passover meal, reminding Jewish people of their Divine deliverance from Egypt, was a celebration of hospitality, and one particular Passover became very significant for Jesus and his friends. Unfortunately, we have changed beyond recognition this sacrament of Divine hospitality with our fast-food wafers and drop of wine, together with rules about who can break the bread and who can eat at the Hospitable One's table; and although this family meal was traditionally prepared by women, it has, until recently, been presided over exclusively by specially ordained males.

The Hospitable One and Preparer of the Feast is a strong image for me, as some of my most "sacred" moments have been spent over the shared preparation and eating of food, especially in countries where language is a barrier between us—sharing food as an act of love, nurture, friendship, and fellowship requires few explanatory words. Many times I have sat at a table where wine has been poured and bread placed on side plates in preparation for the meal, and the urge to take up these elements and say a blessing, free of the rules of who can or cannot do this, is almost overwhelming. The Divine Host, who invited acquaintances to a grand feast only to receive excuses, sent the servants out into the streets to invite the "unworthy" to share the feast, a different image from the Divine Host captured in a wafer. Hospitality is limited without food to share, and not surprisingly, food images have also been used for the Divine. Subsistence living, whatever the region or religion, has linked the Divine with life-giving bread, that ancient staple of different varieties and shapes. Manna was sent from Yahweh to starving Hebrew wanderers (Exod. 16:14–15), and Jesus offered "bread from GOD" that gave "life" (John 6:32–33). Because of its importance, bread also became a metaphor for food in general and a symbol for being able to afford food at all. The pregnant Mary, anticipating the changes her son would bring, said of Yahweh, "*He has filled the hungry with good things, and sent the rich away empty*" (Luke 1:53).

Eating together as friends brings another nongendered anthropomorphic metaphor to mind, the Divine Friend. Friendship, according to seventeenth-century theologian Jeremy Taylor, is "*the greatest love and the greatest usefulness, and the most open communication, and the noblest sufferings, and the most exemplary faithfulness, and the severest truth, and the heartiest counsel, and the greatest union of mind, of which brave men and women are capable.*"[23] Humans were created as friends of the Creator to walk in the cool of the evening, a sensory rich image against the intense heat of a Middle Eastern midday. By making this a story of sin and alienation, however, we have claimed that GOD stopped being friends with us, taking the Divine bat and ball and going home, or at least locking us out of the Divine backyard where the game was being played. Yet this ignores the fact that afterward, GOD made warm vests for Adam and Eve (Gen. 3:21), was present to help Eve give birth (Gen. 4:1), and was called Abraham's friend for something we might question today—driving people off their land to give it to Abraham's progeny (2 Chron. 20:7). Friendship is a two-way commitment, with both sides vulnerable or dependent at times—the Divine need is not just about needing things done in the world but also about satisfying the Divine heart. *"That you need God more than anything, you know at all times in your heart,"* Martin Buber said, *"but don't you know also that God needs you—in the fullness of his eternity, you? How would man exist if God did not need him, and how would you exist? You need God in order to be, and God needs you—for that which is the meaning of your life."*[24]

Friendship also demands accountability on both sides, as Job demonstrated with his challenges to Yahweh. I get irritated when parents have children for their own fulfillment, then later turn it around, filling children with guilt and demanding a lifetime payback for a "debt" the children did not initiate in the first place. If we recoil from such manipulation in human life, we must also recoil from a theology that describes a Creator making humans for the Divine pleasure, then guilting them for eternity if they don't show proper obedience or love. Just as children bring joy to parents, grow up, and leave home, humans also need to grow up and leave home so that the Divine-human relationship can become more like friendship than dependency. *"The rules of friendship mean there should be mutual sympathy between friends,"* the Buddha said, *"each supplying what the other lacks and trying to benefit the other."*[25] Of course, friendship with the Divine will necessarily be asymmetric in some respects, as we are dependent on the Divine differently from Divine dependence on us, but the relationship is still mutual insofar both seek out the other for their needs. Jesus told his followers, *"I do not call you servants any longer, because the servant does not know what the master is doing; but I have called you friends, because I have made known to you everything that I have heard from my Father"* (John 15:15).

There is no limit to anthropomorphic possibilities as Divine images, but I personally would rather settle for a Divine Friend and Hospitable One than a Divine Warrior "marching as to war with the cross of Jesus going on before." I never liked the "battle for souls" that Christians were supposed to be fighting. I can remember my childhood anguish each day on the way to school, knowing that I must engage the person beside me in a conversation, to establish the state of their soul before bus stop 21, and convert them before stop 25. Panic would flood me as I glanced sideways at my prey, followed by even colder panic if they refused to be engaged or my nerves failed. The Divine Warrior was supposed to help but always seemed on a break during my bus ride, thus assigning me a task and setting me up to fail—not like a Friend would act. While some anthropomorphic Divine metaphors appeal to us more than others, depending on our own experiences of life and other human beings (some people refuse to use any because, for them, the Something described does not exist), they are all limited by our human naiveté and must remain what they are—metaphors. As Dorothee Soelle said, *"Every symbol that sets itself up as absolute must be relativized. We cannot live without symbols, but we must relativize them and surpass them iconoclastically."*[26]

13

The Bible
Tells Me So . . .

The Bible itself is made up of hundreds and hundreds of witnesses
to people's experience of what they name as God and there's no
reason why we should confine it to that. Truth is truth. We shouldn't
be afraid of that. Just because it's not put in our formulas doesn't
mean that we have to be oppressive about it.

—*Dorothy McCrae McMahon*[1]

Early religions were not obsessed with exclusive truth, perhaps because
they recognized their fragile insignificance and were glad if Deities
were receptive to them at all. They were able to accommodate many
Divine Beings, either different entities or different incarnations of the
One. Mesopotamian traditions assigned a particular Deity to each
town, not in competition but like town councils today, responsible for
the welfare of that particular group. If greater assistance was required,
Deities beyond one's normal ken could be sought, and if one tribe conquered another, the tribal GOD was conquered as well. Other cultures
shared many Deities by assigning them specific responsibilities to
expand the help-lines in an uncertain world—the Greeks corralled
theirs into a Pantheon or Divine Court. Hinduism reveled in an
astounding diversity of skilled avatars, often with multiple arms and
eyes for more efficiency, but all incarnations of the One, appearing in
various times of special need. The tenth avatar of Vishnu is still to
come, making Hinduism open-ended to further Divine "savior" visits.
When Christianity first went to India, people appreciated Jesus' wisdom but did not see the need to substitute one incarnation for all of

theirs, since the *Bhagavad Gita* said, *"In any way that men love me in that same way they find my love: for many are the paths of men, but they all in the end come to me."*[2] Similarly, when missionaries first told stories about Jesus to Australian Aborigines, some who accepted them did not wish to abandon their own stories, so they simply incorporated Jesus into their already rich heritage. Buddhism did away with Brahman and avatars altogether, seeking release from human suffering through practicing the Four Noble Truths to gain Enlightenment (Buddhahood). Even when Bodhisattvas (enlightened humans postponing Nirvana to help others) emerged in Buddhism, they were not Divine Beings as such, but human rescue figures or saviors.

The heroic savior figure appears in most religions, stretching way back to Egyptian times where, according to Canadian theologian Tom Harpur, many of their figures and stories resembled what was later said about Jesus.[3] The hero reached its noblest, or most hopeless, form in Norse mythology, where the GODS, knowing they would one day all be destroyed by evil, continued to fight for good, recruiting humans to die as heroes and enter the halls of the warrior dead (Valhalla) until a final, inevitable defeat.[4] "Sons of God" were savior figures in Hebrew history, humans commissioned by Yahweh to rescue or "save" Israel at various times. Around Jesus' time, there was an expectation of a king like David who would defeat Israel's oppressors and inaugurate Yahweh's Kingdom again in their midst. The Latin poet Virgil also prophesied a future golden age in his *Eclogues* (39–38 BCE), heralded in by the birth of *"the firstborn child of promise."* This image was attributed to Virgil's contact with Jewish families in Rome and later "adopted" by Greek-influenced Christians as further confirmation of Jesus as their Greek-style hero figure.[5] Heroic savior figures inspire, not because they are ontologically different from humans or do supernatural things, but because they are human and thus we can all imitate them. Paul told his followers to be "imitators" of him as he imitated Jesus the Christ (1 Cor. 11:1). Such imitation becomes a futile mission, however, if the one to be imitated is superhuman or Divine.

After twelve chapters of acknowledging Divine Mystery defying description, we are faced with a claim that this Mystery has been embodied in all its essentialness, once and for all, in a human male form in one small area of the world—Jesus, Jewish sage and Greek hero figure, fully man and fully GOD. If this is so, we need ponder GOD no

longer. Not surprisingly, when Christianity declared its hero savior figure to be GOD, the global religious landscape changed forever, not
because everyone believed it, but because this exclusive claim, rather
than one explanation among others, challenged all religious truth claims
and was followed up by Christianity moving around the world to usurp
Divine "pretenders." Many of us grew up in this culture of religious
exclusiveness that is epitomized by my student in a World Religions
course. After moving from discussions of Judaism and Christianity to
Hinduism and its incarnations of the One, his hand shot up, "That can't
be true because the Bible says Jesus Christ is the only incarnation of
God, the only way, truth, and life." "And why should a Hindu believe
such a claim on such an authority?" I asked, a question totally beyond
his ken, having never even considered that a different sacred text or
GOD-claim might have validity. The transformation of Jesus into GOD
was Muhammad's criticism of Christianity. Through a long history
starting with "In the beginning," GOD had sent human savior messengers—Moses, Elijah, Amos, Jesus and Muhammad—but Christianity
had corrupted this tradition by divinizing Jesus, thus a new revelation
(the Qur'an) was needed:

> He [Allah] sent down upon you the Book in truth, confirming what went
> before it, and he sent down the Torah and the Gospel before this as a guide
> to all people (Surah 3:2) . . . He is God, alone, God the absolute. He does
> not beget, he is not begotten, and there is none in any way equal to him
> (Surah 112) . . . They do blaspheme who say: "God is Christ the son of
> Mary." But said Christ: "O Children of Israel! worship God, my Lord and
> your Lord." Whoever joins other Gods with God, God will forbid him the
> garden, and the Fire will be his abode (Surah 5:72).

Sallie McFague critiques this one-and-only claim, this "scandal of
uniqueness," from within the Christian tradition on its "incredible,
indeed absurd" cosmology:

> God is embodied in one place and one place only: in the man Jesus of
> Nazareth. He and he alone is "the image of the invisible God" (Col. 1:15).
> The source, power, and goal of the universe is known through and only
> through a first-century Mediterranean carpenter. The creator and redeemer
> of the fifteen-billion-year history of the universe with its hundred billion
> galaxies (and their billions of stars and planets) is available only in a

thirty-year span of one human being's life on planet earth. The claim, when put in the context of contemporary science, seems skewed, to say the least.[6]

We therefore need to investigate the evidence on which Christianity makes its claim because it seriously affects what we can think about GOD. Some will simply say "the Bible says so," but things are not so tidy—councils of bishops four centuries after Jesus were still debating whether Jesus was GOD or "like" GOD, a world of difference. What is this Bible that has kept us "drawing within the lines" in Christian theology for so many centuries, and what authority does it have to make such claims about Jesus? If I were to identify significant challenges in the last fifty years that have necessitated rethinking Divine images, those made to claims of the literal nature and infallibility of the Bible would be at the top of my list. While the Bible is the source of much of what we say about GOD, it is also the reason why we have been so limited in what we say about the Divine. Some people claim the teachings of our ancient forefathers (and a rare foremother) to be unchanging truths, but this is contrary to life experience in general—we would hardly make such claims about Aristotle's science. "*If a religion establishes a relationship between man and God*," Leo Tolstoy said, "*but does so through affirmations which are so contrary to the level of knowledge people have reached that they cannot believe in them, then neither is this a religion, but merely a semblance of one.*"[7]

Recently I dined with a group of people, some not known to me. When the conversation turned to recent terrorist attacks, one man made a definitive statement that the Qur'an incites violence. Surprisingly to him, I disagreed, saying there was much about peace in the Qur'an and added that the Hebrew Bible and Christian Old Testament also have their share of violence against their enemies (Ulphila flashed through my mind, that fourth-century apostle to the Goths who omitted the book of Kings when translating the Bible into Goth because they were warlike enough without any encouragement from scripture).[8] The man replied with a dismissive sniff, "Oh, but no one takes any notice of the Bible anymore." Another person at the table, knowing I taught World Religions, interrupted to comment on the lovely weather, anything to stop a serious discussion, GOD forbid, at a dinner party. So many issues surfaced, however, in this brief exchange—assumptions about another's sacred text in an authoritative but unnuanced way from media information disseminated, often in uninformed generalizations; dismissal of the Hebrew Bible's warring culture and the political oppression of New Testament times that led to Jesus' crucifixion; and the claim that the Bible is no longer influential in our culture. Although many people never open a Bible today, public debates wherever we live are fueled at some point by vocal, influential lobbies claiming their authority from the Bible. Community-splitting debates about same sex marriage are not so much about the people involved, but about what the Bible says, or does not say, about homosexuality. Debates about abortion, the drug RU486, and stem cell research are not so much about mother or fetus, but about what the Bible does, or does not say, about when life begins. The debate about teaching creationism or intelligent design alongside evolution in schools is not about scientific method, but about what the Bible says, or does not say, about how the world began.

This is not new. Victorians supported slavery and denied women the right to their children, money, property, and the vote on biblical arguments, and our Western systems of government and law were constructed on arguments supported by the Bible. *"A Bible and a newspaper in every house, a good school in every district—all studied and appreciated as they merit,"* Benjamin Franklin said, *"are the principal support of virtue, morality and civil liberty."*[9] Although few people have read the Bible through and fewer know its origins and history, these same people will base their faith on this book and make exclusive claims about it. Any other book of such magnitude and influence would invite many searching questions about authorship and origins, but these are discouraged of the Bible. It has become for many a talisman magical in itself, regardless of its background, simply because people claim it is the inspired Word of GOD. The "simple" Gospel is often quoted, meaning that the best Christians "just believe" without question. As someone once said, if the Bible was written today, it would be a four-page pamphlet in words of no more than two syllables, on blue paper (because blue sells), with a scratch and sniff section to stimulate a spiritual experience, and a coupon for a Christian music CD.

What then is this book? How did it come about, and what authority does it carry in itself and indirectly over other religions as the "truth" about GOD? Christians, Jews, and Muslims all claim a revealed religion, meaning that the Divine has somehow communicated with human beings. The Jews believed Yahweh made a covenant with them, formulated laws, acted in their favor, and, at certain intervals, sent additional or revised messages through prophets. The Law (Torah) was revealed to Moses and later written down as the first five books of the Hebrew Bible, with narrative, songs, prophetic utterances, and exhortations later filling the rest. The Hebrew scriptures were not claimed as Yahweh's dictation but rather the record of many peoples' experiences of the Divine, thus rabbis could apply these stories in different times and places and find multiple meanings in them. These midrashic (Hebrew, "to search, inquire, and interpret") interpretations focused on individual words and grammar forms, not to determine one correct meaning on which great doctrinal towers could be constructed, but with the assumption that *"the biblical text has an inexhaustible fund of meaning that is relevant to and adequate for every question and situation."*[10] While the Mishnah contained rabbinic laws, the Palestinian and Babylonian Talmuds were commentaries on these laws, full of dramatic and detailed embellishments of the Hebrew stories and characters. Unlike legal documents, imagination could work freely as long as it stayed within the parameters of what the religious community would accept.[11]

Rabbis had long discussions about everything, such as Eve being constructed from Adam's rib. Did that mean she was made from stolen goods, and what does that say about Divine integrity? Why was theft necessary to create Eve when GOD had already created many different creatures—why not another from scratch? Did losing a rib make Adam incomplete, and was that why a man searches for a woman, not vice versa, because he has lost something? And which rib was it, left or right, and why a rib, not some other body part? One rabbinic answer put on Yahweh's lips in such discussions was:

> I will not create her from (Adam's) head, lest she be swelled-headed; nor from the eye, lest she be a coquette; nor from the ear, lest she be an eavesdropper; nor from the mouth, lest she be a gossip; nor from the heart, lest she be prone to jealousy; nor from the hand, lest she be light-fingered; nor from the foot, lest she be a gadabout; but from the modest part of man, for even when he stands naked, that part is covered.[12]

From this one topic, we see the willingness to hold conflicting ideas without identifying one correct position, recognizing that no one can authoritatively look into the Divine cards. Where the Torah was not specific, no one would be hauled off to prison for suggesting a different interpretation. This makes sense of the rabbinic debates in which Jesus was involved, and also raises questions as to whether the various Gospel stories, written so long after Jesus' death and not always agreeing, were also "midrash"—stories expanding on limited information and memories about Jesus for the next generation. Such inclusiveness also allowed different sects to be accommodated within Judaism until the unsuccessful Jewish War of 70 CE, when Jewish leaders pondered Yahweh's "disfavor" and consequently weeded out nonorthodox teaching, including the followers of Jesus.

Muslims also recognize Divine revelation in the Tawrat (Torah) and Injil (Christian Gospels), but see the Qur'an (Arabic for "recitation" or "reading") as the final disclosure through the prophet Muhammad. *Ahl al-Kitab*, Arabic for a religious community with written scriptures, occurs some fifty-four times in the Qur'an and is applied to all people to whom GOD has sent a scripture (which should in itself produce dialogue across these religions):

> Lo! Those who believe (in that which is revealed unto thee, Muhammad), and those who are Jews, and Christians, and Sabaeans—whoever believeth in Allah and the Last Day and doeth right—surely their reward is with their Lord, and there shall no fear come upon them neither shall they grieve (Surah 2:62).

A covenant attributed to Caliph Umar was elaborated in Sharia law by the mid-ninth century, allowing any "people of the Book" to live peacefully under Islamic rule and uphold their own religious duties and laws, provided they did not proselytize.[13] What is different with Muslims, however, among "people of the Book" is their belief that the Qur'an is Allah's actual words in Arabic, passed unaltered through the conduit Muhammad to scribes who wrote them down exactly as the incarnate Word. In comparisons between Islam and Christianity, therefore, the Qur'an as incarnate Word for Muslims is like Jesus, the incarnate Word for Christians, rather than the Bible.

As Allah's actual unmediated words, the Qur'an is the complete and final guide for Muslims in all aspects of human life, and is thus not open to challenges or critique like those made by Hebrew and Christian scholars of the Bible's cultural limitations. As thirteenth-century Sufi Shams-i-Tabrizi said, "*All theologies are straws that His Sun burns to dust: Knowledge takes you to the threshold, but not through the door."*[14] Since the Qur'an's Arabic is considered so perfect that only a Divine revelation could have produced it, earliest efforts at interpretation to explain difficult wording and grammar was done with great trepidation, and translation of the Qur'an into other languages happened more through scholarly pressure than Muslim desire to share scriptures (translations are called paraphrases or interpretations, not the Qur'an). Muslim scholars today who try to use methodologies of textual criticism borrowed from biblical criticism are thought blasphemous by many. Feminist Islamic scholars have a particularly bad press, because they also challenge traditional ideas of women's subordination thought to come from the Qur'an, but which, in fact, come more from later Islamic law and interpretation.[15] Fundamentalist Christians who claim an infallible, inerrant, and Divinely inspired Bible should be sympathetic with Islamic reverence for their infallible Qur'an, but, of course, those who believe in biblical infallibility and Christian uniqueness would see Islamic "truth" as false. *"It is a complete fallacy to think that when faith speaks to faith to bring about harmony and reconciliation between people it speaks the same language,"* says religion scholar Mona Siddiqui, speaking of global politics that use religious terms as if they have universal meaning. *"There is an obvious treading on eggshells so as to create a context for discussion but in which very often the real issues that polarize even the most liberal of us end up being ignored or moved into different spaces."*[16]

Christians believe GOD spoke through the events recorded in the Hebrew scriptures and also through the Jewish Jesus, as recorded in the New Testament. The Christian Bible is therefore an eclectic story of Divine communication over two thousand years of history written in poetry, allegory, correspondence, and narrative. Even though writing was known in Abraham's time, the Hebrew Bible began as oral stories passed down the generations, and when the Hebrews settled in one place, the stories were recorded on scrolls of papyrus stored in libraries ("bible" means a library of scrolls or "little scrolls"). After the Jewish exile in Babylon in the sixth century BCE, scribes collected oral and written traditions together and compiled them into the five scrolls of the Pentateuch containing all necessary law, instruction, and guidance (Torah). Other scrolls were added later, encompassing almost two thousand years of Hebrew traditions. Jesus and his followers used these scrolls, but by the end of the first century when Jesus' followers were mostly Gentile, the Septuagint (a Greek translation of the Hebrew scriptures containing an apocrypha of additional books) was used.

As for the New Testament, stories and sayings of Jesus circulated around isolated Mediterranean communities after his death, carried by wandering apostles and trades people. Different communities later wrote down their stories, hence the various "gospels" (good news). These were copied by hand for sharing between communities (Romans 16:22 includes a greeting from Paul's scribe Tertius), and they supplemented the Hebrew scriptures, retrospectively linking Jesus back to Hebrew Bible predictions. Their memories of Jesus varied and often contradicted each other. Luke has Mary and Joseph returning to Nazareth after Jesus' birth in Bethlehem, and yet Matthew says they fled to Egypt. John's Gospel has many differences, including no breaking of bread at the last supper, a three-year ministry for Jesus with many trips to Jerusalem (the others record one year and one trip), and Jesus cleansing the temple at the beginning of his ministry, not the end. I grew up learning that the four gospels were written by the disciples as eyewitness accounts, thus proving the literal and historical accuracy of the events recorded, but biblical scholars now agree that the gospels were not written by disciples but were later community faith statements, like long sermons urging belief. Each Gospel chose and arranged its material to make a specific argument to a specific community rather than a comprehensive narrative—John's Gospel says it only included selected stories that would make people believe (20:30–31). If a community was originally Jewish, their gospel assured them that Yahweh was still their GOD, and if the audience was mostly Greek, the universality of Jesus was preached—Paul told the philosophers of Athens that their Unknowable One had now been revealed through a man, with no mention of his Jewishness or a Jewish GOD (Acts 17:22–32). Apostles' names were not assigned to the Gospels until the late second century by Bishop Irenaeus, to distinguish them rather than naming the author. Irenaeus also limited the authorized gospels to four because there were four winds, four compass points, four living creatures in Revelation 4:6, and four Divine covenants—strange logic today. Not all Irenaeus' colleagues agreed with his choice. Marcion thought Luke was the only true Gospel, Justyn Martyr accepted three but not John, and Tatian produced a gospel merging all three (*Diatessaron*). Other surviving gospels include the Gospel of Thomas, the Gospel of Mary, and the Infancy Stories of Jesus, all used by early Christian communities even though they did not make the final fourth-century canon.

There were early attempts to collect Paul's letters together once the codex format (pages bound as a book) replaced scrolls. However, some letters now labeled as Paul's were not written by him but later, perhaps by someone "of his school," because there are discrepancies of ideas between these later letters and Paul's, reflecting a different stage of the emerging church. Come to think of it, the whole Bible is mostly anonymous—Job is not by Job, Samuel is not by Samuel, and although the Pentateuch was thought to have been written by Moses, the text does not say that and Moses' death is included within it. As biblical scholar William Schniedewind points out, there is no word in classical Hebrew for "author," as the authority for the story was the community that passed it on to their children (Deut. 6:6–7)—the nearest word would be *sofer* (scribe), the one who wrote down the community's story.[17] This is why the "infallible Bible" argument based on inspiration of the writers is strange, as we do not know who they were, nor whether any of these writings were composed by one person at a single sitting. Genesis contains conflicting story fragments from different periods, like an anthology or scrapbook: in Genesis 1, the animals are created before humans, but in Genesis 2, Adam is created before the animals; Adam and Eve are created together in Genesis 1 and Eve after Adam in Genesis 2. Scholars see these books as composites of different tribal traditions rather than a single story, just as Holocaust survivors would hold different memories and interpretations of their experiences.

The biblical writings were added to and adapted over time as they were copied and circulated. We do not have any original scrolls, and early copies vary in their texts, challenging claims that GOD miraculously inspired each word of the Bible (yet did not ensure that the originals were preserved). As biblical scholar Bart Ehrman says:

> How does it help us to say that the Bible is the inerrant word of God if in fact we don't have the words that God inerrantly inspired, but only the words copied by scribes—sometimes correctly but sometimes (many times!) incorrectly? What good is it to say that the autographs (i.e. the originals)

were inspired? We don't have the originals! We have only error-ridden copies, and the vast majority of these are centuries removed from the originals and different from them, evidently, in thousands of ways.[18]

Early copyists around the Mediterranean were often trained household slaves or professional public scribes, as few people were literate. Standards could vary, as Roman poet Martial indicates: *"If any poems in those sheets, reader, seem to you either too obscure or not quite good Latin, not mine is the mistake: the copyist spoiled them in his haste to complete for you his tale of verses."*[19] Many early Christian manuscripts would have been done, not by professional copyists, but by literate community members wanting to obtain and share different texts for reading in worship. According to Ehrman, ancient Greek texts (like early Christian writings) had no punctuation marks, no distinction between upper and lower case, and no spaces separating words, all of which made it difficult to interpret the text accurately.[20] *"The differences among the manuscripts have become great, either through the negligence of some copyists or through the perverse audacity of others,"* third-century theologian Origen said of the Gospel copies he accessed, *"they either neglect to check over what they have transcribed, or, in the process of checking, they make additions or deletions as they please."*[21] Bishop Dionysius (second century CE) declared that false believers had *"filled with tares"* his writings, *"taking away some things and adding others"*; while Latin Christian scholar Rufinus considered the problem large enough to tell transcribers, under warning of hellfire, to *"add nothing to what is written and take nothing away from it, and make no insertion or alteration,"* carefully comparing their transcription with the copy from which it was made.[22] Ehrman lists numerous reasons for alterations of New Testament texts in the first few centuries, giving many examples that I will leave you to read for yourself: accidental mistakes; explanatory add-ons, even whole passages (John 21 and Mark 16:9–20 are not in the oldest manuscripts); links back to the Hebrew scriptures—"this was done to fulfill what was spoken by the prophet"; alteration of awkward or unusual statements to improve the sense; and changes to support evolving orthodox theological positions.

As original witnesses died out, the test for orthodoxy was whether a teaching could be traced back to an original apostle—later, orthodoxy became a way to guard against what was deemed heresy. Some copyists promoted their community's theological position (or their own) by editing biblical verses that might support an opposing argument. As Jesus' Divinity evolved, for example, verses that originally named Joseph as his father were altered—the King James Version (1611) says of Simeon's prophecy about the baby Jesus, "*Joseph and his mother marveled at those things*" (Luke 2:33), whereas the New Revised Standard Version (1989), having studied the earliest texts, has returned the translation to "*And the child's father and mother were amazed at what was being said about him.*"[23] When the Docetists claimed that Jesus was not a fully flesh-and-blood human, verses not in the earlier manuscripts described Jesus sweating while praying (Luke 22:43–44) to support the fully human, fully Divine orthodox position.[24] As Judaism became defined over against Christianity, anti-Jewish additions also emerged. For example, while some copies say Pilate flogged Jesus then "*handed him over to be crucified*" (Matt. 27:26), others handed him "*to them (i.e. to the Jews) in order that they might crucify him.*"[25] Ehrman also discusses the difficulty of establishing which copy was closest to the original, as an earlier copy from an altered manuscript could become the official one while a later copy from the original might remain uncopied. As for Paul and his scribes, did he dictate his letters to them in full or simply spell out salient points in haste for their elaboration; and even if letters did leave the scribe's hand as Paul dictated, what of communities copying them for circulation, adding their own explanations and comments? The earliest fragment of Galatians dates from about 200 CE, one hundred and fifty years after it was written, so how many scribes, in haste to get out Paul's comments, lie in between? This discussion of textual changes in the early centuries is not to devalue the Bible but to indicate its human origins, as we should expect if we think about it seriously without supernatural claims to make its origins otherwise. Biblical scholars have long recognized that the Gospels of Luke and Matthew depend heavily on borrowings from the earlier Gospel of Mark added to and put in their own words, just as we say "in other words" to clarify a point, yet Matthew and Luke have not been rejected as "altered texts."

Many writings circulated in the first few centuries amongst scattered Mediterranean communities, and there were many more Gospels than four, arguing different things about Jesus and his teachings. Once Christianity became defined by doctrinal creeds in the fourth century, however, there was a need to "authorize" certain writings into a canon, excluding those that did not represent "orthodoxy." At the end of the fourth century, Bishop Athanasius' list of books won the day over church historian Eusebius' list (Eusebeus was unsure of James, Jude, 1 and 2 Peter, and 3 John, and was baffled by Revelation). There is a difference, however, between a formal and a practical New Testament canon—the Acts of the Apostles was scarcely used, while excluded writings such as the Shepherd of Hermas continued to be read. Judaism had settled on its Hebrew Bible canon at the end of the first century CE, choosing a shorter list of books than those in the Greek Septuagint. The early church followed the Septuagint for their "Old Testament," but when fourth-century theologian Jerome translated the Christian Bible into Latin, he wanted to follow his Jewish colleagues' shortened list and omit the extra "apocryphal" books in the Septuagint. His influential colleague Augustine disagreed, and so the extra books were bracketed in, only to be removed later by the Reformers, who then did not reorder the Old Testament books to conform to the Jewish scriptures. The Protestant Bible format, therefore, had actually never been used before, showing that any discussion of GOD's Word depends on the particular edition about which you are talking. Eastern church Bibles have other additions—the book of Enoch mentioned in Jude was unknown until an ancient copy of it was discovered in ancient Ethiopian scriptures in the Ge'ez language.

Despite all this well-documented history of editing and compilation, some folk still insist that all the words of the Bible should be read literally as GOD's dictated words. Where does this claim come from? Jewish rabbis and early church fathers did not read scripture literally but saw layers of meaning behind the verses, narrative (literal), poetic, allegorical, spiritual. The literal reading was the least preferred, as it was considered mundane and bland. This Latin verse reflected the difference:

> The letter shows us what God and our fathers did;
> The allegory shows us where our faith is hid;
> The moral meaning gives us rules for daily life;
> The anagogy shows us where we end our strife.[26]

Taking the term "Jerusalem" as an example, the letter (literal) shows its place on the map; the "heavenly" Jerusalem is allegorical; hope for a "new" Jerusalem is moral and social; and the hidden, spiritual allusion (anagogy) shows Jerusalem as an object of ultimate hope. In Jerome's Latin translation (Vulgate), he chose the intention of a text, and today's scholars, looking back on his translation, can see places where a more correct rendition could have been made. Reflecting church dogma at the time, Jerome also changed some Greek names of female church leaders in Romans 16 to Latin male names because church leaders were, by then, all male. These many levels of meaning, with the church determining the correct interpretation, held into the Middle Ages. Was Jonah factual or allegorical? Was Job a real person or a character in a play about Yahweh's dealings with humanity? Thomas Aquinas made changes in his time, declaring the literal-grammatical sense as primary, to which one then added the spiritual sense: "*All the senses of scripture are founded on one, the literal, from which alone any argument can be drawn, and not from those intended in allegory.*"[27] Since Aquinas did not read Greek, his "literal" reading came from Jerome's Latin Vulgate.

Until this point, the Vulgate was the Roman church's Bible and the Greek Bible, from which Jerome's Latin translation was made, that of the Eastern church. Humanist scholar Erasmus published a Greek New Testament for the Roman church in 1516, relying on medieval manuscripts and, in places, translating back from Jerome's Latin into Greek, thus creating Greek readings not in ancient Greek New Testament manuscripts. Interestingly, an addition not in the ancient Greek manuscripts had crept into the Latin New Testament by the Middle Ages (in square brackets): "*There are three that testify:[in heaven, the Father, the Word and the Holy Spirit; and these three are one. And there are three that testify on earth] the Spirit, and the water, and the blood, and these three agree*" (1 John 5:7–8). Erasmus therefore omitted this addition in his Greek translation, but since this omission was important for the church's doctrine of the Trinity, the resulting fuss forced Erasmus to include it in his later edition, the one on which the King James Version (KJV) was based. It is therefore in the KJV, but not in Luther's German Bible, which was based on Erasmus' first edition.[28]

The Reformation installed scripture (*sola scriptura*) as the authoritative guide to faith, rather than the broader collection of theological writings defined as authoritative in the Roman church's 1546 ecclesiastical decree:

This truth and rule are contained in written books and in unwritten traditions which were received by the apostles from the mouth of Christ himself, or else have come down to us, handed on as it were from the apostles themselves at the inspiration of the Holy Spirit.[29]

Such authority given to scripture alone was justified by the Spirit's inspiration of the original writers and also of the current readers. Printing press in hand, Luther translated the Bible into common German for distribution, to be interpreted not in allegorical or spiritual ways but in its commonsense, everyday meaning. Luther did not think of the Bible as infallible but rather, through the words of scripture, the Word was heard with the Spirit's help. He also did not sanction all the biblical books— he ignored James as a book of straw and criticized some of the others. As for the King James Version, when James VI of Scotland became James I of England, he authorized a new translation of the Bible in English, although there were already several translations available. Gathering a group of fifty-four translators from various fields, this translation was based on a composite of sources, including Luther's German Bible, Erasmus' Greek New Testament, Jerome's Latin Vulgate, and some earlier English versions. Despite its cut-and-paste history, the King James Version (1611) became the official English version and is still championed by many today as the only "correct" translation, yet we can see that this idea of the Bible (whether Latin Vulgate or KJV) as a single, unchanged, inerrant volume of books, written somehow under direct Divine pushing of the pen, is patently false.

Not until centuries later did biblical scholars search out the earliest Greek and Hebrew manuscripts for translation purposes and also investigate the biblical social context to dissect its message from layers of cultural and linguistic baggage. As a result, the Revised Standard Version, a revision of the KJV, was published in the 1880s (and an American edition in 1902). Those who were raised on the KJV as GOD's actual words were threatened by changes to the familiar texts and so clung to this old version as literal and inerrant, insisting every word was inspired and not open to error, and that GOD would not allow scripture to lead us astray with contradictions. Five fundamental points of belief were declared in 1895, including inerrancy of scripture and a literal interpretation, and thus "fundamentalism" was born, dividing American Protestants into fundamentalists and modernists according to their acceptance or rejection of new biblical scholarship and the Revised Standard Version. Scholarship changed again in the 1940s when scrolls from biblical times older than those previously known were discovered at the Dead Sea and in Egypt, including some unknown Gospels portraying New Testament events in a new light—the New Revised Standard Version (1989) included scholastic input from these manuscripts. Today, we have at our disposal some 5,700 Greek manuscripts, many only fragments and the earliest an early second-century fragment of John 18; 10,000 manuscripts of the Latin Vulgate; manuscripts in Syriac, Armenian, and Coptic; and writings of early church fathers quoting New Testament texts in their earliest forms. In all these, scholars claim some 200,000 to 400,000 variations.[30]

Given all this, what do people mean by claiming the Bible is inspired? Why are stories on the last page of the Acts of the Apostles more sacred than events that took place the following week? This inspiration claim has prevented biblical critique for years and still does for many, so what is it? Our answer determines how we approach the Bible. Some people say that since the Divine is incapable of error, GOD would not produce an imperfect scripture, dismissing all the editing just described by claiming inerrancy of the "original" documents—a useless argument when we don't have the originals. Others claim the inspired Bible is a textbook for all times and that biblical authors were inspired to write down geographical, cosmological, and scientific information they could not know or understand, yet we don't know who these writers were, so how can we evaluate this claim? When churches are confronted with hard social and moral questions today, church newspapers are full of letters demanding "Go back to the Bible," listing odd texts from here and there, as if this book, enmeshed in ancient desert cosmology and law, is unquestionably applicable for every aspect of twenty-first-century life. Yet these same folk are very selective with the texts they quote. Jesus' command to the rich young ruler to sell all he had and give to the poor in order to be a disciple is rarely preached literally, yet the words from 1 Timothy—"*I permit no woman to teach or to have authority over a man*" (2:12)—are still used to refuse ordination to many women, even though the verses immediately before are dismissed as culturally outdated—that women must not braid their hair or wear gold, pearls, or expensive clothes. On what or whose criteria are some "inspired" verses negotiable, yet verses reflecting Greco-Roman subordination of women eternally binding? We do need to go back to the Bible to find, along with noble thoughts and actions, divinely sanctioned violence, rape, incest, injustice, and deception, all of which must be confronted as unacceptable today. As religious writer Sara Maitland says:

> We must not confuse the community and its sacred texts with God. Communities may legitimately desire protection against all forms of assault, but we cannot afford any longer to pretend that it is God whom we wish to protect. A God who needs this sort of protecting is not a God worth believing in.[31]

Instead of defending the Bible with inerrant, inspired claims, why not let the Bible speak for itself? The word *theopneustos* ("inspired" or "God-breathed") occurs only once in the Bible to describe scripture. Timothy is told to hold fast what he has learned because *"All scripture is inspired by God and is useful for teaching, for reproof, for correction, and for training in righteousness, so that everyone who belongs to God may be proficient, equipped for every good work"* (2 Tim. 3:16–17). The scriptures here were Hebrew scrolls, not the New Testament writings; what "inspired by God" meant in the verse is not recorded; and no claims are made beyond scripture's usefulness as a guide to life. On the other hand, inspired or GOD-breathed appears often in the Bible to describe human beings: the Spirit breathed into clay at creation; prophets inspired by the Spirit "coming upon" them; the Spirit coming upon Jesus, anointing him for a mission; Jesus transferring this Spirit to his followers to guide them into all truth; and the Spirit coming on all of them at Pentecost. This recurring "in-spiration" says that we are all inspired people, not just some unknown scribes compiling the biblical stories of a community. Do we claim to be infallible? Of course not. While the Bible holds a central place for Christians because it contains the story of their founder Jesus, to claim it is the only or final story negates the Bible itself with its promise that the Spirit continues to work, bringing more light and truth to every generation, more stories of divine encounters. The way some folk defend the Bible against anything new, you'd think the Spirit fled on the last page and we are left alone with only a book. We need to distinguish between words of Scripture that can become outdated and the Word encountered both in ancient stories and today, putting the emphasis where the Bible does on the Divine Spirit helping discern what is *"useful for teaching, for reproof, for correction, and for training in righteousness"* (2 Tim. 3:16).

Attempts to twist these ancient desert experiences into timeless rules must be challenged, as Jesus challenged the rules in his day. When Leviticus demands the death of a man who "lies with" another male (20:13), or calls women "impure" and untouchable during menstruation (15:19–24), or forbids the eating of the blood of any animal (17: 14), we need to say, "These rules were made for ancient desert people. Are they still useful in our time and circumstance?" We must also protest when some ancient laws are insisted upon today but not others, like quoting Leviticus against a same-sex relationship while ignoring Levitical prohibitions on blood-sausage. When the Bible (or any sacred text) is used to encourage hate, oppress human beings, incite violence against humanity or the earth, or demand we leave our minds and experience at the door, it behooves inspired or Spirit-breathed humans to go back to that text and liberate it from those who use it in inappropriate, noncompassionate ways. The Bible, like the sacred text of any religious community, is a guide from a particular context, not an eternal archetype into which contemporary experiences and knowledge must fit. In the mid 1800s, a group of Church of England scholars published *Essays and Reviews*, arguing for a more enlightened understanding of religion and the Bible in the face of emerging scientific knowledge (*Origin of Species* was published the year before). Benjamin Jowett, master of Balliol College, Oxford, wrote an essay "On the Interpretation of Scripture," which was refreshingly challenging then and still is today. He summarized his argument:

> Of what has been said, this is the sum: That Scripture, like other books, has one meaning, which is to be gathered from itself without reference to the adaptations of Fathers or Divines; and without regard to a priori notions about its nature and origin. It is to be interpreted like other books, with attention to the character of its authors, and the prevailing state of civilization and knowledge, with allowance for peculiarities style and language, and modes of thought and figures of speech. Yet not without a sense that as we read there grows upon us the witness of God in the world, anticipating in a rude and primitive age the truth that was to be, shining more and more unto the perfect day in the life of Christ, which again is reflected from different points of view in the teaching of His Apostles.[32]

This commonsense approach to the Bible as a guide from another time allows us to read images of the Divine from those ancient deserts and busy Mediterranean market towns, yet not be limited to them or by them. *"The Bible is like a window—looking through it you see the world,"* Frederick Buechner said. *"If you look at the window you see fly specks, dust, and the crack where Junior's Frisbee hit it. If you look through it, you see the world beyond."*[33] While we can make use of the symbolism and ideas available to us, we can and must critique those parts that no longer make sense or, worse still, are harmful and violent. And we can add our own contemporary experiences of encounters with the Sacred in our own poetry and metaphors, always recognizing the elusiveness (or absence, for some) of what is described. Such openness to the Bible allows us to "read" the Divine through others' traditions as well, whether the poetry of the Sufis or the silent meditation of Buddhists.

A group of us read together Jack Miles' book *God: A Biography*. One very enthusiastic member kept telling all her friends that we were reading *God: An Autobiography*. How I wish—but even then, I wonder if there would be fewer questions.

Who Do You
Say I Am?

OM. That Word is the everlasting Brahman:
   that Word is the highest End . . .
It is the supreme means of salvation.

—Upanishads [1]

◌ ◌

We believe in Allah and that which is revealed unto us and that
which was revealed unto Abraham, and Ishmael, and Isaac, and
Jacob, and the tribes, and that which Moses and Jesus received,
and that which Prophets received from their Lord.

— Qur'an, Surah 2:136

◌ ◌

Jesus said . . . "I am the way, and the truth, and the life.
No one comes to the Father except through me."

—John 14:6

Having thought about the Bible and how we might evaluate its message
and authority for today, we return to the Christian claim, still debated
in the fifth century CE, that Jesus the *Messiah* (Greek *Christos*) was fully
man and fully GOD. From where did this come, and how did it develop
through history? The question "Who was Jesus?" has two parts—who
was the man that trudged around Galilee, and who was the Jesus who
became Lord of the church? Most serious scholars recognize this evolution of belief within and beyond the New Testament with the various

gospels and letters written at different times. Paul's seven letters are the earliest (50–60 CE),[2] and Mark is the earliest Gospel (around 70 CE), with Matthew and Luke written 80–90 CE and John 90–100 CE. Some of the other letters, such as the letters to Timothy, were probably written in the early second century CE. Paul's letters and the Gospels were Jewish writings addressed to synagogue worshippers (or recently excluded) and so have to be read within the Jewish context. Three Gospels record a question on Jesus' lips, "Who are people saying I am?" (Matt. 16:13; Mark 8:27; Luke 9:18) to which the disciples gave various answers but all agreed that Jesus was a prophet, like John the Baptist, Elijah, or Jeremiah. Peter says, "*You are the Messiah*," or in Matthew, "*the Messiah, the Son of the Living God.*"

Messiah (*Christos*) is Hebrew for "anointed one" and meant any individual chosen by Yahweh to save Israel or significantly contribute to its destiny, whether kings (Ps. 89:20), priests (Lev. 4:5), or prophets (Jer. 1:5). King Cyrus of Persia was called Yahweh's *messiah* or "anointed one," the only non-Israelite so designated, because he delivered the Israelites from exile (Isa. 45:1, 4), and there was speculation around John the Baptist as to whether he was the longed-for *messiah* (Luke 3:15). *Messiah* status was not something one claimed for oneself but rather was designated by Yahweh and recognized by followers through what one did. Many scholars believe that the Jesus of the Synoptic Gospels (Matthew, Mark, and Luke) did not see himself as a *messiah* during his lifetime and that this statement was placed on Peter's lips when the Gospels were written forty or more years later, reflecting conclusions reached by Gospel communities.[3] Even if the title *messiah* was being applied to Jesus during his lifetime, it had no supernatural implications but meant, like other "anointed ones" in Jewish history, someone called by Yahweh to save Israel, this time from Roman domination.

There was heightened expectation of a *messiah* ("savior") around Jesus' time, yet the Jews did not agree as to how this *messiah* would save them. The Pharisees wanted a religious leader, Essenes favored a dramatic Divine intervention, activist Zealots hoped for a military man (Caesar had been called a "savior" for his political and military efforts), and the poor, not necessarily in the discussion, longed for justice (Luke 1:52–53). While Jesus' followers were convinced, either then or in retrospect, of Jesus' role, the chief priests and scribes, given their insults flung at Jesus on the cross, were not: *"He saved others; he cannot save himself. Let the Messiah, the King of Israel, come down from the cross now, so that we may see and believe"* (Mark 15:31–32). Others at the time were also being evaluated as potential *messiahs*. The prophet Theudas (after Jesus' time) was headed in that direction until his execution, "The Egyptian" rallied followers to circle Jerusalem's walls like a new Joshua, the Jewish uprising of 70 CE had a messianic flavor, and so did Simon the Messiah's revolt in 131 CE. You see the pattern—gather disciples, promise deliverance for Israel, and be killed by the opposition. Jesus gathered followers, talked of initiating a new reign of GOD, was accused of claiming to be a king, and was killed by the Romans. The response on Peter's lips, therefore, was not some otherworldly revelation being beamed in through him, but the community's conviction that Jesus fulfilled their expectations for a *messiah*.

The second part of Peter's statement, *"the son of the living God"* (only in Matthew), is also a Jewish comment. "Son of God" was the honored title applied to anyone, including all of Israel, called into a special relationship with Yahweh: *"Out of Egypt I called my son [Israel]"* (Hosea 11:1). *"You are my son: today I have begotten you"* (Ps. 2:7) was standard language for a king on his coronation day, proclaiming him the adopted "son" of the "father" (the city or nation's Deity).[4] On choosing David as king, Yahweh told his messenger Nathan: *"I will establish the throne of his kingdom forever. I will be a father to him, and he shall be a son to me"* (2 Sam. 7:13–14). The language about King David parallels language later used about Jesus, a "king like David" who would restore GOD's reign in Jerusalem:

> The oracle of David, son of Jesse, the oracle of the man whom God exalted, the anointed of the God of Jacob, the favorite of the Strong One of Israel. The Spirit of the Lord speaks through me, his word is upon my tongue. (2 Sam. 23:1–2)

Although Handel's *Messiah* has forever engraved into our minds *"The people who walked in darkness have seen a great light . . . on them light has shined"* (Isa. 9:2) as an announcement of Jesus, these words were, in fact, the beginning of an oracle for the coronation of a Judean king (perhaps Hezekiah). The imagery of moving from darkness to light was a traditional metaphor for the relief from oppression brought by a good king. This oracle lists the ideals of a Davidic king and describes his Divine birth or adoption as a Divine "Son" on becoming a king:

> For a son has been born for us, a son is given to us; authority rests on his shoulders; and he is named Wonderful Counselor, Mighty God, Everlasting Father, Prince of Peace. His authority shall grow continually, and there shall be endless peace for the throne of David and his kingdom. (Isa. 9:6–7)

Such imagery obviously had nothing to do with biology, but indicated, like *messiah*, a king's special Divine calling in terms of Israel's destiny—the names Wonderful Counselor, Mighty GOD, Everlasting Father, and Prince of Peace were also given to Egyptian kings at their coronations.[5]

Our earliest information about Jesus comes from Paul's letters. Paul said, "*When the time had fully come, God sent forth his Son, born of a woman, born under the law*" (Gal. 4:4, RSV). "*Born of a woman*" described human birth (Job 14:1), "*born under the law*" meant Jewish, and, as already discussed, "*God sent forth his Son*" meant a person called by GOD for a special task. There is no birth story in Paul's writings, no hint of an extraordinary birth, hardly anything about Jesus' life and teachings, and no supernatural overtones about his death—the Romans basically killed their political opposition. According to Geza Vermes, a Catholic priest who reclaimed his Jewish roots and became Oxford's First Professor of Jewish Studies, Jesus was executed because he was doing the wrong thing in the wrong place at the wrong time: "*Had he not been responsible for the fracas in the Temple of Jerusalem at Passover time when Jewish tradition expected the Messiah to reveal himself, very likely Jesus would have escaped with his life.*"[6]

The Jesus of the Synoptic Gospels was also a Jewish man with feet firmly planted in Palestinian soil, a sage or wisdom teacher concerned with how to live, not with Jewish laws. His solutions were pragmatic—have compassion, ignore irrelevancies, avoid legalism, seek justice, and celebrate life. Like others of his day, he was an exorcist or local healer, and like others, his success depended on whether his recipients had faith in him. He was also a person for whom GOD and the spiritual realm were very real, hence his good news that the "reign of God" would soon break into their earthly realm, maybe in his lifetime. This coming reign was not something original with Jesus but a Jewish expectation to accompany a *messiah*. Paul adopted Jesus' urgency about this "soon to come" kingdom, but when it did not come, later writers projected it into an unknown future or, in John's Gospel, as already here:"*Anyone who hears my word and believes him who sent me has eternal life, and does not come under judgment, but has passed from death to life*" (John 5:24).

If Jesus was someone anointed by Yahweh, like prophets and kings, there would be a specific moment when the Spirit of the Lord "came upon him," commissioning him for his task. New Testament variations as to when this actually happened reflect evolving ideas about who Jesus was. As already discussed, Paul, our earliest informant, did not come to belief through an empty tomb (he does not mention this) or a resuscitated body (his vision was formless, and he had to ask whose voice it was). Stories of a bodily resumption of earthly life and an ascension are in later Gospels and not always the earliest manuscripts. The oldest copies of Mark end with terrified women running from an empty tomb (16:8), and Gospel claims on Jesus' lips about rising again in three days do not fit with the disciples running away and not believing the women, hardly signs of expecting a sequel. Paul encountered a noncorporeal "vision" (interestingly, the same word for the later Gospel "resurrection" appearances), a Light and a Voice, the usual formula for Yahweh breaking into the earthly realm (Acts 9:1–5; Gal. 1:15–16). The voice of Jesus addressing Paul from GOD's spiritual "kingdom" was proof to him that this faithful man (and therefore humans in general) survived death ("raised" from death), the big afterlife debate of Paul's day:

> Now if Christ is proclaimed as raised from the dead, how can some of you say there is no resurrection of the dead? If there is no resurrection of the dead, then Christ has not been raised; and if Christ has not been raised, then our proclamation has been in vain and your faith [in your own resurrection] has been in vain. We are even found to be misrepresenting God, because we testified of God that he raised Christ—whom he did not raise if it is true the dead are not raised. (1 Cor. 15:12–16)

For Paul then, Jesus' anointing and commissioning as a "son of God" came after his death, signified by his being "raised" from the mortal state to live on in GOD's spiritual realm, the "*gospel concerning his Son [adopted one] who was descended from David according to the flesh [a man] and was declared to be Son of God with power according to the spirit [Spirit] of holiness by resurrection from the dead*" (Rom. 1:3–4).

The usual commissioning signs are all there—declared a "son of God" by the Spirit "coming on him" with power; and saving Israel, not through military victory but through "proving" an afterlife for the faithful in the kingdom of GOD soon to break into the human realm, bringing the faithful dead with it.

While Paul located Jesus' anointing as *messiah* and adoption, like the kings, as GOD's "son" after his death, Mark, the earliest Gospel, located Jesus' commissioning at his baptism by John at the start of the Gospel—Mark has no birth or childhood stories. This commissioning followed the standard pattern for "sons of God"—an apocalyptic event announcing Yahweh entering the human realm (the heavens torn apart), an anointing by the Spirit, and sanction from a Divine Voice declaring him a "son of God": "*As he was coming up out of the water, he saw the heavens torn apart and the Spirit descending like a dove on him. And a voice came from heaven, 'You are my Son, the Beloved; with you I am well pleased'*" (Mark 1:10–11).[7] Matthew and Luke, written some twenty years after Mark's Gospel, reflect expanding ideas about Jesus' person and mission and include stories about his birth and childhood (the only New Testament Gospels to do so). Here his commissioning happened *in utero*, just as Jeremiah had been commissioned: "*Before I formed you in the womb I knew you, and before you were born I consecrated you; I appointed you a prophet to the nations*" (Jer. 1:5). This commissioning in the womb has all the standard language. The Divine Voice speaks to Mary through an angelic messenger: "*You have found favor with God*" (Luke 1:30). The bewildered Mary protests on the grounds of age and suitability—she is a "virgin" (a young girl not yet of age, perhaps even before puberty) and a peasant girl, hardly the mother of a king who would "*be great, and will be called the Son of the Most High, and the Lord God will give to him the throne of his ancestor David*" (v. 32). The angel reassured Mary on both counts—her "barren" cousin Elizabeth had conceived in her "old" age (v. 36) and the child was Yahweh's choice. The Spirit would "come upon" him in the womb, commissioning him as a "son of God": "*The Holy Spirit will come upon you, and the power of the Most High will overshadow you; therefore the child to be born will be holy; he will be called Son of God*" (v. 35). This was not unique—Elizabeth's husband Zechariah had also been told of his expected child, John the Baptist, "*even before his birth he will be filled with the Holy Spirit*" (Luke 1:15).

These scenarios remind us of Samson's "barren" mother who had an angelic visitation: "*Although you are barren, having borne no children, you shall conceive and bear a son . . . the boy shall be a nazirite [one separated or consecrated] to God from birth. It is he who shall begin to deliver Israel from the hand of the Philistines*" (Judg. 13:3–5). The "barren" Hannah, Samuel's mother, also promised her child to Yahweh as a Nazirite if she could conceive, and her song of praise after Samuel's birth is very similar to Mary's, an ancient poem of thanksgiving appropriate to a change of fortune (1 Sam. 2:1–10).[8] "Barrenness" followed by a Divine opening of the womb (like Abraham and Sarah) was a Hebrew motif for announcing the birth of a special "son of GOD" with a destiny for Israel. It is therefore vitally important to consider these Hebrew motifs and titles in their original context before making unique claims from them about the Jewish Jesus.

Just as Jesus' commissioning moved from after his death to before his birth to reflect evolving beliefs about him, his power also evolved. In Paul's writings, GOD raised Jesus from the dead, an act of GOD (1 Cor. 15:15), yet in the later Gospel of Luke, Jesus predicted he would rise again (Luke 24:7) and he "has risen" (v. 5), suggesting some knowledge and ability within himself. Even though John's Gospel (written at the end of the first or into the second century CE) claimed to have the same purpose as the other Gospels—"*these are written so that you may come to believe that Jesus is the Messiah, the Son of God, and that through believing you may have life in his name*" (20:31)—it represents the final evolutionary stage of the New Testament Jesus. Although the Spirit descended symbolically on Jesus at baptism, indicating him to be the commissioned "*Son of God*" or "*God's chosen one*" as in other Gospels (1:32–34), John's story begins before creation. Rather than the Spirit "coming upon" a Jewish man to lead him in a special task, the *Logos* (translated as "Word"), prior to and present at creation, entered the human realm, "filling" or "becoming enfleshed" in this man Jesus: "*In the beginning was the Word, and the Word was with God, and the Word was God . . . All things came into being through him, and without him not one thing came into being . . . And the Word became flesh and lived among us*" (1:1–3; 14). As for Jesus' powers in John, he is no longer a Jewish "son of God" proclaiming a coming Kingdom, but a Son claiming "oneness" with the Father (10:30), while also calling the Father greater than himself (14:28).[9] John's Jesus makes long, carefully composed speeches not in other Gospels, orchestrates his own death by announcing the hour, controls his trial, gives up his spirit at death, and reappears through closed doors to breathe this spirit into his followers. The only reference to Jesus as "lamb of God" in the Gospels is in John (1:29), associating him symbolically at the beginning of his ministry with the sacrificial Passover lamb, and dying on the day before Passover (the day the lamb was slaughtered) rather than after Passover in the other Gospels. The Kingdom has also come in John's Gospel, brought in by Jesus and expressed as a family metaphor of Father, Son, and the "children of God."

John's Jesus has also acquired some Greek accessories, which is not surprising since this community is no longer in the synagogue and Christianity has become more Gentile—the author is no doubt making metaphorical links to Greek thought. The Greek term *Logos* (translated as Word) is not the Hebrew Creator GOD (Creating Voice), but in the hierarchy of Deities in Greek cosmology, a second-level Divine Principle with a mediatory task within the Divine Order—"*the creative power which orders the world and the intermediary through whom men know God.*"[10] The *Logos* is "with God" before creation but also "God" as part of the Divine Pantheon, a metaphorical borrowing that suggests a "divinity" in Jesus not permitted in the radical Jewish monotheism of Jesus' day. As to how this Divine *Logos* "became flesh," we need to compare Greek anthropology with Jewish anthropology. A human being in Jewish anthropology is an undivided "soul," the Jewish word for both flesh and spirit as a fully integrated person. While the Divine Breath is metaphorically shared with human beings, it is, like breath, something that "enlivens" the whole person, not a part of the person. The "soul" in Greek thought, however, is one part of a dualistic human being made up of "soul" (spirit/mind) and "body" (matter/flesh). This "soul" is an immortal essence prior to its birth into inferior matter (the body), and it returns at death to the spiritual realm. The immortal soul/spirit was the superior and "true" part of a human being, while the body was its inferior vehicle. If we put these two Greek concepts together, *Logos* and "soul," Jesus becomes, in Greek thought, a Divine-human mix of body (matter) and an immortal soul that, in Jesus' case, is the preexistent Divine *Logos* "made flesh" or incarnated to "live among us." This immortal "soul" of GOD will depart at death to the heavenly realms like all migrating immortal souls. While John's

Gospel is borrowing Greek metaphorical language in order to interpret the Spirit "coming upon" a Hebrew "son of God," he is also introducing other Greek theological and anthropological ideas along with the metaphors that will change the whole understanding of who Jesus was. While the idea of Yahweh inhabiting a human being was offensive in Jewish thought (Divine-human mixing caused the flood), a Divine-human mix of soul and matter was possible in Greek anthropology and common amongst its Deities, as GODS had sex with human women to produce Divine-human offspring.

The metaphors in John's Gospel were intended to bridge conceptual gaps between Judaism and Hellenistic (Greek) thought—Jewish philosopher Philo (20 BCE–50 CE) had also interpreted Hebrew scripture using terms from Greek philosophy, including *Logos*. However, another link would be made later in terms of Jesus' identity by aligning a passage found only in Matthew's Gospel with this "Greek" anthropology and *Logos* theology. Although Paul, Mark, and John do not record a birth story, and Luke's birth story can be read as a Hebrew commissioning in the womb, Matthew's birth story alone focuses on Joseph. According to Matthew, Joseph discovered Mary was pregnant with a child not his own (even though Matthew's first chapter traces Jesus' genealogy from David through "*Joseph, the husband of Mary, of whom Jesus was born*"). Joseph had every legal right to have Mary stoned (Deut. 22:20), but like the Hebrew Bible's faithful Divine husband, decided instead to "dismiss her quietly." An angel then tells him that "*the child conceived in her is from the Holy Spirit*" (1:20), that is, chosen by GOD before birth and commissioned *in utero* by the Spirit "coming upon" Mary, like both Jeremiah (Jer. 1:5) and John the Baptist (Luke 1:15). Joseph marries Mary, takes the family to Egypt, and after a dream, brings her back to settle in Nazareth. Although Jesus' paternity (if not Joseph) is not revealed, the story can be read, like the only other birth story in Luke, as the birth of a child commissioned *in utero* as a "son of God."[11]

However, the compiler of the Gospel of Matthew was also intent on linking his stories about Jesus back to the Hebrew Bible with explanatory phrases such as "*All this took place to fulfill what had been spoken by the Lord through the prophet*" (1:22). In support of the angel's instructions to Joseph to marry Mary, Matthew borrows a passage from Isaiah (which is not in Luke's birth story): "*The young woman is with child and shall bear a son, and shall name him Immanuel"* (7:14). Unfortunately, Matthew used the Greek word *parthenos* for "young woman" when quoting from Isaiah, a word that could also mean "a woman who had not had intercourse." The original Hebrew word in Isaiah was *almah* meaning "young woman" (*betulah* was Hebrew for a woman who had not had intercourse). Given this "hint" of a woman who had not had intercourse in close proximity to Matthew's comment that the child was not Joseph's, talk of a "virgin" birth (like Greek GODS mating with human women) arose, even though later Greek translations of Matthew's Gospel corrected the error to *neanis* (young girl).[12] Thus the commissioning Spirit "coming upon" Mary (only recorded in Matthew and Luke) would evolve into the Divine act of fertilization of a virginal woman to explain how the "only" Divine *Logos* of GOD "became flesh" in Jesus—a "biological" Son of GOD the Father, rather than a Jewish "son of GOD" commissioned for a Divine task. This may not be how the Christmas story was taught in your church school, and you are at liberty to read these stories in a different way, yet we have to take careful note when so much Christian doctrine is built on so few sentences in one Gospel only, from a birth story not even mentioned in the two other Gospels nor in our earliest New Testament writings, the writings of Paul.

In order to explain his revelation about Jesus, Paul borrowed the pictorial account from Genesis of how humans (*adam*) became mortal, arguing that *adam* (humankind) had now regained immortality, as Jesus had said, demonstrated by Jesus alive in GOD's realm: *"Therefore just as one man's trespass led to condemnation for all [that is, mortality or death], so one man's act of righteousness leads to justification and life for all"* (Rom. 5:18).[13] Paul's contrasting *adam* (humankind) metaphor would become a literal distinction between two men, Adam and Jesus, even though Jesus never called himself the second Adam or linked his mission to the Garden or mentioned the first couple except as an example of marriage (Matt. 19:4). By the fourth century, church dogma argued a literal Adam passing defective genes ("original sin") through tainted seed to all humans, corrupting everyone through sexual activity (conception) except Jesus, by now declared as conceived in a woman who had not had intercourse (virgin) by GOD Himself, avoiding Adam's corrupted seed. In time, Mary would also be declared immaculately conceived and ever-virgin, to remove her from both tainted seed and sex, with her other children now named as Jesus' cousins (Matt. 13:55). "*There were moments in my education from the Irish Christian Brothers,*" George O'Brien says, "*when I had the distinct impression that the entire point of creation of the sun, the moon, the stars, the journeys of the patriarchs, the flight out of Egypt, the proclamation of the prophets, the New Testament, and the pageant of the Popes was to stamp out smooching. Never has so much earnestness been devoted to so little effect.*"[14]

Why could this transformation of Jesus happen? Scholars give many reasons. Since Paul was not a disciple, he interpreted Jesus' mission outside of its context and apart from the Jerusalem church. His focus was in and on the wider Mediterranean world where Jesus was interpreted in Greek concepts before belief in his Jewish *messiah* status had fully matured in the Jewish context. The Jewish War (70 CE) and subsequent persecution of marginal Jewish groups practically extinguished the Jerusalem church, centering Christianity in Gentile-friendly and later, anti-Jewish areas where it was exposed to many other religious and philosophical influences: Roman sacred rites, the dying-rising Saviors of mystery religions, human perfectibility and sexual control (celibacy) in Stoicism and Epicureanism, and Gnostic dualism of light and darkness, spirit and matter, good and evil worlds. All this led to a plethora of theologies about Jesus, and as a result, Christianity became concerned too early about defining orthodoxy against heresy. Once theological ideas were declared heresy, as we shall see, they were eliminated or forced underground.

When Constantine became the sole Roman emperor in the early fourth century, he declared Christianity a tolerated religion in his empire and assembled Christian bishops from around the Mediterranean to define orthodox doctrine and practice. If my discussion so far in this chapter sounds like "heresy" to you, it is vitally important to realize that, almost three hundred years after Jesus' death, his Divinity was still not established among Christian bishops. Although elevated far above a Jewish "son of GOD," major issues remained unresolved—was he, as Son of GOD, fully divine like the Father GOD or a lesser being, the same or similar? This is an understandable question since, as discussed, *Logos* was a second-level Divine Being in Greek cosmology. Bishop Arius (256–336) argued the Son (*Logos*) was created by GOD, albeit the greatest creature, but therefore not fully GOD. According to his colleague Bishop

Athanasius, while the Son was begotten of the Father, this did not mean "created" but "emanated," thus the Son was actual GOD-matter, not a secondary product. A second question followed—if Jesus was both divine and human, how could divine and human matter exist in the same human body? This would hardly keep us awake at night, but it was illogical in Greek thought, as Arius pointed out. Athanasius won the day and at the Council of Nicaea in 325 CE, Jesus was declared fully GOD and fully human, even though the bishops could not explain how. The emperor following Constantine reverted to Arius' position; some theologians were arguing that Jesus was merely a human shell filled with GOD-substance and a GOD-mind (difficult to explain in the baby Jesus); others said Jesus sometimes operated with a GOD-mind and sometimes with a human mind (explaining the baby Jesus); and still others argued that the divine and human natures were totally merged, something anathema to Greek ideas about different substances. Although strongly political by now, a council in 381 CE reiterated that Jesus was fully GOD and fully man, one person in two natures, without mixture, change, division, or separation, even though it could not be explained—the first of many mysteries "to be believed."

With such declarations, Mary became a problem. Was she the mother of the human part of Jesus or also of the Divine part? A compromise labeled her *Theotokos* (GOD-bearer), suggesting that in some way she gave birth to GOD, thus reintroducing the old questions. After a fiasco council of 431 CE where opposing bishops deposed each other and forced each other into exile, theological rivalry began to threaten imperial unity, and so the Council of Chalcedon in 451 CE reaffirmed a fully human, fully divine Jesus with the Trinity metaphor describing the Divine relationship, leaving each side to read it as they wished. The resulting creed was excessively wordy, virtually a legal brief to exclude all "heresies" that suggested Jesus was less than GOD and reads in part:

> [We] confess one and same Son, our Lord Jesus Christ, the same perfect in divinity and also perfect in humanity; truly God and truly man, of a reasonable soul and body; of the same substance with the Father according to Divinity, and of the same substance with us according to the humanity; in all things like unto us, without sin; begotten for all ages of the Father according to the Divinity, and in these latter days, for us and for our salvation, born of the virgin Mary, the Mother of God, according to the

Manhood; one and the same Christ, Son, Lord, Only-begotten, to be acknowledged in two natures, inconfusedly, unchangeably, indivisibly, inseparably; the distinction of natures being by no means taken away by the union, but rather the property of each nature being preserved, and concurring in one Person and one Subsistence, not parted or divided into two persons, but one and the same Son, and only-begotten, God the Word, the Lord Jesus Christ . . .

This creed claimed a consensus of bishops, adding that *"no one shall be permitted to bring forth a different faith, nor to write, nor to put together, nor to excogitate, nor to teach it to others."* The punishment for bishops was deposition, and for monks and laity, anathematization.[15] Thus Jesus the Jewish builder's son was defined by Christian bishops four centuries after his death.

The creed said *"for us and our salvation,"* spawning centuries of atonement theories as to how Jesus' death "saved" us and from what. Second-century bishop Irenaeus said that had human "mortality" continued, it would suggest a Divine defeat and evil's triumph. GOD corrected the problem by Jesus dying and being bound in hell for three days by the Devil, thus setting Adam (humanity) free, a victory over evil powers holding humankind bondage to sin and death.[16] Later church fathers substituted a ransom theory—humans in bondage to evil powers had to be redeemed with a ransom payment, and the Devil, lured by the bait of Jesus coming to hell, was tricked when GOD raised the sinless Jesus, breaking the Devil's power over humanity. In both these theories, Jesus' death and resurrection ended human bondage, enabling humans to progress to perfection or become deified (the Eastern church's position). Western theology, centered in Rome and influenced by Augustine, went in a different direction. Humans are not warring against an evil Being (Devil) but against "moral" evil, the opposite of good. The perversity of the human will is twisted away from GOD toward inferior things. Since Augustine could never overcome his perverse will, especially in sexual matters, he concluded that humans had not been freed from the bondage of sin by Jesus' death and resurrection, as Eastern Christians said, but were eternally bound by this perversity of will, inherited like a bad gene from Adam's tainted seed after the "fall"—the Adam metaphor continues to grow. GOD "became flesh" as the Second Adam, untainted by human "seed" through his "virgin birth," in order to save us from the consequences of this aberration (something we couldn't do ourselves), but not from the aberration itself. Augustine's theology won in the West, declaring all humans permanently flawed from conception (through sex), while their Orthodox cousins were freed from the devil's bondage.

In the eye-for-an-eye Middle Ages, English theologian Anselm rejected transaction-with-the-devil theories and talked instead of the feudal, majestic GOD outraged by human sin and needing to be appeased, either by human punishment (suffering and damnation) or satisfaction (making up for the offence through voluntary suffering). Since no mere human was good enough, Anselm's Father GOD solved His legalistic problem by sending His Divine Son in the form of a man as a substitutionary blood sacrifice, satisfying the Father's offense and clearing the Divine books. Anselm's Parisian contemporary Abelard rejected such violent theories, saying that, rather than talking about good and evil acts, sin was contempt for GOD's wishes, and Jesus was the supreme example of incarnated Divine love. Jesus went to the cross because he would not waver in his message of love and reconciliation, and his suffering aroused love in human beings as their "salvation." While Abelard would gain a hearing today, by denying a retributive explanation for Jesus' death, he was way out of step in an era of feudal lords and wayward peasants and he spent much of his life condemned by the church.[17] Anselm's substitution theory was later adapted by changing offended Divine honor demanding sacrifice to Divine wrath demanding punishment, which Jesus took on himself in death. Later reformers emphasized the victory of the cross, where GOD defeated evil through this cruel event, yet Jesus was still the scapegoat. Such theories and adaptations have dominated Christian theology for centuries and still do, often in combinations and with mightily mixed metaphors—there are enough Divine images in the Bible to take off in countless explanatory directions depending on the verses you choose.

Enlightenment philosophers rejected the cruel medieval GOD demanding scapegoats and threatening people with hell, dismissing any doctrines that went against human reason. Nineteenth-century author Leo Tolstoy agreed, *"There can be nothing as immoral as those dreadful teachings, according to which an angry and vengeful God punishes everyone for the sin of Adam, or that he sent his son to earth to save us, knowing beforehand that men would murder him and be damned for it.*"[18] The challenge continues today to move beyond theologies that make us eternally accountable and eternally wrong. Feminist scholars challenge atonement doctrines that glorify killing, suffering, torture, and punishment, abuses against which we now legislate. With watch-dogs today checking inhumane slaughtering of animals, how can we expect people to be impressed with a loving GOD insisting on the cruel slaughter of His only Son in a ritual paralleling the sacrifice of a captive lamb, yet many Christian leaders continue to exalt such violence, and many in the pews know no other options. Cosmic battles and tainted genes make little contemporary sense unless we leave our minds at the door, yet these metaphorical arguments based on outdated, often harm-ful worldviews are written into Christian creeds, hymns, and liturgies, thus cementing them as eternal and literal "truth." As biblical scholar John Dominic Crossan says, "*My point . . . is not that those ancient people told literal stories and we are now smart enough to take them symbolically, but that they told them symbolically and we are now dumb enough to take them literally.*"[19]

This long and detailed discussion has been necessary because the man Jesus became GOD in Christianity, and thus the source of all we need to know of GOD. Yet we hardly have enough information to form a complete image of Jesus, let alone GOD. "*Would that Jesus had beaten Paul to it,*" Jewish scholar Vermes says, "*and had himself sum-marized the salient traits of his preaching in a letter or two!*"[20] For some, my discussion of Jesus will seem scandalous in light of traditional doctrines, but I have offered it as logically and as simply as I can, to show how many reputable scholars and people of faith "read" Jesus of Nazareth today. This man Jesus engaged his contemporaries with the fearless courage of a prophet, unceasing compassion for the outcasts, and a sense of humor and turn of phrase that left the best Jewish minds, like Nicodemus, floundering. He acted like other "holy men" of the period between the Hebrew Bible and the New Testament, living fru-gally, detaching themselves from mundane concerns, being pragmatic about religious rules, and performing miracles and healings. Jesus con-tinued his revolutionary journey even when it was glaringly obvious that his path could only end in death. "*The face of this Jesus, truly human, wholly theocentric, passionately faith-inspired, and under the imperative impulse of the here and now,"* Vermes says, *"impressed him-self so deeply on the minds of his disciples that not even the shattering blow of the cross could arrest its continued real presence. It compelled them to carry on in his name with their mission as healers, exorcists and preachers of the Kingdom of God. It was only a generation or two later, with the increasing delay of the Parousia, that the image of Jesus famil-iar from experience began to fade, covered over first by the theological and mystical dreamings of Paul and John, and afterwards by the dog-matic speculations of church-centered Gentile Christianity."*[21]

One might expect an ex-Catholic priest and now Jewish scholar to take this approach, but it is also the approach of an increasing number of Christian scholars who recognize the problems with our inherited story of Jesus. A new Christianity is evolving, uncovering the human Jesus so long buried under centuries of dogma that celebrated only supernatural virgin births, miracles, and a bodily resurrection as evi-dence of the Divine with us. In an essay on Muhammad, a student inad-vertently revealed that on which she based her faith in Jesus:

> Another factor about Muhammad that surprises me is the fact that he has no supernatural powers. This man seemed so real and down to earth that it is amazing that he could convert all the people he did. The only miracle that he proclaimed was that of the Qur'an. He did not heal the sick, or walk on water. He lived in a clay house and still would perform daily duties that all men would perform.

Recovering Jesus' humanity not only allows his teachings to be heard in fresh, contemporary ways, but also allows other "truths," both in Christianity and other religions, to be taken seriously. *"Those who rely on physical miracles to prove the truth of spiritual things forget the ever-present miracle of the universe and of our own lives,"* Upanishads scholar Juan Mascaró said. *"The lover of the physical miracle is in fact a materialist: instead of making material things spiritual, as the poet or the spiritual man does, he simply makes spiritual things material, and this is the source of all idolatry and superstition."*[22] E. Stanley Jones (1884–1978), a Christian missionary to India for many years, discovered the message of Jesus again in Indian life, a culture so much closer to the dust of Palestine. *"I have come not to abolish [the law] but to fulfill"* (Matt. 5:17) challenged what was stultified in Hinduism as much as what was stale in the Judaism. Jesus was a new avatar for Hinduism, just as

Buddha had been in his time. "*The thing that strikes me about Jesus is his imaginative sympathy,*" a Hindu scholar told Jones. "*He entered into the experience of men and felt with them. He could feel the darkness of the blind, the leprosy of the leper, the loneliness of the rich, the degradation of the poor, and the guilt of the sinner.*" Yet such devout Hindu thinkers did not feel the need to sacrifice their rich religious history in order to heed the wisdom of another messenger from the One.[23]

The Divine Word, narrowed into one Word "made flesh" in Christianity, needs to be liberated to speak wherever It wills, in whomever It chooses, as It always has. The Greeks talked of *entheos*, the Divine creativity within, Hindu Upanishads talk of One who rules the universe but is also a tiny seed in every heart, Judaism's central statement is "*the Lord is our God, the Lord is one,*" Christian creeds begin with "*We believe in one God,*" the first pillar of Islam says "*There is no God but Allah,*" and the Sikh evening prayer opens with "*You alone are the Creator. All that exists comes from you, without you, nothing else could exist.*" With such a consensus of One discovered in different ways and forms across millennia of human experiences, we need to think seriously about claims of the only true GOD revealed in a single revelation to a small nation in one small part of the world. As biologist and philosopher Jean Rostand (1894–1977) said, "*I am inclined to judge a belief quite differently according to whether it asks the right to be one or insists on being the only one.*"[24] Are other experiences of the Divine simply wrong because Christians say so? It is the task of each of us to weigh up all the evidence in light of our twenty-first-century culture and knowledge, including today's open exposure to religions other than our own. "*God is at work in and through all things,*" theologian Charles Bayer says from within Christianity. "*No religion or religious statement can possibly describe the extent of this purpose or plan. We can never say that we have somehow an exclusive claim on God, and thus we can never marginalize or exclude anyone else from sharing in the divine initiative.*"[25]

The doctrine of the Trinity (GOD as Father, Son, and Holy Spirit) is a central statement distinguishing Christianity from its cousins Judaism and Islam, yet it is not spelled out as such in the Bible and was still debated in the fifth century. The doctrine explained different ways of being GOD, especially Father and Son, while still maintaining Oneness. Like any metaphor, it borrowed from philosophical and social orderings of its day (which would later fuel a rift between Eastern and Western

Christianity). The three components described as *hypostases* or *personae* were translated into English as "persons," shoring up in peoples' imagination both "three-ness" and also the anthropomorphism of Father and Son (although leaving the "dove" somewhat out on a limb). In nineteenth-century Protestantism, the doctrine lost its prominence with questions from biblical criticism about the "divinity" of Jesus (it was relegated to an appendix in Friedrich Schleiermacher's *The Christian Faith*). It was revived in twentieth-century discussions, and today, in association with a renewed interest in the Spirit, it is filling endless new books. Those who wish to preserve the Trinitarian metaphor describe, not the three entities, but the internal relationships of love, sociability, community, mutuality, and interdependence between different experiences of the Divine. I personally find it metaphorically satisfying to return to the universal image of Divine Formlessness or Spirit, experienced in many ways within the universe (and beyond which I cannot know). The ongoing Creating Spirit is the Spirit that "inspired" the man Jesus and his followers and "fills" everything as Ground of Being or Persuasive Lure—what Elizabeth Johnson describes as *"beyond, with, and within the world; behind, with, and ahead of us; above, alongside, and around us."*[26] This move goes beyond three and *"infinitizes the Trinity,"* according to theologian Nancy Victorin-Vangerud, *"widening the Spirit's We to its most inclusive status."*[27]

Many Christians do not find such "inclusivism" threatening, given statistics about attitudes to other religions—the voices that shout the loudest in public do not necessarily represent the majority. People can be fully committed to the GOD they discover through Jesus, a man so distinctively open to the Divine Spirit in his day, without having to make absolute claims, especially when his immediate followers did not make such claims. We can be totally committed to our "truths" about GOD while still recognizing that any human grasp on truth is relative. We can take Jesus' teachings as the Word for us without saying it is the only Word for everyone. Interestingly, those who make exclusive claims usually quote a verse found only in John's Gospel: *"Jesus said to him, 'I am the way, and the truth, and the life. No one comes to the Father except through me'"* (John 14:6), without considering whether, in its original context, it was intended as a universal claim or simply an assurance for a band of followers wondering how to access GOD outside the synagogue. The same people ignore Jesus' response when the disciples complained about someone (not trained in their seminary) casting out demons in his name: "*Whoever is not against us is for us*" (Mark 9:40). These two statements, both attributed to Jesus, represent different ways of answering "Who do you say I am?" It is up to each of us to decide which way to respond.

What Is Truth?

Traditional images of God seem to have lost their appeal in modern American and European culture. It is not that God's existence has been disproved—philosophers continue to debate the proofs inconclusively, and no informed and honest observer of the philosophical scene really thinks a case has been established either way. Or ever will be. No, God has simply become boring and irrelevant. We no longer care for big men with white beards. We no longer feel the weight of tremendous guilt that drove the Pilgrim on his Progress.

—Keith Ward[1]

One thing we have learned in our contemporary world is that while we can speak for ourselves and define what is true for us, we cannot do it for everyone and for all time because we are forever limited by the relativity of our own culture, worldview, and knowledge. The grand old days of universal truths are gone, even though we might, in faith, still clutch some that seem almost universal and certainly work for us. When Jesus told Pontius Pilate that his GOD-given mission was *testifying to the truth,*" Pilate made his famous response "*What is truth?*" (John 18:37–38). We would have needed a camera rolling to decipher whether Pilate's response was one of interest, invitation to dialogue, cynicism, despair, ridicule, or hopelessness about the ability to define truth. However, this is still the struggle in thinking about GOD—what is truth? Is Something true because of our experiences (or lack of them) or because a particular set of doctrines says so, even if they may not make sense? English author Rudyard Kipling (1865–1936) wrote a delightful vignette of a woman he once dated:

She has the face of an angel, the voice of a dove and the step of a fawn. I worshipped her blindly till I found she was the Cantonment Chaplain's daughter. My love was proof against this also and I said, "I will go and listen to Papa on Sundays." I went once . . . He preached. I went a second time for I saw she was lovely and I hoped peradventure that her Papa might have been drunk. But he preached a second time and I drove home . . . and laid the mangled heads of her Papa's sermon before my Papa. And he said, "My Son—there must be hereditary insanity in that family. Avoid it." And I avode for I was of the same opinion as my Papa.[2]

When the Buddha was approached by someone wanting answers to all his intellectual questions before following the Buddhist way, the Buddha described a person, wounded by an arrow, insisting on knowing the caste, occupation, and motivation of the attacker before allowing the arrow to be removed. *"In exactly the same way,"* the Buddha concluded, *"anyone who should say, 'I will not follow the teachings of the Blessed One until the Blessed One has explained all the multiform truths of the worlds'—that person would die before the Buddha had explained all this."*[3] Ultimate truth about GOD is never found—the message of this book. All truth is evolving, correctible, and open to more truth as new factors constantly enter our changing experience, individually and globally—even the confident theologian Karl Barth said they would be laughing in heaven over the volumes of inadequate theological tomes in his wheelbarrow. We talk about the Divine in and for our time and context, trying to be as objective as possible, but knowing that we will certainly fall short. Does this make it a hopeless, relativist exercise? Some might say "yes," but I believe it is in our nature to try and make sense of our experiences in light of current knowledge and the new information we twist around our minds every day. *"We can do theology, doing the best we can with our bag of categories,"* theologian Paul Sponheim says. *"There will be no perfect, complete theology. But in our speaking of God, we can do better, rather than worse. In this it will be essential to recognize the reality of ineradicable ambiguity."*[4] This is very different from the past where Divine truth was declared without hesitation or qualification (although some religious leaders today have not realized this type of confidence has been found wanting). A minister I knew regularly began his sermon, *"I had prepared something else for today but on the way God told me to say this instead."* A string of cobbled together disheveled clichés followed, hardly a Divine composition, but what could be expected when it was a ten-minute drive from his home to church? I always expected a booming Voice to drown him one day with, "*I said nothing of the sort.*"

Creative hesitation to name truth for ourselves, but not for everyone else, opens up the possibility of finding other truths that may not negate but rather expand our own, the difference between traveling a road winding to a distant horizon and being holed up in our backyard defending our turf. With the freedom of the last chapters, we can appreciate the Bible as an inspiring record of human experiences written down in varying forms at different times as a guide for those continuing in the tradition, and culminating in the hope of a special person commissioned by the Spirit, a *messiah* to point the way to the longed-for reign of GOD. When Jesus, whom his followers identified as the commissioned one, told his disciples he was going away, Thomas reminded Jesus that they did not know where he was going so how could they know the way? Jesus replied, "*I am the way, the truth and the life. No one comes to the Father except through me*" (John 14:6). Rather than reading these words spoken in a small corner of the world as a revelation to the universe about the person of Jesus, we can hear a man, totally open to GOD, assuring his followers that his message pointed the way to GOD and that they would not be abandoned but would have the Spirit of truth that inspired him "*whom the Father will send in my name*" and who "*will teach you everything, and remind you of all that I have said to you*" (John 14:26). The apostles claimed that Spirit within them as the source of their teaching and healing, and Paul reminded the Greek philosophers of Athens of the universal Spirit "within them" about which their poets had written:

> From one ancestor, he [God] made all nations to inhabit the whole earth, and he allotted the times of their existence and the boundaries of the places where they would live, so that they would search for God and perhaps grope for Him and find him—though indeed he is not far from each one of us. For "In him we live and move and have our being"; as even some of your poets have said, "For we too are his offspring." (Acts 17:26–28)[5]

If we take these words of Jesus about the indwelling Spirit seriously, we have both recognized Jesus as the one who showed us something of

GOD, and we can also listen to other "sons and daughters of GOD," filled with the Spirit and open to the Divine Word.

Such Divine inclusiveness takes us back to the Formless One, the Something More described by what It is not, the "I am who I am," or the "I will become what I will become," the One not confined to one human form but incarnated in us all and in the world, in whom "we live and move and have our being," as Paul's Greek poets said. The *Svetasvatara Upanishad* says:

> This is the God in fire and in the waters;
> The whole world has He entered;
> In healing plants is He, He it is in the trees:
> To this God all hail, all hail![6]

These images sit naturally with twenty-first-century people who feel (or yearn for) an interconnectedness with the universe, even if we do not all describe it in religious terms. Why should we have to believe limiting "truths" from past worldviews that make us wiggle and squirm to make them fit? A fish does not drown in water or a bird fall from the sky, Mechtild of Magdeburg said, because they are living where and how they were meant to be, "*Each creature God made / Must live in its own true nature.*"[7] In the best-selling book *Tuesdays with Morrie*, which contains conversations between a dying sociology professor and a past student, Morrie described feeling part of something bigger than himself in a story of a little wave bobbing happily on the ocean until it saw a huge wave crash against the shore. Panicking, the little wave said to a bigger wave, "*All of us waves are going to crash, to be nothing. Isn't it terrible?*" The big wave said, "*No, you don't understand. You're not a wave, you're part of the ocean.*"[8]

This is foreign territory to those who have frozen the whole of Divine history into one event, text, and time from which everything else must be measured. The 1999 Southern Baptist International Mission Board Prayer Guide targeted Hindus, asking members to pray that the world's nine hundred million Hindus might be "convicted of sin and see Jesus as the Light of the World" during Divali, their annual Festival of Lights, and similar prayer guides were issued targeting Jews between Rosh Hashanah and Yom Kippur. This is offensive to many people today, yet it reflects Christian exclusivist culture over centuries. Why are people so afraid of religions other than their own? Are we afraid of being caught up in something that might "do something" to us or "take control of us" in some magical way? Are we afraid of being inappropriate, such as standing on the grave of someone's GOD or messing up the rituals and thus offending the worshippers? Or are we simply terrified of offending our GOD, attracting the Divine Wrath by giving a half-nod to another Deity?

Interestingly, the Hebrew Bible has no distinct word for what is translated as "truth." The Hebrew words mean constant, faithful, and reliable, something proved "true" through time within relationships. The Greek word for truth, on the other hand, means intellectual truth or correct knowledge. According to biblical scholar Joanna Dewey, both meanings are used in the New Testament, but Paul's writings and John's Gospel build more on the Hebrew understanding of experiencing what is "truly real" rather than possessing correct knowledge.[9] None of us can prove the truth about GOD in the Greek "intellectual" way—anything said about the Divine is a faith statement from our own experience, or if "correct knowledge" is demanded, from believing someone else's experience. There is nothing wrong with faith—most things about life are acts of faith, usually based on a combination of reason, experience, and advice from others. Paul Sponheim says:

> The Christian "reads" the world in faith, not by proof. The Christian does not claim to offer pure objectivity, a "view from nowhere." To stand somewhere, or—better—to start from somewhere, can be part of a circle that is not vicious but virtuous as one stays open to insights and input from outside.[10]

The problem arises, as I have said repeatedly, when a particular group believes that their faith statement is the only truth, the correct knowledge, and their GOD the only description of the Divine, like a personal possession. Yet it is illogical to claim exclusive possession while also claiming GOD as the Creator and Sustainer of all creation—"*The God who is present to each is the God who is present to all*," Sponheim reminds us, "*those whom we would exclude are brought along, for they are present with God.*"[11]

Until recently, the Christian interest in other religions was conversion, based on the biblical injunction to make disciples of the entire world, the claim that Jesus is the only way to salvation, and the dogma that there was no salvation outside the church. In a rather circular argument, Karl Barth, while acknowledging Christianity's imperfections as with any religion, called it the "true" one because GOD chose it for GOD's revelation in Jesus, yet such an argument could be used by any religion with a sacred text claiming an exclusive Divine revelation. Others have argued an exclusivist position in a different form. Since a religion and its symbols arise out of a particular culture, that religion is part of that culture and makes best sense in that culture. Doctrines people map out for themselves are "true" if they are adequate in getting people from one point to another in their religious journey; they are the "only way" because they work for that culture's particular description of who they are. Each religious tradition is therefore relative but absolutely valid for its particular adherents, and although talking between religions may be interesting and informational, each remains the "truth" for its followers.

A second group of people are happy to admit revelations in other religions but are less enthusiastic when it comes to salvation. While early church fathers were somewhat open about this, Augustine tipped the scales toward "no salvation outside the church," reinforced in the Middle Ages with an "at all." The Council of Florence (1442) declared that *"no persons, whatever almsgiving they have practiced, even if they have shed blood for the name of Christ, can be saved, unless they have remained in the bosom and unity of the Catholic Church."*[12] With colonization of other lands, however, Christianity encountered thousands who had never heard of Christ. Were they automatically consigned to hell through no fault of their own? The Council of Trent (1545–63) therefore declared that if "heathens" followed their consciences and lived morally, they were implicitly expressing a desire to join the true church and thus could receive salvation, not through their own religion but vicariously through Catholicism. The Second Vatican Council (1962–1965) expanded this to suggest (not explicitly) that other religions were also ways of salvation even though they had never heard of Christ, producing what theologian Karl Rahner (1904–1984) called "anonymous Christians." However, once an anonymous Christian heard the Gospel, they then had to become Christian for their salvation to continue to count. Rahner's colleague Hans Küng opposed this *"sweeping the whole of good-willed humanity into the backdoor of the holy Roman Church,"* since he detected no underlying orientation of

Buddhists or Hindus toward Christianity.[13] Küng did say, however, that Christ was normative, not only for Christians but for all faiths, the archetypal human relationship with the Divine and thus a necessary critical analyst of all faiths. While Küng may not have been sweeping all religions into Rahner's Christian backdoor, he was measuring them against Christianity as the counterweight of the scale.

An ever-increasing group of people see many religions as valid ways to salvation, different paths leading to the One. The *Bhagavata Purana* says, "*Just as rivers come from many sources, yet all become one with the ocean, so all the Vedas, all sacred writings, all truth, though they are different in the way they come into being, all come home to God.*"[14] This is not necessarily a claim that all are equally valid, but who can decide that for everyone for all time and on what universal authority? Even if the criterion was whether a religion makes human transformation (salvation/liberation) possible, we would differ on what "salvation" means and how it is attained. Instead, the aim of interreligious dialogue is to share theological ideas for transformation, not in order to construct some blended religious soup, but to find commonalities and fresh language without slipping into generalities such as "all Muslims think this . . ." Talking between religions, or even between different versions of the same religion, offers a connectedness that "we are not alone." In a group I facilitated, a woman was taking revolutionary theological steps that were still miles from where I stood, yet I experienced more "aha" moments listening to her excitement than I did with group participants whose theology lined up with mine. Why? Because I identified, not with her theology, but with her evolving process of wriggling free from harmful religious ideas. I had also done such wriggling and understood her struggle, even though her "freedom" was being expressed differently from mine. Dialogue is more likely to happen when we are not making exclusive claims or erecting doctrinal idols to worship rather than looking for the One with many names, contexts, and attributes. It is simply not true that the church has always got it right, and those who defend the traditions on the basis of their long history should also consider slavery and patriarchy, both of which lasted for centuries because those holding power kept them in place. "*If Tradition is already perfect and whole, if the Bible is inerrant, if dogma is immutable, if the pope is infallible, and if only one interpretation is lawful,*" religious scholar Don Cupitt says, "*then there can be no question of reinterpreting, reimagining, reinventing, or reminting religious belief. The System already knows all the answers. The theologian's task is merely to give us grounds for assenting to the Truth, by demonstrating the strength of the credentials of its mouthpiece and by showing the error of all its opponents and critics."*[15]

If GOD is the universal One, where do we find GOD? Certainly not confined to an otherworldly heaven, if we listen to the many voices describing the One, but rather transcendent and immanent, closer than our breath yet sweeping the corners of the universe. Yahweh was everywhere, filling the very structures of the created order: *"Am I a God near by, says the Lord, and not a God far off? Who can hide in secret places so that I cannot see them? says the Lord. Do I not fill heaven and earth?"* (Jer. 23:23–24). Hebrew people eventually built a temple, yet they knew this could never contain the Divine (1 Kings 8:27), since Yahweh was also the *Alpha* and *Omega*, the beginning and the end (Rev. 21:6), stretched between the limits of our imagining and beyond. The *Maitri Upanishad* spells this Divine expansiveness out further:

> His [Brahman's] infinity is everywhere. In him there is neither above, nor across, nor below; and in him there is neither east nor west. The Spirit supreme is immeasurable, inapprehensible, beyond conception, never-born, beyond reasoning, beyond thought. His vastness is the vastness of space. At the ends of the worlds, all things sleep; he alone is awake in Eternity.[16]

In the Qur'an, GOD is the Creator, the ongoing Monitor, the All-Seeing, and All-Present: *"He knows what enters into the earth and what comes forth from it, what comes down from heaven and what goes up to it. He is with you wherever you are, and he sees whatever you do"* (Surah 57:3). *"Where can I go from your Spirit?"* the psalmist said. *"Or where can I flee from your presence?"* (139:7). As a visual person, such ever-present Energy free of time and space is easier to imagine now that electronic communication has demonstrated how time and place become irrelevant. I write an email in a time and space convenient for me, even at 3 a.m., knowing its recipients will read it in their time and space without restrictions set by my circumstances. As Charlie Brown said, *"The world cannot come to an end because it is already tomorrow in Australia."*

GOD with us also includes GOD within us (John 14:17). Emily Bronte talked of the *"God within my breast,"*[17] and Buddhism talks about Enlightenment filling the physical body: "*A body may be thought of as a receptacle; then, if this receptacle is filled with Enlightenment, it may be called Buddha.*"[18] The Divine within can also be imagined metaphorically as us in the Divine, integral parts of a pulsating World Body—"*In the One you are never alone,*" Dag Hammarskjöld said, "*in the One you are always at home.*"[19] Divine immanence does not deny Divine transcendence, however, because the physical world is not the limit of the Divine but rather the limit of what humans can experience of the Divine: "*He has made everything suitable for its time; moreover he has put a sense of past and future into their minds, yet they cannot find out what God has done from the beginning to the end*" (Eccles. 3:11). Yet the limits of what we can know, or at least surmise, are always expanding as we learn about the further reaches of space through science. While many scientists want to keep science and religion as separate discussions, this does not stop us borrowing their language and images to expand our metaphors for GOD. "*We now know of one trillion galaxies, so God's home is much bigger than we ever imagined and populated by all kinds of beings we're just getting to know,*" Matthew Fox says. "*Every being is a revelation of divinity, if we listen with an open heart . . . now we can also see divinity in terms of black holes, in terms of interconnectivity and as the mind of the universe.*"[20]

One of the most useful theologies for accommodating the Divine in a contemporary world is process theology, briefly mentioned already in relation to Divine power. While "theism" sees GOD as entirely separate, transcendent and independent of the world and its activity, an all-powerful Being interacting with the world from without, "pantheism" sees GOD and the world as the same entity with nothing beyond this. "Panentheism" (process theology's category) sees the world and everything in GOD (or GOD immanent in the world), but GOD is also more than the world—transcendent—thus what human beings experience of the Divine does not exhaust the reality of GOD. Alfred North Whitehead, a mathematician turned philosopher, recognized the need to talk of all life—aesthetics, ethics, religious intuitions, and science—in the same scheme of thought, rather than the language of Western philosophy with its static, discrete beings, enduring substances, and essences. Science was also moving from a mechanistic view of the world toward the world as an interacting organism, and so

Whitehead's cosmology could not only accommodate the new science but also could talk of a GOD space (free of religious baggage, however). The traditional, theistic GOD was a discrete, unchanging Being different from all other categories and substances, which is why fourth-century church fathers had problems describing Jesus as GOD, two different substances in one entity. Whitehead's philosophy, however, described everything, including GOD, in the same terms—momentary events instead of enduring substances, all interacting with each other and affecting each other in an interconnected, changing universe. "*As a net is made up by a series of knots,*" the Buddha said, "*so everything in this world is connected by a series of knots. If anyone thinks that the mesh of a net is an independent, isolated thing, he is mistaken. It is called a net because it is made up of a series of connected meshes, and each mesh has its place and responsibilities in relation to other meshes.*"[21] However, humans, animals, plants, and GOD are not just one series of events, constantly becoming and dying in every moment, but a multiplicity of series at any one time in the brain, the digestive system, photosynthesis, the emotions, not all "experienced consciously" but all contributing to the process of becoming at any moment. In this same process for rocks, frogs, and wheat, some have more complex and numerous series of events than others, like a human compared to a rock, but all share this common process of constantly becoming in an interconnected world. "*Everything has its coming forth and passing away; nothing can be independent without any change,*" the Buddha said. "*It is the everlasting and unchanging rule of this world that everything is created by a series of causes and conditions and everything disappears by the same rule; everything changes, nothing remains constant.*"[22]

Each emerging event in each series of events in the universe is influenced by the previous event, but this is not all its "information," otherwise new events would simply repeat the past. Each becoming event has an "initial aim" (what process theologians identify as the Divine Lure or Persuasion), suggesting optimal possibilities for each new moment. Becoming events are not "predestined" to accept this Divine lure but make choices, being urged toward this optimal choice for transformation. When an event does not choose this lure but clings to the past, this, projected into millions of events in our interconnected world, affects the whole universe, and subsequent aims must be formulated within the limited situation our choices have created, thus limiting Divine Action.

Even so, the Divine lure for every becoming event is still the maximum possibility in the limits of the moment. When we accept the Divine Lure in each new event, we are in process, moving to richer experiences and becoming more "like GOD," as it were. If everything is this single type of reality, GOD is also a series of events, not Something unchanged, unchangeable, of different stuff and external to the world, and since GOD is involved in every event in the universe as the Divine Lure, every event is part of the Divine experience and thus not lost to the world but in the Divine collective memory and available for future events. GOD therefore changes with the incorporation of new experiences, growing in richness. "*To say God grows is not to say that God becomes wiser or more loving,*" process theologian David Griffin says, "*it means only that, as new creatures arise and new experiences occur, the objects of the divine love have increased and therefore the divine experience has been enriched.*"[23]

Whitehead described two poles for GOD—a transcendent pole beyond our ken, what the Hebrews recognized as an unknowable Divine Essence and what Sallie McFague calls the invisible face of GOD: "*That aspect or dimension that we never see, never know. It is what God is when God is not 'being God'; it is the mystery, the absoluteness, that relativizes all our notions and models of God; it is the goodness of God; it is the silence that surrounds all our paltry and pathetic attempts to speak of God; it is the big no to all our little yeses.*"[24] The immanent pole or Divine Lure is what we encounter within our universe, these poles described in the Trinitarian metaphor as mystery of GOD, physicality of GOD (the world as GOD's body), and mediation of the invisible and visible (Spirit).[25] In summary then, all life is in process, becoming and dying in an interconnected web of life, with the Divine participating in all this change and also changing. Since our choices decide what GOD is able to do in the world, the Divine Lure is not all-powerful as in power-over, but all-powerful as in all-luring toward harmony and richness. What we do and how we choose affects Divine Purpose, and when we work with the Divine Lure to mend creation and tend the vineyard, we are not estranged, tainted creations but co-creators in an ever-changing universe the Creating Voice called good:

> The sea of Divine Attention
> laps my soul,
> but not only mine.

Others feel its stroking
on the other side of the ocean.
By sharing these waters
the world is connected.[26]

This is the tip of the Whiteheadian iceberg and the theology that emerged from his philosophy—if you like it, you can read more in the works of John Cobb, Charles Hartshorne, and Marjorie Suchocki.

Like the Greek metaphorical-philosophical categories of different substances by which GOD and humanity were described in early Christian theology, process theology is another metaphorical-philosophical scheme to help us imagine our world, a framework for "explaining" our experiences within the universe. We have always lived and thought within philosophical frameworks, but the advantage of this process metaphorical scheme is that it dispenses with the theistic Being "out there," over against us and different from us, pulling our strings from outside and manipulating the created universe over and against its scientific laws, a nonsensical image for a scientific world. The process imagery can support science and an evolutionary universe by imagining the Divine Lure as the essential Persuasive Power of the universe, limited by human choices and not something external, or alternately, imagining the whole universe within the Divine "body." Whitehead's principle called GOD (a three-letter symbol for something identified within the universe) could equally be called something else by science or ethics for those not willing to introduce a Divine dimension. Such a Principle within and around, however, gives us new images and returns us to some of the old ones clothed in different language—GOD is the air between and around us, vital for our life together; the water that not only touches all our surfaces but also invades us; the light that floods all space as does the darkness; the sound that is all-pervasive; energy, in whatever form, driving our world processes; and music as both the sound and the silent spaces between.

Process imagery also allows us to rethink "eternal" life beyond boiling caldrons or golden streets elsewhere, focusing instead on the "eternal" GOD here with us. While "eternity" is a time category, a duration of infinite length, "eternal" is a state of existence outside of time with no beginning or end. Our genes remind us that we are eternal, showing up for centuries to keep "us" and our "traits" alive, which gives a new dimension to the way we raise children, treat friends, and order our lives. We plant eternal seeds and make life count in more practical ways than living in some world hereafter. This does not negate possibilities beyond death, but that is a faith statement, something we can't know or prove, although some experiences make us suddenly say "maybe." Australian scientist Paul Davies will neither rule it out nor vouch for it:

> The best hope we have for the survival of the soul is that, just as, when my computer blows a fuse, I can run the software on another machine, so it's not inconceivable that some aspects of our mental life could be run on another machine. Another body, another system. It doesn't hold out much hope for survival after death but it's not logically impossible.[27]

Such honest openness is refreshing compared with the traditional doctrines embellished with all sorts of verbal and visual flourishes—we have made religion into the unknown afterlife rather than the reality we know, life in this world. It may surprise you that many celebrated Victorian poets, Wordsworth, Shelley, Blake, Coleridge, Browning, Tennyson, and others, believed in reincarnation because it seemed such a waste of the human mind and spirit, finely honed and matured through a lifetime, to be relegated to a place in the clouds with halo and harp. When Australian poet Oodgeroo (Kath Walker) became an Aboriginal tribal elder on a visit to western Australia, they told her this was her *"fifth time around."* When she asked why five "reincarnations," they said, *"With the knowledge you have and the compassion you have, you could not learn that in one, two, three, four generations. This is your fifth trip."*[28] Florence Nightingale also believed in reincarnation, not by returning to earth as a gnat or a cow, but a more openminded curiosity as to what an active "heaven" and "other worlds" might mean. Because of this conviction, she did not despair about reforms she could not accomplish in one lifetime: *"If I could be permitted to return and accomplish this [reform] in another being, if I may not in this, I should need no other heaven . . . If it would please God to give me, with a nearer consciousness of his presence, the task of doing this in the next life."*[29]

No doubt some might close the book, even at this late stage, claiming I am promoting reincarnation, which good Christians have assigned to the "pagans," but I am rather reminding us that people have used different metaphors to talk about the unknown beyond death. If heaven is where GOD is, and we believe the Divine is in our midst, being with the Eternal One after death means being where GOD is, here in this world—which puts a different metaphorical slant on things. Imagine being surrounded by all those now in the memory of that traveling, ever-present One in this world and other "worlds" of the universe, the many dwelling places. The letter to the Hebrews, after listing those dead and with GOD—Abel, Enoch, Noah, Abraham, Moses, and others—said that we are surrounded by *"so great a cloud of witnesses"* (12:1). In the process model, life is a series of momentary events continually dying to make way for new ones, with the Divine Lure active in every event. If physical death happens in one moment, where is the Divine Lure in the next moment? Are there "me" events still in process? And if the many events of "me" have become part of the eternal, collective memory of GOD, am "I" now part of the Divine Lure in the plethora of emerging events throughout the universe in the next moment? When a fetus pushes through into the world, it immediately adapts to a new set of circumstances, even breathing through lungs it did not use before. Is there a parallel process at death? *"Before I was born, waiting in the womb, I felt terribly afraid,"* Rumi wrote. *"I thought that birth would be death, since it would force me to leave my familiar surroundings. Then at my birth I realized that my fears were unjustified. Far from being death, birth was release from prison, into a world of bright colors and sweet smells."*[30] Islamic mystics saw death as a moment they had been working toward all their life, *"a final consummation of love, the realization of the union of the Lover with the Beloved, the 'I' with 'God,'"*[31] something process thinking might describe as being in the memory of GOD, becoming "immortal." With talk of sound waves, neurophysiology, and all sorts of ideas as to how mind and consciousness works from psychologists and psychiatrists, surely our metaphors and philosophical frameworks trying to describe our GOD experiences (or not) must also change.

Changing metaphors has helped the conversation between science and religion. In 1633, the church forced Galileo to recant his "absurd" scientific ideas under threat of torture. Now the shoe is on the other foot, with science effectively forcing the church to recant its absurd theological ideas, also under threat of extinction. As we have seen, Charles Darwin changed the science-religion debate in the mid-nineteenth century by challenging the prevailing "theological" science that species were independently created. He offered a new Divine "plan of creation," that all organic beings were descended from one primordial form into which life was first breathed, an explanation ennobling the Creator's work. *"There is grandeur in this view of life,"* he said, *"with its several powers having been originally breathed into a few forms or into one; and that, whilst this planet has gone cycling on according to a fixed law of gravity, from so simple a beginning endless forms most beautiful and most wonderful have been made, and are being evolved."*[32] Darwin's ideas might have happily percolated on in odiferous laboratories and anthropology museums, but like Galileo, he had taken on GOD and the ultimate "scientific" text, Genesis. In early twentieth-century America, Darwin's ideas spawned Social Darwinism and Eugenics, the belief that only well-educated elites and physically fit people should reproduce. By the 1920s, twenty-four states had passed laws permitting eugenic sterilizations, and some twelve thousand had been performed. As a result, many people who initially accepted evolution as an explanation for Divine Creation stepped back, with the Tennessee legislature banning the teaching of evolution in public schools. Scientists and theologians wanting to reconcile religion and evolutionary theory supported a 1925 test trial of science teacher John Scopes, but it backfired, cementing fundamentalist opposition to evolution as neither proven fact nor religiously neutral.[33]

The spectrum of "science and religion" positions is broader today, from atheistic science, to science and religion as separate categories with "different" integrities, to creationist "science" defending the biblical creation story, and all points in between. What process theology adds to the debate is Divine Persuasion, however it might be described, operating within the natural world as an integral activity in every event, rather than a GOD-Being external to it. With quantum physics allowing for spontaneity and chance within natural laws, process theologians can apply the metaphor GOD to such "creativity," opening the science-religion debate in a new direction with new language. The Divine Life-Breath in everything also puts a different slant on the intrinsic value or integrity of all creation (not just human beings), the *"value of all creatures in and for themselves, for one another, and for God, and their interconnectedness in a diverse whole that has unique value for God."*[34]

But the old debate stays loudly with us—is the Bible a scientific text-book about creation and GOD's involvement in the world? Rabbi Harold Kushner thinks this debate denigrates both the Bible and science: "*To search for truth instead of relying on ancient guesswork is a religious affirmation, not a repudiation. What religion worthy of its name would base itself on the hope that people would be too intimidated to find out how the world really works?*"[35] The term "Intelligent Design" is thrown around today (instead of the older term Creationism), causing confusion, deliberate or accidental, since this term was originally used for the universal design, making evolution the ongoing method of creation, thus accommodating both evolution and religious beliefs, depending on whether one added a "Designer" to the formula. Today, the term means an Interventionist Designer with a certain plan from the beginning (although many using it deny this)—what Paul Sponheim describes as a GOD that "*starts the ball rolling only to disappear until a sudden intervening entrance is needed to rescue a project gone badly.*"[36] Yet any scientific conclusions from Genesis make little sense if the Bible is the story of people trying to understand the Divine in their time and place with their pool of images and no inclination to write a thesis on cosmology. As biblical scholar Jaroslav Pelikan said:

> The Bible is not intended to be a universal history of the whole human race, much less a cosmogony that accounts for the structures and laws of the entire physical and biological universe. How could even a minimal cosmogony, one that was based on the sophisticated and well-informed astronomy of the ancient Near East, be content to throw in the phrase "and the stars" as an explanation for what a later chapter of Genesis itself acknowledge to be stars without number, and leave it at that? Rather, the Bible consistently directs out attention away from cosmogony, be it mythical or scientific, to the special relationship between God and the human race.[37]

Science studies the natural world and seeks explanations through observable events and measurements, its definition and limits. Good science does not launch into philosophical or religious arguments involving metaphysical or supernatural speculation beyond these limits. Since we cannot do experiments to prove GOD, the Divine cannot be a question within the scientific endeavor. We can, however, look at scientific discoveries and ponder from our faith perspective where a GOD-space might fit in the scientific scheme of things. Science cannot deny us permission to do this, since metaphysical and spiritual ideas are beyond their job description, but this does not prove GOD scientifically, nor can we make any such claim.

In the end, talking about GOD and choosing our Divine metaphors come down to faith statements, and different people come up with different answers from the same material. Rumi, who has been with us throughout this book, seemed fairly confident that Divine truth could be distinguished from falsehood with the right effort, and *"as a person grows in holiness, night turns into day."*[38] Yet, as I have said from the beginning, night does not turn to day for everyone, or night might turn to day occasionally but then revert back to night with despairing regularity and for extended periods. The search for GOD is ongoing, even for those who have decided that GOD is not at all, because even that conviction in an ever-evolving world is necessarily always open to contradiction, just as certainty about a Divine Presence is also open to evolutionary disillusionment. Theologian Keith Ward calls the journey *"a quest for a fuller dawning of a light once dimly seen, of creative powers obscurely felt, of haunting intimations of a personal ground of being, a hope for a time when we might no longer see transcendence as in a glass darkly, but finally meet face to face."*[39] This book has highlighted conclusions of past adventurers, whether Native American, Australian Aboriginal, Buddhist, Muslim, or Christian, thrown back over their shoulders as hints and visions, but always dressed in metaphors and allusions from another age that need careful unpacking if they are to guide us on our path.

Such a book might be expected to end with a confident "yes" about GOD to make us all feel secure, the *"I once was blind but now I see"* conclusion. My experience (and what I hear from the many with whom I speak) tells me, however, to believe more in the journey and the questions, not always knowing where one is headed but going anyway because of who we are. *"For as long as I can remember, God and I have not been able to leave each other alone,"* Mary Jo Meadow writes. *"I have searched with all my heart for God and have often not liked the God I found. I have bent myself in 'sweet surrender' and have angrily challenged. I have pursued the 'Hound of Heaven' and have struggled in the grip of a god who deserves to be rejected. Through it all, one thing has become clear. I am so constructed—genes? Early experiences? Temperamental inclination?—that the search will not, cannot be abandoned. Images of God may be found and rejected, replaced and revamped, sometimes absolutely lacking—but the search goes on.*"[40]

The question is . . . can you live with that . . . can I live with that? I think I can, because I can do no other. It is the way I live with everything else, an ongoing juggling of a few certain facts, constant new experiences, some diverse opinions, and faith in many things, some scientifically verifiable and others not—it is the adventure of being alive. I leave you with the words of Henry David Thoreau:

> How many a man [or woman] has dated a new era in his [or her] life
>   from the reading of a book!
> The book exists for us, perchance, which will explain
>   our miracles and reveal new ones.
> The at present unutterable things we may find somewhere uttered.
> These same questions that disturb and puzzle and confound us
>   have in their turn occurred to all the wise men [and women];
>   not one has been omitted; and each has answered them,
>   according to his [her] ability, by his [her] words and life.[41]

Notes

Preface

1. By the author.
2. Quoted in Dag Hammarskjöld, *Markings*, trans. Leif Sjöberg and W. H. Auden (New York: Alfred A. Knopf, 1965), 3.
3. Marjorie Suchocki, "Weaving the World," *Process Studies* 14 (Summer 1985): 84.

Chapter 1: Is Something Out There?

1. Paul Tillich, *Biblical Religion and the Search for Ultimate Reality* (Chicago: University of Chicago Press, 1965), 9.
2. Rig-Veda, quoted in Dominic Goodall, ed., *Hindu Scriptures*. (London: Phoenix Giant, 1996), 17.
3. Quoted in Martin Buber, *Eclipse of God: Studies in the Relation Between Religion and Philosophy* (Atlantic Highlands NJ: Humanities Press, 1979), 29.
4. Charles Bayer and Gordon Stirling, "Is God Almighty? A Dialogue on Theodicy," *Journal of Theology and Ministry* (Australia) (Spring 1999): 14.
5. Harold S. Kushner, *When Bad Things Happen to Good People* (New York: Avon Books, 1981), 128.
6. Quoted in Lorraine Kisly, ed., *Ordinary Graces: Christian Teachings on the Interior Life* (New York: Bell Tower, 2000), 8.
7. William Wordsworth, "Ode: Intimations of Immortality from Recollection of Early Childhood," in *The Poetic Works of Wordsworth*, ed. Thomas Hutchinson (London: Oxford University Press, 1959), 460.
8. Susan Howatch, *A Question of Integrity* (London: Warner Books, 1997), 655–56.
9. *The Brothers Karamazov*, quoted in Manning Clark, *The Puzzles of Childhood: His Early Life* (Ringwood, Australia: Penguin, 1989), 145.
10. Quoted in William James, *The Varieties of Religious Experiences: A Study in Human Nature* (New York: Collier Books, 1968), 392.
11. Robert Van de Weyer, ed., *Rumi* (London: Hodder and Stoughton, 1998), 82.
12. Hammarskjöld, *Markings*, vii.
13. Karen Armstrong, *The Spiral Staircase: A Memoir* (London: Harper Perennial, 2005), 2.
14. Ibid., 244.
15. Huston Smith, *Why Religion Matters: The Fate of the Human Spirit in an Age of Disbelief* (New York: HarperSanFrancisco, 2001), 28–29.
16. Quoted in John Bowker, *God: A Brief History* (London: DK Publishing, 2002), 339.

Chapter 2: Metaphorically Speaking . . .

1. Sara Maitland, "Children of the Book Come of Age," in *Books and Religion: A Quarterly Review* (New York: Trinity Church, 1990), 40.
2. John K. Hutchens, *New York Herald Tribune*, September 10, 1961.
3. Van de Weyer, *Rumi*, 70.

4. Florence Nightingale, *Suggestions for Thought by Florence Nightingale: Selections and Commentaries*, ed. Michael D. Calabria and Janet A. Macrae (Philadelphia: University of Pennsylvania Press, 1994), 28.

5. Ibid., 17.

6. Don Haddon, *Birds and Bird Lore of Bouganville and the Northern Solomons* (Alderley, Australia: Dove Publications, 2004), 88, 239–40.

7. See Karen Armstrong, *A History of God: The 4,000 Year Quest of Judaism, Christianity and Islam* (New York: Ballantine Books, 1993); Jack Miles, *God: A Biography* (London: Simon and Schuster, 1995); Bowker, *God*.

8. Jonathan Z. Smith, ed., *The Harpercollins Dictionary of Religion* (New York: HarperSanFrancisco, 1995), 1068.

9. Frederick Buechner, *Wishful Thinking* (London: Collins, 1973), 91.

10. Quoted in Amantha Trenoweth, *The Future of God: Personal Adventures in Spirituality with Thirteen of Today's Eminent Thinkers* (Newtown, Australia: Millennium Books, 1995), 257–58.

11. Sallie McFague, *Models of God: Theology for an Ecological, Nuclear Age* (Philadelphia: Fortress Press, 1987), xi.

12. Abd al-Hakeem Carney, "Imamate and Love: The Discourse of the Divine in Islamic Mysticism," *Journal of the American Academy of Religion* 73, no. 3 (September 2005): 708.

13. Armstrong, *History of God*, 239.

14. Bowker, *God*, 364.

15. Primo Levi, *Survival in Auschwitz* (New York: Simon and Schuster 1996), 123.

16. Quoted in R. B. Appleton, *The Elements of Greek Philosophy From Thales to Aristotle* (London: Methuen, 1922), 31.

17. Elizabeth A. Johnson, *She Who Is: The Mystery of God in Feminist Theological Discourse* (New York: Crossroad, 1992), 7.

18. Quoted in Bowker, *God*, 98.

19. George Dennis O'Brien, *God and the New Haven Railway: And Why Neither One is Doing Well* (Boston: Beacon Press, 1986), 4.

20. Sallie McFague, *The Body of God: An Ecological Theology* (Minneapolis: Fortress Press, 1993), 152.

21. Buber, *Eclipse of God*, 136.

22. Thomas Merton, *Seeds of Contemplation* (Norfolk, CT: New Directions Books, 1949), 134.

Chapter 3: The GOD Who Is Not . . .

1. Quoted in Robert Cecil, Richard Rieu, and David Wade, comp., *The King's Son* (London: Octagon Press, 1981), 22.

2. Quoted in Armstrong, *A History of God*, 220.

3. Quoted in Marcus Borg, *The God we Never Knew: Beyond Dogmatic Religion to a More Authentic Contemporary Faith* (New York: HarperSanFrancisco, 1997), 48.

4. Quoted in Johnson, *She Who Is*, 45.

5. Rudolf Otto, *The Idea of the Holy* (1923; repri., Oxford: Oxford University Press, 1958), xvi.

6. Quoted in Otto, *Idea of the Holy*, xviii–xix.

7. Van de Weyer, *Rumi*, 83.

8. Quoted in Bowker, *God*, 220.

9. Ibid., 218.

10. Ibid., 220.

11. Buber, *Eclipse of God*, 28.

12. Thomas Merton, *No Man Is an Island* (New York: Harper Brace, 1955), 245.
13. Quoted in Mary Lee Wile, "Serene Light, Unspoken Word," *Daughters of Sarah* 21, no. 4 (1995): 12.
14. Quoted in ibid., 10.
15. Quoted in Bowker, *God*, 250.
16. Quoted in Shama Futehally, *In the Dark of the Heart: Songs of Meera* (London: HarperCollins, 1994), 111.
17. Quoted in Jane Hirschfield, ed., *Women in Praise of the Sacred: 43 Centuries of Spiritual Poetry by Women* (New York: Harper Perennial, 1994), 94.
18. Quoted in Bowker, *God*, 291.
19. Armstrong, *History of God*, 219.
20. Quoted in Paul Clasper, *Eastern Paths and the Christian Way* (Maryknoll, NY: Orbis Books, 1982), 45–46.
21. Ibid., 41–42.
22. A comment made by Jürgen Moltmann in a public lecture.
23. This idea is developed in my book, *In Defense of Doubt: An Invitation to Adventure* (St. Louis, MO: Chalice Press, 1995).
24. Mary Jo Meadow and Carole A. Rayburn, *A Time to Weep, a Time to Sing: Faith Journeys of Women Scholars in Religion* (Minneapolis: Winston Press, 1985), 239.
25. Elie Wiesel, *Night* (New York: Pyramid Books, 1961), 81.
26. Quoted in John Hick, ed., *The Existence of God* (New York: Macmillan, 1964), 225.
27. G. F. Maine, ed., *A Book of Daily Readings: Passages in Prose and Verse for Solace and Meditation* (London: Collins, n.d.), 154.
28. By the author.

Chapter 4: To Be . . . or Not to Be?

1. Quoted in Philip Yancey, *Reaching for the Invisible God* (Grand Rapids, MI: Zondervan, 2000), 37.
2. Quoted in Hick, *Existence of God*, 31. I acknowledge my indebtedness to Hick for his drawing together centuries of commentary on this question, something I would otherwise have had to collect for myself.
3. Quoted in Robert E. Van Voorst, ed., *Readings in Christianity* (Belmont, CA: Wadsworth, 1997), 139.
4. Quoted in Hick, *Existence of God*, 46–47.
5. Ibid., 15.
6. A discussion of the Victorian poets is found in Val Webb, *Florence Nightingale: The Making of a Radical Theologian* (St. Louis, MO: Chalice Press, 2002), 197–98.
7. Quoted in Maine, *Book of Daily Readings*, 151.
8. "Dover Beach," quoted in Keith Ward, *God: A Guide for the Perplexed* (Oxford: Oneworld Publications, 2002), 177.
9. Quoted in Hick, *Existence of God*, 115.
10. Quoted in F. G. Hamish, *Ideas of Order: Anglicans and the Renewal of Theological Method in the Middle Years of the Nineteenth Century* (Assen, The Netherlands: Van Gorcum, 1974), 136.
11. Charles Darwin, *The Origin of Species* (New York: Barnes and Noble Books, 2004), 525–26.
12. Quoted in Randal Keynes, *Darwin, His Daughter, and Human Evolution* (New York: Riverhead Books, 2001), 53.
13. Ibid., 283.

14. Ibid., 45.
15. Ibid., 43.
16. Ibid., 304.
17. Ibid., 147, 270, 278.
18. Quoted in Appleton, *Elements of Greek Philosophy*, 31.
19. Donald Musser and Joseph L. Price, eds., *A New Handbook of Christian Theology* (Nashville: Abingdon Press, 1992), 37.
20. Armstrong, *History of God*, 287.
21. Quoted in Keynes, *Darwin*, 200.
22. O'Brien, *God and the New Haven Railway*, 157.
23. Musser and Price, *New Handbook of Christian Theology*, 37. Some Christian persuasions would add even more qualifiers.
24. Quoted in ibid., 41.
25. Ibid., 22.
26. Quoted in Yancey, *Reaching for the Invisible God*, 37.
27. Quoted in Ward, *God*, 138.
28. Elie Wiesel, *Memoirs: All Rivers Run to the Sea* (New York: Schocken Books, 1995), 84–85.
29. Smith, *Why Religion Matters*, 60.
30. John A. T. Robinson, *Honest to God* (London: SCM, 1963), 16.
31. Quoted in Musser and Price, *New Handbook of Christian Theology*, 121.
32. From an interview with Van Buren recorded in Ved Mehta, *The New Theologian* (London: Weidenfeld and Nicholson, 1966), 50–56.
33. John Hick, ed., *The Myth of God Incarnate* (London: SCM Press, 1977).
34. Quoted in Nigel Leaves, "The God Problem," *The Fourth R* 18, no. 3 (May–June 2005): 4, 6.
35. Quoted in ibid., 4.
36. John Shelby Spong, *A New Christianity for a New World: Why Traditional Faith Is Dying and How a New Faith Is Being Born* (New York: HarperCollins, 2001), 71.
37. Musser and Price, *New Handbook of Christian Theology*, 396.
38. Hans Küng, *Why I am Still a Christian* (Nashville: Abingdon Press, 1986), 45–46.
39. Edward Schillebeeckx, in conversation with Huub Oosterhuis and Piet Hoogeveen, *God Is New Each Moment* (New York: Seabury Press, 1983), 104.
40. Ibid., 103.
41. Ibid., 57.
42. Johnson, *She Who Is*, 39.
43. Otto, *Idea of the Holy*, 7.
44. Martin Marty, quoted in Lisa Miller, "Spirituality in America," *Newsweek*, September 5, 2005, 65.
45. Leo Tolstoy, *A Confession and Other Religious Writings,* trans. Jane Kentish (Harmondsworth, UK: Penguin, 1987), 134, 137.
46. Quoted in Hick, *Existence of God*, 17.
47. Quoted in Maine, *Book of Daily Readings*, 57.
48. Quoted in Bowker, *God*, 218.
49. Yet GOD did change the Divine Mind about creating human beings and sent a flood (Gen 6:6–7).
50. Paul Tillich, *Systematic Theology* (Chicago: University of Chicago Press, 1951), 1:237.
51. Quoted in Trenoweth, *Future of God*, 176–77.

52. Tolstoy, *Confession and Other Religious Writings*, 63.

53. Yancey, *Reaching for the Invisible God*, 38.

54. David Marr, *Patrick White: A Life* (Sydney: Random House Australia, 1992), 282–83.

55. Hick, *Existence of God*, 19.

56. Gordon Kaufman, "On Thinking of God as Serendipitous Creativity," *Journal of the American Academy of Religion* 69, no. 2 (June 2001): 415–16. His recent book on this discussion is *In Face of Mystery: A Constructive Theology* (Boston: Harvard University Press, 1993).

57. Harold Kushner, *Who Needs God?* (New York: Summit Books, 1989), 23.

58. Armstrong, *Spiral Staircase*, 4–5.

59. Robert E. Egner, ed., *Bertrand Russell's Best* (London: George Allen and Unwin, 1958), 30.

Chapter 5: What's in a Name?

1. Tao-Te King, quoted in Robert O. Ballou, ed., *The Portable World Bible: A Comprehensive Selection from the Eight Great Sacred Scriptures of the World* (1944; repr., New York: Viking Press, 1969), 542.

2. Van de Weyer, *Rumi*, 23.

3. Quoted in Hick, *Existence of God*, 211.

4. Mary E. Mills, *Images of God in the Old Testament* (Collegeville, MN: Liturgical Press, 1998), 24.

5. Although Genesis 1 used the generic *Elohim* for GOD, Genesis 2 uses the specific name *Yahweh*, signifying different strains of Hebrew tribal traditions that became incorporated into the Hebrew Bible.

6. Buber, *Eclipse of God*, 7–9.

7. Quoted in Bowker, *God*, 248–49.

8. Martin Buber, *I and Thou*, trans. Walter Kaufmann (New York: Charles Scribner's Sons, 1970), 160–61.

9. Michael Moran, *Beyond the Coral Sea: Travels in the Old Empires of the South West Pacific* (London: HarperCollins, 2003), 36–37.

10. Quoted in Graham Hancock, *The Sign and the Seal: The Quest for the Lost Ark of the Covenant* (New York: Crown Publishers, 1992), 299.

11. From a television interview with Karen Armstrong.

12. John Mbiti, *African Religions and Philosophy*, 2nd ed. (Oxford: Heinemann International, 1990), 35.

13. *Mundaka Upanishad*, quoted in Juan Mascaró, trans., *The Upanishads* (Middlesex, UK: Penguin Books, 1971), 75.

14. *Tulsi Das*, quoted in Bowker, *God*, 129.

15. *Katha Upanishad*, quoted in Mascaró, *Upanishads*, 59.

16. *Adi Granth*, quoted in Bowker, *God*, 124.

17. Buber, *I and Thou*, 160.

18. Quoted in Smith, *Why Religion Matters*, 30.

19. Tolstoy, *Confession and Other Religious Writings*, 31.

20. Buber, *I and Thou*, 123–24.

Chapter 6: Feathers on the Breath of GOD

1. Bukkyo Dendo Kyokai (Buddhist Promoting Foundation), ed., *The Teaching of Buddha* (Tokyo: Toppan Printing, 1987), 138.

2. *Katha Upanishad*, quoted in Mascaró, *Upanishads*, 65.

3. Quoted in Bukkyo Dendo Kyokai, *Teaching of Buddha*, 52–56.

4. By the author.

5. Quoted in Armstrong, *History of God*, 243.

6. Bukkyo Dendo Kyokai, *Teaching of Buddha*, 48.

7. Schillebeeckx, *God Is New Each Moment*, 29.

8. *Svetasvatara Upanishad*, quoted in Mascaró, *Upanishads*, 87.

9. Quoted in Bowker, *God*, 254.

10. Sabina Flanagan, *Hildegard of Bingen: A Visionary Life* (New York: Barnes and Noble, 1989), 143.

11. Quoted in Terence E. Fretheim, *God and World in the Old Testament: A Relational Theology of Creation* (Nashville: Abingdon Press, 2005), 66.

12. David Suzuki and Amanda McConnell, *The Sacred Balance: Rediscovering Our Place in Nature* (Sydney: Allen and Unwin, 1997), 38.

13. Adrian Room, *The Concise Dictionary of Word Origins* (New York: Quality Paperback Book Club, 1995), 54.

14. Wayne A. Meeks, ed., *The HarperCollins Study Bible: New Revised Standard Edition* (New York: HarperCollins, 1993), 2103.

15. Jaroslav Pelikan, *Whose Bible Is It? A History of the Scriptures Through the Ages* (New York: Viking, 2005), 25.

16. Clement of Alexandria, "The Song of the Word," in *Exhortation to the Heathen* (Society of Biblical Literature Seminar Papers, Alanta, GA, 1993), 809.

17. Tillich, *Biblical Religion*, 5.

18. Quoted in Carney, "Imamate and Love," 709.

19. St. Augustine, *Confessions*, trans. R. S. Pine-Coffin (Middlesex, UK: Penguin, 1961), 10:1, 207

20. Quoted in Hirshfield, *Women in Praise of the Sacred*, 129.

21. Quoted in Trenoweth, *Future of God*, 158.

22. William Corlett and John Moore, *The Islamic Space* (New York: Bradbury Press, 1979), 149.

23. Rabindranath Tagore, quoted in Maine, *Book of Daily Readings*, 19.

Chapter 7: Where Can I Go from Your Spirit?

1. Caroline Jones, *An Authentic Life: Finding Meaning and Spirituality in Everyday Life* (Sydney: ABC Books, 1998), 16–19.

2. Philip Sheldrake, SJ, *Spirituality and History* (New York: Orbis Books, 1995), 6.

3. Mascaró, *Upanishads*, 64.

4. Rabindranath Tagore, *Gitanjali: A Collection of Indian Songs* (New York: Macmillan, 1971), 42–43.

5. Mascaró, *Upanishads*, 120.

6. Ibid., 81.

7. Quoted in Bowker, *God*, 339.

8. See also 1 Cor. 3:16; 1 John 3:24.

9. See also Judg. 3:10; 11:29; Isa. 61:1; Ezek. 11:5; Ezra 1:5; Neh. 9:30; Joel 2:28–29; Matt. 10:20; Luke 1:41; John 14:26; 16:13; and Acts 2:4, 17; 4:31.

10. As discussed later, the Gospels do not agree about when the commissioning Spirit "came upon" Jesus.

11. Mascaró, *Upanishads*, 67.

12. Don Cupitt, *After God: The Future of Religion* (New York: HarperCollins, 1997), 51–52.

13. Johnson, *She Who Is*, 128.

14. Ibid., 130–31.

15. For this analysis of contemporary pneumatology, I am indebted to Nancy Victorin-Vangerud's excellent book *The Raging Hearth: Spirit in the Household of God* (St. Louis, MO: Chalice Press. 2000). Victorin-Vangerud cites the work of Colin Gunton, Elizabeth Johnson, Sallie McFague, Jürgen Moltmann, Jose Comblin, Krister Stendahl, Michael Welker, Mark I. Wallace, Peter Hodgson, and many others.

16. Ibid., 23.

17. Quoted in Kisly, *Ordinary Graces*, 7.

18. Mark I. Wallace, *Fragments of the Spirit: Nature, Violence and the Renewal of Creation* (New York: Continuum, 1996), 136.

19. Quoted in David L. Edwards, *Christian England: From the 18th Century to the First World War* (Grand Rapids, MI: W. B. Eerdmans, 1984), 3:141.

20. Quoted in Armstrong, *History of God*, 358.

Chapter 8: Nature Speaks

1. Quoted in Rachael Kohn, *The New Believers: Re-imagining God* (Sydney: HarperCollins, 2003), 153.

2. Quoted in F. C. Happold, *Mysticism: A Study and an Anthology* (Harmondsworth, UK: Penguin, 1963), 253.

3. John Calvin, *Institutes of the Christian Religion*, ed. John T. McNeill (Philadelphia: Westminster Press, 1960), 1:52.

4. Quoted in Smith, *Why Religion Matters*, 48.

5. Rabindranath Tagore, *Fruit-Gathering* (Madras: Macmillan India, 1985), 18.

6. Quoted in Trenoweth, *Future of God*, 247.

7. Quoted in Musser and Price, *New Handbook of Christian Theology*, 328.

8. Handwritten note in Florence Nightingale's copy of Thomas à Kempis' *Imitation of Christ*, pages 26–27, in the Florence Nightingale Museum, St. Thomas' Hospital, London.

9. McFague, *Body of God*, 208.

10. Quoted in Jonathan Z. Smith, *HarperCollins Dictionary of Religion*, 733.

11. Trenoweth, *Future of God*, 70.

12. Handwritten note in her Bible at the Florence Nightingale Museum, St. Thomas' Hospital, London.

13. See entries on "Enlil," "Ninlil," and "Nippur" in Paul J. Achtemeier, ed., *Harper's Bible Dictionary* (New York: HarperSanFrancisco, 1985), 267, 708.

14. Quoted in Trenoweth, *Future of God*, 32.

15. Tagore, *Fruit-Gathering*, 55.

16. Bukkyo Dendo Kyokai, *Teaching of Buddha*, 65–66.

17. Quoted in Mascaró, *Upanishads*, 14.

18. *Svetasvatara Upanishad*, quoted in Goodall, *Hindu Scriptures*, 201.

19. Bukkyo Dendo Kyokai, *Teaching of Buddha*, 78.

20. Tolstoy, *Confession and Other Religious Writings*, 65, 128.

21. This phrase is not in the New Revised Standard Version but listed as an addition after verse 13 in some ancient authorities.

22. Achtemeier, *Harper's Bible Dictionary*, 661.

23. Mascaró, *Upanishads*, 20.

24. O'Brien, *God and the New Haven Railway*, 5.

25. Achtemeier, *Harper's Bible Dictionary*, 232.

26. Others suggest the dove returning the olive branch to Noah was the sign of the Spirit, yet the rainbow was the Divine sign in the Noah story.

27. Rainbow Spirit Elders, *Rainbow Spirit Theology: Towards an Australian Aboriginal Theology*, ed. Robert Bos and Norman Habel (Victoria, Australia: HarperCollins Religious, 1997), xii.

28. Ibid., 24.

29. Ibid., 32.

30. Ibid., 88.

31. Quoted in Trenoweth, *Future of God*, 256–57.

Chapter 9: Divine Attributes: God Is Like . . .

1. Johnson, *She Who Is*, 45.

2. Shems Friedlander and Al-Hajj Shaikh Muzaffereddin, *Ninety-Nine Names of Allah: The Beautiful Names* (New York: HarperSanFrancisco, 1993), 7. Islam sees the revelations of Judaism and Christianity as part of their history, one story of God from the beginning.

3. Ibid.

4. Geoffrey Faber, *Jowett: A Portrait with Background* (Cambridge, MA: Harvard University Press, 1957), 143.

5. Quoted in Ward, *God*, 56.

6. Augustine, *Confessions*, 136.

7. Goodall, *Hindu Scriptures*, 47.

8. Bukkyo Dendo Kyokai, *Teaching of Buddha*, 64.

9. Rumi quoted in Van de Weyer, *Rumi*, 21.

10. This phrase is chanted in five Psalms (100, 106, 107, 118, 136); three passages in Chronicles (1 Chron, 16:34; 2 Chron. 5:13; 7:3); and once in Jeremiah (33:11). Variations of this one phrase occur in twelve other Psalms (25, 34, 52, 54, 69, 73, 86, 109, 119, 135, 143, 145), 2 Chron. 30:9, Lam. 3:25, and Nah. 1:7.

11. "Letter from Jefferson to Ezra Styles, President of Yale, June 25, 1819" (www.church-statelaw.com/historical materials).

12. Frank McCourt, *Angela's Ashes: A Memoir* (New York: Touchstone, 1996), 179.

13. Quoted in Hick, *Existence of God*, 120.

14. Tagore, *Gitanjali*, 89.

15. Alfred North Whitehead, *Process and Reality: An Essay in Cosmology* (New York: Free Press, 1978), 346.

16. Hammarskjöld, *Markings*, 118.

17. Quoted in Happold, *Mysticism*, 253.

18. Mascaró, *Upanishads*, 10.

19. Edith Hamilton, *Mythology* (Boston: Little, Brown and Company, 1942), 77–78.

20 Mascaró, *Upanishads*, 33.

21. Tagore, *Gitanjali*, 49.

22. Quoted in Bowker, *God*, 221.

23. Tagore, *Gitanjali*, 88.

24. Quoted in Hirshfield, *Women in Praise of the Sacred*, 88.

25. Ibid., 104.

26. Ibid., 45.

27. O'Brien, *God and the New Haven Railway*, 112.

28. Mitch Albom, *Tuesdays with Morrie* (New York: Random House, 2002), 174.

29. Eighth-century poet Shantideva, quoted in Bowker, *God*, 73.

30. From *ED-Jubilee*, e-newspaper of the 8th Assembly of the World Council of Churches, Harare, Zimbabwe 3–14 December 1998.

31. Jonathan Z. Smith, *HarperCollins Dictionary of Religion*, 498.

32. *ED-Jubilee*, 8th WCC.

33. Levi, *Survival in Auschwitz*, 124.

34. Tolstoy, *Confession and Other Religious Writings,* 21.

35. Terry Tempest Williams, quoted in Miriam Therese Winter, ed., *Good Company* (Cleveland, OH: Pilgrim Press, 1996), no page number.

Chapter 10: The Power of the One

1. Carol P. Christ, *She Who Changes: Re-imagining the Divine in the World* (New York: Palgrave Macmillan, 2003), 39.

2. Miles, *God*, 6.

3. Anna Herriette Leonowens, *Anna and the King of Siam. From the English Governess at the Siamese Court: Being Recollections of Six Years in the Royal Palace at Bangkok* (London: Trübner and Co., 1870), 112. It must be noted that Anna Leonowens' depiction of Thailand's King Rama IV is considered demeaning by Thai people in terms of the true history of this man so beloved by them.

4. Otto, *Idea of the Holy*, 19.

5. Richard Rodriguez, *Hunger of Memory: The Education of Richard Rodriguez* (New York: Bantam Books, 1982), 85.

6. Nightingale, *Suggestions for Thought*, 149.

7. Quoted in Anna Case-Winters, *God's Power: Traditional Understandings and Contemporary Challenges* (Louisville, KY: Westminster/John Knox Press, 1990), 151.

8. Quoted in Maine, *Book of Daily Readings*, 33–34.

9. Albert Camus, *The Plague* (Middlesex, UK: Penguin 1979), 186.

10. Quoted in J. Polkinghorne, *Science and Providence: God's Interaction with the World* (London: SPCK, 1989), 59.

11. Kushner, *When Bad Things Happen*, 4.

12. This description of ancient Palestine is summarized from William G. Dever, *Did God have a Wife? Archeology and Folk Religion in Ancient Israel* (Grand Rapids, MI: W. B. Eerdmans, 2005), 12–31.

13. Ibid., 15.

14. Case-Winters, *God's Power*, 52.

15. Van de Weyer, *Rumi*, 63.

16. Irshad Manji, *The Trouble with Islam* (New York: St. Martin's Press, 2003), 213.

17. Quoted in Case-Winters, *God's Power*, 133–34.

18. Quoted in Musser and Price, *New Handbook of Christian Theology*, 396.

19. Quoted in Trenoweth, *Future of God*, 147.

20. Ibid., 147.

21. Susan Howatch, *Ultimate Prizes* (New York: Fawcett Crest, 1989), 343–44.

22. *Adi Granth*, quoted in Bowker, *God*, 123.

23. Meister Eckhart, *Breakthrough: Meister Eckhart's Creation Centered Spirituality in New Translation* (Garden City, NY: Doubleday, 1980), 103, 118.

24. Letter by David Hosick in *Christian Century*, June 14, 2003.

25. Bukkyo Dendo Kyokai, *Teaching of Buddha*, 74.

Chapter 11: Imago Dei

1. Van de Weyer, *Rumi*, 32.
2. John M'Clintock and James Strong, eds., *Cyclopaedia of Biblical, Theological and Ecclesiastical Literature* (New York: Harper and Brothers Publisher, 1871), 4:499.
3. Johnson, *She Who Is*, 71.
4. M'Clintock and Strong, *Cyclopaedia*, 501.
5. Henricus Cornelius Agrippa, *Declamation on the Nobility and Preeminence of the Female Sex*, trans. and ed. Albert Rabil (Chicago: University of Chicago Press, 1996), 47.
6. Calvin, *Institutes of the Christian Religion*, 1:14:2; 1:15:1, 3.
7. Ibid., 1:11:1.
8. Quoted in Cupitt, *After God*, 108.
9. Van de Weyer, *Rumi*, 33.
10. A summary of these arguments can be found in Webb, *Florence Nightingale*, 50–53.
11. Keynes, *Darwin*, 284, 315.
12. Justin D. Kaplan, ed., *The Pocket Aristotle* (New York: Pocket Books, 1958), 280.
13. Interestingly, this often quoted verse appears in a different form in the New Revised Standard Version: "*He subdues the ancient gods, shatters the forces of old*," a good example of how things change in translation when new sources are available.
14. Bukkyo Dendo Kyokai, *Teaching of Buddha*, 356.
15. For this discussion see Borg, *God We Never Knew*
16. Brian Wren, *What Language Shall I Borrow? God-talk in Worship: A Male Response to Feminist Theology* (New York: Crossroad, 1993).
17. As a side note, when Saladin, the Kurdish warrior from Tikrit (northern Iraq), conquered Jerusalem back for the Muslims in 1187 after eighty-eight years of Christian rule, he allowed the remnant of the crusader army and the resident Catholics to leave the city without harm.
18. Mona Siddiqui, "When Reconciliation Fails: Global Politics and the Study of Religion," *Journal of the American Academy of Religion* 73, no. 4 (December 2005): 1148.
19. Quoted in *Rochester Post Bulletin*, August 18, 2002.
20. Tolstoy, *Confession and Other Religious Writings*, 158.
21. Dorothee Soelle, *Against the Wind: Memoirs of a Radical Christian* (Minneapolis: Fortress, 1999), 24.
22. Quoted in Robert McAfee Brown, *Religion and Violence*, 2nd ed. (Philadelphia: Westminster Press, 1987), 55.
23. Swami Prabhavananda and Christopher Isherwood, trans., *Bhagavad-Gita: The Song of God* (New York: Mentor Book, 1972), 1:34.
24. Ibid., 1:38.
25. Tolstoy, *Confession and Other Religious Writings*, 228–29.
26. Quoted in Brown, *Religion and Violence*, 29.
27. Kushner, *Who Needs God?* 201.
28. Johnson, *She Who Is*, 18.
29. Ibid., 57.
30. Quoted in Trenoweth, *Future of God*, 211.

Chapter 12: In the Family Way

1. Julian of Norwich (1342–1416), quoted in Elizabeth Clark and Herbert Richardson, eds., *Women and Religion: A Feminist Sourcebook of Christian Thought* (New York: Harper and Row, 1977), 108.

2. Achtemeier, *Harper's Bible Dictionary*, 14.

3. Athalya Brenner, "Some Reflections on Violence against Women and the Image of the Hebrew God: The Prophetic Books Revisited," in Jane Schaberg, Alice Bach, and Esther Fuchs, *On the Cutting Edge: The Study of Women in Biblical Worlds* (New York: Continuum, 2004), 79.

4. C. S. Lewis, "Priestesses in the Church?" in C. S. Lewis, *God in the Dock: Essays on Theology*, ed. Walter Hooper (London: Fount, 1979), 92–93.

5. Quoted in Elisabeth Schüssler Fiorenza, *In Memory of Her: A Feminist Theological Reconstruction of Christian Origins* (New York: Crossroad, 1989), 255.

6. Quoted in ibid., 258.

7. 1 Tim. 2:11–15; 1 Pet. 3:1–7; Col. 3:18; 1 Cor. 14:34–35 (a non-Pauline addition to a Pauline letter).

8. Quoted in Val Webb, *Why We're Equal: Introducing Feminist Theology* (St. Louis, MO: Chalice Press, 1999), 125.

9. Muriel Porter, *The New Puritans: The Rise of Fundamentalism in the Anglican Church* (Melbourne, Australia: Melbourne University Press, 2006), 90. The meaning of this Corinthians verse is disputed by scholars, coming in a discussion of whether women should wear veils. Some believe "head" should be translated as "source"—the source of the Son is the Father; the source of woman is man, based on Eve created from Adam in the Genesis 2 story.

10. Mills, *Images of God*, 3, 14.

11. Translation by Pelikan, *Whose Bible Is It?* 25.

12. For more on *Sophia*-Wisdom, see Johnson, *She Who Is*; and Elisabeth Schüssler-Fiorenza, *Jesus, Miriam's Child, Sophia's Prophet: Critical Issues in Feminist Christology* (New York: Continuum, 1994).

13. *The Wisdom of Confucius* (Mount Vernon, NY: Peter Pauper Press, 1963), 9.

14. Kwok Pui-lan, *Chinese Women and Christianity, 1860–1927* (Atlanta, GA: Scholars Press, 1992).

15. Clark and Richardson, *Women and Religion*, 86.

16. For more on women's subordination, read Webb, *Why We're Equal*.

17. John Edger Wideman, "Russell Means: The Profound and Outspoken Activist Shares Some of His Most Ardent Convictions," *Modern Maturity* 38:5 (September–October 1995), 70.

18. Dever, *Did God have a Wife?* 311, 317.

19. Bukkyo Dendo Kyokai, *Teaching of Buddha*, 28.

20. Henri Nouwen, *The Return of the Prodigal Son: A Story of Homecoming* (New York: Doubleday, 1992), 102.

21. Dorothee Soelle, *Theology for Skeptics: Reflections on God*, trans. Joyce L. Irwin (Minneapolis: Fortress, 1995), 25.

22. Johnson, *She Who Is*, 53–54.

23. Quoted in Maine, *Book of Daily Readings*, 119.

24. Buber, *I and Thou*, 130.

25. Bukkyo Dendo Kyokai, *Teaching of Buddha*, 432.

26. Quoted in Soelle, *Theology for Skeptics*, 27.

Chapter 13: The Bible Tells Me So . . .

1. Quoted in Trenoweth, *Future of God*, 134.

2. Mascaró, *Upanishads*, 23.

3. For this discussion, see Tom Harpur, *The Pagan Christ: Is Blind Faith Killing Christianity?* (Crows Nest, NSW, Australia: Allen and Unwin, 2005),

4. Hamilton, *Mythology*, 443–46.

5. For a discussion on Jesus as a Greek hero figure, see Gregory J. Riley, *One Jesus Many Christs: How Jesus Inspired Not One True Christianity but Many* (Minneapolis: Fortress Press, 2000).

6. McFague, *Body of God*, 159.

7. Tolstoy, *Confession and Other Religious Writings*, 89.

8. Pelikan, *Whose Bible Is It?* 214.

9. John P. Bradley, Leo F. Daniels, and Thomas C. Jones, *The International Dictionary of Thoughts* (Chicago: J. G. Ferguson Publishing, 1969), 79.

10. Achtemeier, *Harper's Bible Dictionary*, 635.

11. Ibid., 366.

12. Kristen Kvam, Linda Shearing, and Valarie Ziegler, eds., *Eve and Adam: Jewish, Christian, and Muslim Readings on Genesis and Gender* (Indiana, PA: Indiana University Press, 1999), 81.

13. Smith, *HarperCollins Dictionary of Religion*, 836.

14. Quoted in Bowker, *God*, 344.

15. Smith, *HarperCollins Dictionary of Religion*, 514–18.

16. Siddiqui, "When Reconciliation Fails," 1141–53.

17. William M. Schniedewind, *How the Bible Became a Book; Textualization of Ancient Israel* (Cambridge: Cambridge University Press, 2004), 7.

18. Bart D. Ehrman, *Misquoting Jesus: The Story Behind Who Changed the Bible and Why* (New York: HarperSanFrancisco, 2005), 7.

19. Ibid., 47.

20. Ibid., 48.

21. Ibid., 52.

22. Ibid., 53–54.

23. Ibid., 158.

24. Ibid., 164. These verses are bracketed in the New Revised Standard Version, indicating their absence in other ancient authorities.

25. Ibid., 194.

26. Pelikan, *Whose Bible Is It?* 131.

27. Quoted in ibid., 127.

28. Ibid., 156.

29. Ibid., 19.

30. Ehrman, *Misquoting Jesus*, 88–89.

31. Maitland, "Children of the Book Come of Age," 40.

32. Faber, *Jowett*, 143.

33. Buechner, *Wishful Thinking*, 12.

Chapter 14: Who Do You Say I Am?

1. Mascaró, *Upanishads*, 59.

2. 1 Thessalonians, Philippians, Philemon, Galatians, 1 and 2 Corinthians, and Romans. Others ascribed to Paul were written later and not by Paul.

3. For more on messianic claims in the Gospels, see "Messiah" in Achtemeier, *Harper's Bible Dictionary*, 630–31.

4. Note on 2 Sam. 7:14 in Meeks, *HarperCollins Study Bible*, 477.

5. Meeks, *HarperCollins Study Bible*, 1025–26.

6. Geza Vermes, *The Changing Faces of Jesus* (New York: Penguin 2000), 280.

7. Paul's commissioning was also described as Voice and Light, followed later by laying on of hands and filling by the Spirit.

8. Meeks, *HarperCollins Study Bible*, 420.

9. I argue in my book *John's Message: Good News for the New Millennium* (Nashville: Abingdon Press, 2000) that this Son-Father language is about a shared mission or task also handed on to his followers, not a biological relationship.

10. "Philo," in E. A. Livingstone, ed., *The Concise Oxford Dictionary of the Christian Church* (Oxford: Oxford University Press, 1977), 400.

11. For further discussion on this, see John Shelby Spong, *Born of a Woman: A Bishop Rethinks the Birth of Jesus* (New York: HarperSanFrancisco, 1992).

12. Vermes, *Changing Faces of Jesus*, 224–28.

13. "Act of righteousness" or "obedience," suggesting Jesus' faithfulness as opposed to *adam's* (humankind's) unfaithfulness. Note on Rom. 5:18 in Meeks, *HarperCollins Study Bible*, 2123.

14. O'Brien, *God and the New Haven Railway*, 82–83.

15. The Chalcedonian Creed, quoted in Van Voorst, *Readings in Christianity*, 93.

16. This early explanation focusing on human "mortality" affirms my argument that Paul's interest in Jesus was about mortality and immortality.

17. Abelard is best known today for his love of Heloise, which led to his castration by her angry uncle's henchmen.

18. Tolstoy, *Confession and Other Religious Writings*, 95–96.

19. Quoted in Harpur, *The Pagan Christ*, 1.

20. Vermes, *Changing Faces of Jesus*, 208.

21. Ibid., 276.

22. Mascaró, *Upanishads*, 40.

23. E. Stanley Jones, *The Christ of the Indian Road* (New York: Abingdon, 1925), 205–6.

24. Quoted in Bradley, Daniels, Thomas, *International Dictionary of Thoughts*, 75.

25. Bayer and Stirling, "Is God Almighty?" 14.

26. Johnson, *She Who Is*, 191.

27. Victorin-Vangerud, *Raging Hearth*, 208.

Chapter 15: What Is Truth?

1. Ward, *God*, 1.

2. Judith Flanders, *A Circle of Sisters* (London: Penguin, 2001), 215.

3. Jack Kornfield, ed., *Teachings of the Buddha: Revised and Expanded Edition* (New York: Barnes and Noble Books, 1996), 26.

4. Paul Sponheim, *Speaking of God: A Relational Theology* (St Louis, MO: Chalice Press, 2006), 153.

5. The first quote, "In him . . . we have our being," may have come from Epimenides, sixth century BCE, and the second, "For we too are his offspring," is from Aratus, third century BCE. Meeks, *HarperCollins Study Bible*, 2093.

6. Goodall, *Hindu Scriptures*, 191.

7. Quoted in Hirshfield, *Women in Praise*, 87.

8. Albom, *Tuesdays with Morrie*, 179.

9. Quoted in Achtemeier, *Harper's Bible Dictionary*, 1100.

10. Sponheim, *Speaking of God*, 138.
11. Ibid., 31.
12. Quoted in Paul F. Knitter, *No Other Name? A Critical Survey of Christian Attitudes Toward the World Religions* (Maryknoll, NY: Orbis Books, 1992), 122–23.
13. Ibid., 131.
14. Quoted in Bowker, *God*, 83.
15. Cupitt, *After God*, 113.
16. Mascaró, *Upanishads*, 101.
17. Quoted in Hirshfield, *Women in Praise of the Sacred*, 182.
18. Bukkyo Dendo Kyokai, *Teaching of Buddha*, 60.
19. Hammarskjöld, *Markings*, 154.
20. Quoted in Trenoweth, *Future of God*, 257–58.
21. Bukkyo Dendo Kyokai, *Teaching of Buddha*, 82.
22. Ibid.
23. Quoted in Musser and Price, *New Handbook of Christian Theology*, 387.
24. McFague, *Body of God*, 192.
25. Ibid., 150, 193.
26. By the author.
27. Quoted in Trenoweth, *Future of God*, 113.
28. Ibid., 72.
29. I. B. O'Malley, *Florence Nightingale, 1820–1856: A Study of Her Life Down to the End of the Crimean War* (London: Thornton Butterworth, 1931), 116.
30. Van de Weyer, *Rumi*, 45
31. Corlett and Moore, *Islamic Space*, 86.
32. Darwin, *Origin of Species*, 525–26
33. Edward B. Davis, "Science and Religious Fundamentalism in the 1920s: Religious Pamphlets by Leading Scientists of the Scopes Era Provide Insight into Public Debates about Science and Religion," *American Scientist* 93 (May–June 2005): 253–60.
34. World Council of Churches statement, quoted in McFague, *Body of God*, 165.
35. Kushner, *Who Needs God?* 20
36. Sponheim, *Speaking of God*, 42
37. Pelikan, *Whose Bible Is It?* 29
38. Van de Weyer, *Rumi*, 36.
39. Ward, *God*, 253
40. Meadows and Rayburn, *Time to Weep*, 233.
41. Henry David Thoreau, *Walden* (New York: New American Library: Signet Classic, 1960), 77.

Index

abba, 161
Abel, 223
Abelard, 204
Abimelech, 83
Aboriginal people, 23, 95, 106–7, 114, 124, 173
Abraham, 55–56, 59, 95, 107, 168, 170, 179, 191, 197, 223
Abram, 59
absence, 31–32
Acts, 59, 71, 86, 90, 97, 103, 107, 180, 184, 195, 212
adam, 72, 87, 200
Adam and Eve, 15, 85, 170, 177, 181, 200, 203–4
Adonai, 61
adultery, 155
Agni, 54
agnosticism, 41, 43, 53, 63
Agrippa, Henricus Cornelius, 138
air, 94, 97
Aladdin, 6
al-Arabi, Ibn, 16
Alcheringa, 106
Al-Ghazali, 27–28
al-Hallaj, Akhbar, 7, 82
Al-Khaliq the Creator, 62
Allah, 27, 54, 62, 76–77, 100, 109, 111, 121, 128, 147, 149, 174, 178, 191, 207
Allen, Woody, 25

almah, 200
Al-Malik the King, 62
aloha, 70
Alpha, 217
Amiel, Henri Frédéric, 50
Ammonites, 56, 144
Amos, 174
Anath, 55
Anaxagoras of Clazomenae, 41–42
Angela's Ashes, 113–14
Anglican Articles of Religion, 151
Anglican Communion, 159
anima, 69
Anna and the King of Siam, 123–24
An-Nur, 100
Anselm, Saint, 37–38, 43–44, 204
anthropology, 198–99
anthropomorphism, 171, 208
apophatic, 28
Apsu, 97
Aquila heliaca, 105
Aquinas, Thomas, 27, 115, 164, 185
Aram, 56
Aristotle, 88, 137, 140, 158, 164
Arius, Bishop, 201–2
Arjuna, 145
Armstrong, Karen, 7, 52, 60
Arnold, Matthew, 40

Ar-Raheem the Merciful, 62
Ar-Rahman the Compassionate, 62
Asherah, 55, 164–65
asherim, 164
Astarte, 56, 105
Athanasius, Bishop, 184, 201–2
atheism, 41, 53
Athirat, 55
Augustine, Saint, 27, 77, 111,
    184, 203–4, 215
Aum, 61
Axial Age, 112

Baal, 55–56, 100
Babylonian exile, 57
Baluba, 61
baptism, 99
Barth, Karl, 94, 211, 215
Basil, Saint, 26
Bathsheba, 148
Bayer, Charles, 3, 207
Beguine, 119
betulah, 200
Bhagavad Gita, 145, 173
Bhagavata Purana, 216
Bhakti, 31
Bible, 13, 172–90, 225
    Acts, 59, 71, 86, 90, 97, 103,
        107, 180, 195, 212
    2 Chronicles, 170
    Colossians, 158
    1 Corinthians, 86–87, 90, 159,
        173, 195, 197
    2 Corinthians, 101
    Daniel, 59, 84, 86
    Deuteronomy, 56, 65–66, 97,
        100, 104, 116, 121, 141,
        155, 181, 199

Ecclesiastes, 26, 71–72, 218
Ephesians, 90, 157–58
Exodus, 26, 54, 56, 60,
    62, 70, 74, 97, 101, 104,
    116, 123, 134, 143, 154,
    169
Ezekiel, 72–73, 84, 101, 155
Ezra, 112
Galatians, 158, 194–95
Genesis, 56, 59, 61, 68, 70,
    72, 74, 83, 85, 95–96, 98,
    107, 111, 136, 165, 168,
    170, 225
German Bible, 186
gospels, 180
Greek New Testament, 186
Hebrews, 83, 101, 137
Hosea, 105
Inspiration (*theopneustos*),
    187–189
Isaiah, 28, 99, 103, 105, 116,
    124, 140, 142, 146–48, 150,
    156, 166, 193–94, 200
James, 184, 186
Jeremiah, 71, 104–5, 116,
    127, 142, 165, 192, 196,
    199, 217
Job, 26, 71, 83–84, 98, 194
John, 3, 45, 68–69, 75, 84,
    88, 98, 101, 103, 113,
    117, 133, 147, 161–63,
    169, 171, 180, 182, 184,
    187, 191–92, 195–97,
    199, 208, 210, 212, 214,
    217
1 John, 85, 100, 116–17, 185
Joshua, 57, 143
Jude, 184

Judges, 57, 83, 197
King James Bible (KJV), 183, 185–86
1 Kings, 3, 74, 97, 217
2 Kings, 71, 164
Lamentations, 142
Latin Vulgate, 186
Leviticus, 105, 116, 189, 192
Luke, 70, 83–84, 86, 105, 113–14, 116, 161, 167, 169, 180, 183, 192, 196–97, 199–200
Mark, 57, 70, 90, 99, 103, 113, 182–83, 192–93, 195–96, 199, 209
Matthew, 70–71, 73, 83, 86, 90, 98, 100–101, 103, 105, 113, 146, 161, 169, 183, 192, 196, 199–201, 206
Micah, 146, 148
New Revised Standard Version (1989), 183, 187
New Testament, 13, 180, 182, 184–85, 187, 205, 214
Numbers, 50, 84, 106
Old Testament, 184
Paul, 87, 199
Peter, 87, 90, 113, 158184
Protestant Bible, 184
Proverbs, 71, 105, 124–25, 162
Psalm, 4, 6, 19, 29, 31–32, 70–71, 74, 80, 94, 98, 100–105, 121, 125, 127, 133, 142, 148–49, 168
Revelation, 70, 148, 180, 184, 217
Revised Standard Version, 186

Romans, 84–85, 87, 89, 92, 161, 180, 185, 195, 200
1 Samuel, 83–84, 148, 197
2 Samuel, 84, 103, 193
Timothy, 90, 187, 188, 192
Titus, 90
Vulgate, 184–85
Zechariah, 97–98
Zephaniah, 148
birds, 104–5
Black-winged Night, 117
Blake, William, 222
Blandina, 168
Bodhisattva, 120, 173
Bolsec, Jerome, 138–39
Bonhoeffer, Dietrich, 45
Borg, Marcus, 142
Bowker, John, 16
Brahman, 61–62, 66, 76, 173, 191
bread, 169
Breath, 69, 83, 97, 198
Brenner, Athalya, 156
Brhadaranyaka Upanishad, 111
Bronte, Charlotte, 42
Bronte, Emily, 217
Brown, Charlie, 217
Browning, Elizabeth Barrett, 92, 222
Buber, Martin, 21, 29–30, 58–59, 62, 64, 170
Buddha, 30–31, 65–67, 93, 111, 135, 166, 170, 207, 211, 219
Buddhism, 30–32, 63, 73, 98, 100, 102, 112, 134–35, 141, 173, 211, 217
Buddhist Enlightenment, 111
Buechner, Frederick, 14, 190
Bultmann, Rudolf, 45

Caesar, 192
Cain, 85
Calvin, John, 92, 128, 138
Camus, Albert, 126
Carney, Abd al-Hakeem, 16
Catherine of Sienna, 88
Catholicism, 215
Ch'i, 70
Chaos, 117
Charismatic persuasions, 89
China, 163
Chinese art, 102
Chou emperors, 102
Christ, Carol P., 123
Christian Century magazine, 134
Christian Faith, The, 208
Christianity, 57, 62, 67–68, 207,
    215–16
  art, 68, 71, 88, 142
  exclusivist culture, 213–14
  images, 20
  scripture, 37
  writings, 182
Christos, 192
2 Chronicles, 170
Church of England, 189
Clement of Alexandria, 58, 76
Cobb, John, 221
Coffin, William Sloan, 134
Coleridge, Samuel Taylor, 222
Colonna, Vittoria, 78
Colossians, 158
commandments, 116
communication, 76–78
Communism, 151
Confessions, 77
Confucianism, 112
Constantine, 100, 146, 201–2

conversion, 214–15
Cook, Captain, 70
Copernicus, 138
1 Corinthians, 86–87, 90, 159,
    173, 195, 197
2 Corinthians, 101
Council of Chalcedon, 202
Council of Florence, 215
Council of Nicea, 202
Council of Trent, 215
Cozart, Bernadette, 153
creation, 14
creationism, 225
Crossan, John Dominic, 205
Crusades, 143
Cupitt, Don, 42, 45–46, 216
*Cyclopaedia of Biblical,
    Theological and Ecclesiastical
    Literature*, 136
Cyrus, King, 86

Dakota Indians, 131–32
Daniel, 59, 84, 86
Daoism, 55, 98, 112
dark ages, 62
Darwin, Charles, 40–41, 43,
    139–40, 223–24
David, King, 84, 148, 193–96
Davies, Paul, 222
Day, Dorothy, 120
death, 222–23
Death-of-God movement, 45
Deborah, 152
Decalogue, 48
de Chardin, Pierre Teilhard, 89
*Declamation on the Nobility and
    Preeminence of the Female
    Sex*, 138

Descent of Man, The, 41
Designer, 225
Deuteronomy, 56, 65–66, 97, 100, 104, 116, 121, 141, 155, 181, 199
Dever, William, 127, 164–65
Devil, 203
Dewey, Joanna, 214
Dharma, 93, 98
Diatessaron, 181
Dickenson, Emily, 43
Dionysius, Bishop, 182
Divali, 213
Divine attributes, 109–22
Dixon, John, 141
Docetists, 183
Dodson, Patrick, 107
dokein, 15
Dostoevsky, Fyodor, 6
dove, 71, 84, 105–6, 208

Ea, 97
eagle, 104–5
earth, 94
Earth Mother, 95–96
Ecclesiastes, 26, 71–72, 218
Eckhart, Meister, 15, 133
Eclogues, 173
Eden, 85
Egyptian, The, 193
Ehrman, Bart, 181–83
El, 55, 57, 61, 164
El Elyon, 61
elements, 94
Eliezer ben Judah of Worms, 66
Elijah, 71, 74, 174, 192
Elizabeth, 196
Elohim, 55–57

El Rachum, 121
El Shaddai, 95–96, 165
Endalandala, 61
Enlightenment, 32, 135, 173, 204, 218
Enlil, 96–97
Enoch, 184, 223
entheos, 82, 207
Enuma Elish, 97
Ephesians, 90, 157–58
Epicurieanism, 201
Epicurus, 126
Erasmus, 185–86
Erebus, 117
Eskimo artists, 82
Essays and Reviews, 189
Essenes, 192
Esther, 152
eternal life, 221
eternity, 221
Ethiopian scriptures, 184
Eugenics, 224
Euripides, 2
Eusebius, 184
Eve, 15, 85, 170, 177, 181, 200, 203–4
evil, 126, 128, 203–4
evolution, 224
existence of God, 37–53, 55
Exodus, 26, 54, 56, 60, 62, 70, 74, 97, 101, 104, 116, 123, 134, 143, 154, 169
eye symbol, 142
Ezekiel, 72–73, 84, 101, 155
Ezra, 112

fall, 15
father metaphor, 159–61, 163, 165

father rule, 90
Fazil, 115
female images, 165
Ferré, Frederick, 42–43
Feuerbach, Ludwig, 6
Fiorenza, Elisabeth Schüssler, 48
fire, 94
Flew, Anthony, 35
Formlessness, 65–79, 208, 213
    Communication, 76–77
    Sound, 74, 76
    Voice, 76
    Word, 76
Four Noble Truths, 173
Fox, George, 97
Fox, Matthew, 15, 108, 218
Franklin, Benjamin, 176
Frazer, James, 60
Fuji, 96
Fundamentalism, 186

Gaia, 95
Galatians, 158, 183, 194–95
Galileo, 138, 223–24
Gandhi, 111
Ganges River, 99
Ge'ez language, 184
gender, 152–53
Genesis, 56, 59, 61, 68, 70, 72,
    74, 83, 85, 95–96, 98, 107,
    111, 136, 165, 168, 170, 225
Geneva Catechism, 128
Gnostic dualism, 201
God: A Biography, 190
God: An Autobiography, 190
God as Love, 16, 109
God as Power, 16, 68, 109,
    115, 131

Golden Bough, The, 60
Golden Plover, 12, 15
Gomer, 155
Good Shepherd, 113
gospels, 180, 192
Goulder, Michael, 46
Greek concepts, 75, 87–88, 172
    dieties, 198
    dualism, 81
    epics, 87
    Hellenism, 199
    New Testament, 185
    philosophers, 62, 88
    stories, 117
    texts, 182
    theology, 199
Gregory the Great, 31
Griffin, David, 220
Guadalupe, Nuestra Senora de,
    124–25

hã, 70
Habakkuk, 92
Hadewijch of Antwerp, 119
"Hadith of the Hidden Treasure,"
    77
Hagar, 76
Hamilton, William, 45
Hammarskjöld, Dag, 7, 115,
    218
Handel, George Frideric, 193
Hannah, 197
Han period, 102–3
haole, 70
Harpur, Tom, 173
Hartshorne, Charles, 125,
    129, 221
Hebrew prophets, 112

Hebrews, 83, 101, 137
Hebrew scripture, 13, 20, 26, 28, 37, 46, 48, 50, 55–57, 63, 67–68, 70, 73, 83–85, 87, 90, 99, 115, 140, 156, 177, 180, 182, 184, 205, 214
Hellenism, 199
henotheism, 56
Hesiod, 41
Hezekiah, 193
Hick, John, 52
Hildegard of Bingen, 72–73, 93
Hinduism, 31, 35, 37, 61–62, 66, 76, 112, 117, 145, 172, 174–75, 206–7, 213
    images, 20
    temples, 99, 103
    Upanishads, 66, 69, 82, 98, 191, 206–8
HMS Beagle, 40
Hokmah, 162, 165
hokmah/sophia, 89
Holocaust, 44–45, 131, 181
Holy Spirit, 207
Homer, 13, 41
homosexuality 176, 189
Honest to God, 45
Hosea, 105, 155, 166
Hospitable One, 169, 171
hospitality, 168–69
Howatch, Susan, 6, 131
Huang Po, 30
Hume, David, 39
husbands, 154–59
Hutchens, John K., 9
Huxley, T. H., 43
hypostases, 26, 208

icons, 21
Imago Dei, 72, 136–53
immanence, 81, 217–18
immortality, 86, 223
Inanna, 95, 105
Incas, 100
inclusivism, 208
index, 21
indwelling, 89
Injil, 178
Institutes of the Christian Religion, 92
intelligent design, 225
interreligious dialogue, 212–17
Irenaeus, Bishop, 180, 203
Isaac, 191
Isaiah, 28, 99, 103, 105, 116, 124, 140, 142, 146–48, 150, 156, 165–66, 193–94, 199–200
Ishmael, 191
Ishtar, 95, 105
Isis, 95
Islam, 27, 62, 76, 99, 128, 139, 179, 207, 223
Israel, 59

Jacob, 59, 191
Jainism, 112
James, 184, 186
James I, 186
James VI, 186
Jami, 92
Jefferson, Thomas, 113
Jephthah, 144
Jeremiah, 71, 104–5, 116, 127, 142, 165, 192, 196, 199, 217
Jerome, 184–86

Jerusalem, 127, 155, 184
Jesus, 14, 45, 67, 83–84, 87–88,
    93, 101, 103, 113, 155,
    174–75, 183, 188, 191–209,
    212
  baptism, 105
  birth, 180
  infancy stories of, 181
Jewish War of 70 CE, 178, 193,
    201
Joan of Arc, 88
Job, 26, 71, 83–84, 98, 130, 149,
    170, 181, 185, 194
John, 3, 45, 68–69, 75, 84, 85,
    88, 98, 100, 101, 103, 113,
    116–17, 133, 147, 161–63,
    169, 171, 180, 182, 185, 187,
    191–192, 195–99, 206, 208,
    210, 212, 214, 217
John of Damascus, 37
Johnson, Elizabeth, 18, 48, 88,
    109, 137, 152, 168, 208
John the Baptist, 84, 98, 192,
    196
Jonah, 185
Jones, Caroline, 81, 207
Jones, E. Stanley, 206
Joseph, 180, 183, 199–200
Josephus, 158
Joshua, 57, 143, 148, 193
Jowett, Benjamin, 40, 111, 189
Judaism, 158, 178, 207, 213
Jude, 184
Judges, 57, 61, 83, 152, 197
judgment, 148–52
Judith, 152
Junayd, Ibn, 77
Justyn Martyr, 180

Kali, 95
kami, 102
Kant, Immanuel, 1, 38
Katha Upanishad, 81, 85
Kaufman, Gordon, 52
Keane, Bill, 25
Khnum, 72
Kierkegaard, Sören, 55
King metaphor, xi, 18, 118, 128,
    132, 140, 142, 148
King, Martin Luther, 120, 145
Kingdom of God, 86
1 Kings, 3, 74, 97, 217
2 Kings, 71, 100, 164
King James Bible (KJV), 183,
    185–86
Kipling, Rudyard, 210–11
knowledge, 27–28
Krishna, 117, 145
Küng, Hans, 47–48, 215–16
Kushner, Harold, 5, 52, 68, 78,
    126, 130, 151, 225

Lady Wind, 96
lamb of God, 198
lambs, 140
Lamentations, 142
Lao-tzu (Lao Tze), 55
Latin New Testament, 185
Left Behind, 151
Leonowens, Anna, 123–24
letters, 192
*Letters on the Laws of Man's
    Nature and Development*, 42
Leuba, James, 6
Levi, Primo, 17, 121
Leviathan, 26
Leviticus, 105, 116, 189, 192

Lewis, C. S., 156
Logos, 75, 107, 162, 197–201
Logos-Wisdom, 162
Logos-Word, 163
Lono, 70
Lord's Prayer, 161
Lord Wind, 96
Luke, 70, 83–84, 86, 105, 113–
    14, 116, 161, 167, 169, 180,
    183, 192, 196–97, 199–200
Lunda tribe, 61
Lure, 219–21, 223
Luther, Martin, 14, 31, 33, 186

MacIntyre, Alasdair, 49
mahabbah, 27
Mahabharata, 145
Maimonides, Moses, 28–29, 50,
    111
Maitland, Sara, 9, 188
Maitri Upanishad, 217
male images, 165
mana, 70, 131
Manji, Irshad, 129
Marriage, 60, 118, 157, 176, 200
Maori traditions, 131
Marcion, 13, 180
Marduk (Merodach), 97
Mark, 57, 70, 90, 99, 103,
    113, 182–83, 192–93, 195–96,
    199, 209
Marrkapmirr, 114
Martial, 182
Martineau, Harriet, 42
Marx, Carl, 6
Mary, 169, 180, 196–97,
    199–200, 202
Gospel of, 181

Mascaró, Juan, 117, 206
Masereka, Zebedee, 121
masks, 26–27
Massai, 61
Master of Heaven, 163
Matarusvan, 54
Matthew, 70–71, 73, 83, 86, 90,
    98, 100–101, 103, 105, 113,
    146, 161, 169, 180, 183, 192,
    196, 199, 200–201, 206
Mawalawiya, 6–7
McFague, Sallie, 15–16, 20, 94,
    174, 220
McMahon, Dorothy McCrae, 172
Meadow, Mary Jo, 33, 226
Means, Russell, 164
Mechtild of Magdeburg, 31, 119
memory, 27
Mendelssohn, Fanny, 60
Mersenne, Marin, 42
Merton, Thomas, 24, 30
Messiah, 192–93
metaphor, 17–20, 171
*Methodist and Ecumenical
    Hymnbook*, 142
Micah, 146, 148
Michelangelo, 141
Miles, Jack, 123, 190
Mill, John Stuart, 40, 114
Mills, Mary, 55, 160
Milton, John, 126
Mishnah, 177
Moab, 56
Moltmann, Jürgen, 32
monotheism, 45, 56–57
Moses, 56–57, 60, 84, 101,
    111, 143, 148, 174, 177, 181,
    191, 223

Mot, 55
Mother Earth, 95–96
mother metaphor, 161, 163–68
Mount Fuji, 96, 102
Mount Meru, 103
Mount Saint Helen, 104
Mount Sinai, 102–3
Mount Zion, 103
Muhammad, 27, 76, 128, 174, 206
Mundaka Upanishad, 82
Muslim. *See* Islam
Myth of God Incarnate, The, 45

Nam, 62
namasti, 82
name of God, 54–64
Nathan, 193
natural religion, 93
nature, 92–108
Neamt Monastery, 142
Nebuchadnezzar, 59, 84
nephesh, 83
nesher, 104
New Revised Standard Version (1989), 183, 187
New Song, 76
Newsweek, 48
New Testament, 13, 180, 182, 184–85, 187, 205, 214
Ngali, 61
Ngombe, 61
Nibbana, 32
Nicodemus, 205
Nietzsche, Friedrich, 6, 46, 91
Nightingale, Florence, 11, 94–95, 125, 222
Nineteen Eighty-Four, 10

Ninlil, 96
Nirvana, 32, 120
Njambi-Kalunga, 61
Noah, 86, 223
Noble Path, 100
Noble Truths, 32, 134–35, 173
Norwich, Julian of, 154
Nouwen, Henri, 167
Numbers, 50, 84, 106
Numinous, 27

O'Brien, George, 19, 42, 103, 120, 201
Olam, 61
Old Testament, 184
Om, 61–62, 76, 191
Omega, 217
omnipotence, 128, 135
"On the Interpretation of Scripture," 189
Oodgeroo (Walker, Kath), 95, 222
Origen, 146, 182
original sin, 200
Origin of Species, The, 40–41, 189
Orwell, George, 10
Otto, Rudolf, 27, 124
ousia, 26

Pachamama, 95
Palestine, 127
Paley, William, 39–40
Pallis, Marco, 93
Pannenberg, Wolfhart, 109
pantheism, 218
Paradise Lost, 126
paraphrases, 179

Pascal, Blaise, 27
Pastoral Epistles, 158
paterfamilias, 90
Paul, 30, 59, 76, 85, 87, 90, 92,
    125, 158, 161, 173, 180–81,
    183, 192, 194–97, 199–201,
    205–6, 212–14
peace, 146–47
Peleiades, 105
Pelikan, Jaroslav, 75, 225
Pentateuch, 179, 181
Pentecost, 71, 89–90, 97, 105
Pentecostal persuasions, 89
Perpetua, 168
Persephone, 95
personae, 26–27, 208
Persuasion, 219
Peter, 87, 90, 113, 158, 184, 192
Pharaoh, 83
Pharisees, 86, 192
Philip, 99
Philistines, 57, 197
Philo, 199
pigeon, 105
Pilate, Pontius, 183, 210
Plague, The, 126
Plato, 88, 111–12, 114
pneuma, 69, 89
Politics, 140
polytheistic, 60
popes, 90, 161, 201, 216
Pope John XXIII, 47
prāna, 70, 85
Preparer of the Feast, 169
Prince of Peace, 146
Process theology 47, 218–21
prodigal son, 167
Promise-seekers, 152

Protestantism, 186, 208
    Bible, 184
    traditions, 89
Proverbs, 71, 105, 124–25, 162
Psalm, 4, 6, 19, 29, 31–32,
    70–71, 74, 80, 94, 98,
    100–105, 121, 125, 127, 133,
    142, 148–49, 168
Psalms of David, 109
Pseudo-Dionysus, 30

Qur'an, 27, 38, 54, 56, 62,
    65, 76, 78, 81, 93, 109, 147,
    149, 174–75, 178–79, 191,
    206, 217
Surah, 56, 62, 78, 81, 100, 121,
    128, 148–49, 178, 191

Rabi'a, 119
Radha, 117
Rahner, Karl, 109, 215–16
Rainbow Serpent, 95
Rainbow Spirit, 107
Ramakrishna, Shri, 35
ransom theory, 203
rape, 155, 156, 168, 188
Rapture, 150–51
Rayi, 85
redemption, 15
Reformation, 185
reincarnation, 222
religio, 3
Religious Right, 167
Rembrandt, 167
resurrection, 195, 203
Return of the Prodigal Son, 167
Revelation, 70, 148–49, 180,
    184, 217

Rig-Veda, 54, 62, 117
Robinson, John A. T., 45–46
Rodriguez, Richard, 124
Romans, 84–85, 87, 89, 92, 161,
  180, 185, 195, 200
Rosh Hashanah, 213
Rostand, Jean, 207
ruach, 68, 69, 72, 83, 89–90, 143
Ruether, Rosemary Radford, 48,
  109
Rufinus, 182
Rumi, 6, 10, 28, 55, 128, 136,
  223, 226
Russell, Bertrand, 37, 53

Sadducees, 86
Samson, 197
Samuel, 181, 197
1 Samuel, 83–84, 148, 197
2 Samuel, 84, 103, 193
Sarah, 168, 197
Sartre, Jean Paul, 42
Sat Naam, 62
Saul, 59, 83–84, 148
Schillebeeckx, Edward, 47–48, 67
Schleiermacher, Friedrich, 208
Schniedewind, William, 181
science, 39, 40, 45, 223–25
Scopes, John, 224
scribe, 181
scrolls, 179–80, 188
Second Vatican Council, 47, 215
semiotics, 21
Septuagint, 180
serendipitous creativity, 52
sex, 86, 118–19, 155, 204,
Shakti, 117
shalom, 61, 146

shangi, 163
Shaw, George Bernard, 44–45
Shawnee, 95
Shekinah, 89, 95, 165
Sheldrake, Philip, 81
Shelley, Percy Bysshe, 222
Shemesh, 55
Sheol, 86–87
Shepherd of Hermas, 184
Shiva, 99, 117
Siddiqui, Mona, 143, 179
Sidon, 56
Sieunarine, Everson T., 121
signs, 21
  icons, 21
  index, 21
  symbols, 21–22
Sikhism, 62, 207
Simeon, 183
Simon the Messiah, 193
sin, 15, 203–4,
single mothers, 167
Sistine Chapel, 141
Sky Father, 96
Sky God, 96
Smith, Huston, 7, 44
Soelle, Dorothee, 144–45, 167,
  171
sofer, 181
sola scriptura, 185
Solomon, 3, 148
Solzhenitsyn, Aleksander, 149
Song of Solomon, 105, 118–19,
  155
Songs of Praise, 142
Sophia, 48, 89, 162
Sophia-Wisdom, 95, 162–63
soul, 198

Sound, 74, 76
Source, 26
Southern Baptist International
  Mission Board Prayer Guide,
  213
Spider Woman, 95
Spielberg, Steven, 38
spirit, 26, 80–91, 208
spirituality, 80–81
"Spirituality in America," 48
spiritus, 89
Spong, John Shelby, 42, 46
Sponheim, Paul, 211, 214, 225
sterilization, 224
Stoicism, 201
Suchocki, Marjorie, 221
Sufi, 6–7, 10, 16, 27–28, 77, 82,
  92, 111, 178
sun (*ni*), 99–102
Supreme Ruler, 163
Surah, 56, 62, 78, 81, 100, 128,
  148–49, 178, 191
Suzuki, David, 73
Svetasvatara Upanishad, 213
Sydney Diocese, 159
symbols, 21–22
Synoptic Gospels, 192, 194

Tabrizi, Shams-i-, 178
Tagore, Rabindranath, 81, 93,
  96, 115, 117, 119
Talmud, 28, 177
Tamil Veda, 19
Taoism, 55, 98
Tatian, 180
Tawrat, 178
Taylor, Jeremy, 169
Ten Commandments, 116

Tennyson, Alfred Lord, 39, 222
Teresa of Avila, Saint, 98
Tertius, 180
Tertullian, 146
theism, 42, 46, 218
theodicy, 114, 126,130–31
theology, 13–15, 43
Theotokos, 202
Theudas, 193
Thiering, Barbara, 50–51
Thomas, 133, 212
  Gospel of, 181
Thoreau, Henry David, 5, 227
Tiamat, 97, 164
tianzu, 163
Tillich, Paul, 1, 42, 45, 50,
  77, 109
Timothy, 90, 188, 192
1 Timothy, 187
2 Timothy, 188
Tiruvaymoli, 19
Titus, 90
Tolstoy, Leo, 49, 51, 63–64, 101,
  122, 144, 148, 175, 204
Torah, 109, 177, 179
translations, 179
Trinity, 26–27, 81, 88, 90, 142,
  159, 202, 207–8, 220
Trojan Women, 2
True Name, 62
truth, 210–27, 214
Tuesdays with Morrie, 120, 213
turtledove, 105

Ulphila, 175
Uluru, 23, 102
Umar, Caliph, 178
Unexplainable, 61

Unknown, 61
Upanishads, 66, 69, 81–82, 85, 98, 111, 191, 206–7, 213, 217
Uriah, 148
U Thittila, 32

Valhalla, 173
Van Buren, Paul, 45
Vatican Council (1870), 94
Vedas, 2, 37, 61, 216
Vermes, Geza, 194, 205–6
Victoria, Queen, 41
Victorin-Vangerud, Nancy, 208
Views of the Evidences of Christianity, 39
viraha, 31–32
Virgil, 173
virgin birth, 199–200, 203
Vishnu, 172
Vishwakarma, Lord, 126
Voice, 76, 97
Vulgate, 184–87

Walker, Kath (Oodgeroo), 95, 222
war, 143–46, 171
Ward, Keith, 210, 226
Warrior metaphor, xi, 18, 44, 132, 142–46, 171
water, 94, 97–99
Watery Void, 164
Wesley, John, 7, 97
Whewell, William, 40
Whirling Dervish, 6–7
White, Patrick, 51–52

Whitehead, Alfred North, 115, 129, 218–21
Wiesel, Elie, 33–34, 44
Wilberforce, Samuel, 140
will, 27
Willy Wigtail, 12
wind, 69–70, 96–98
wisdom, 89
wives, 154–59
Woman Wisdom, 164
Word, 26, 76, 162, 197–98
Wordsworth, William, 5, 39, 91, 222
Wren, Brian, 142

Xenophanes, 18, 41

Yahweh, 10, 13, 26, 31, 50, 55–57, 59–61, 71–72, 83, 88, 96–97, 101, 115–16, 121, 127, 129, 134, 142–44, 149, 154–55, 164–65, 168, 177–78, 193, 199, 217
Yama, 54
Yancey, Phillip, 51
Yareah, 55
YHWH. *See* Yahweh
Yom Kipppur, 213
Yoruba Yemaja, 95

Zealots, 192
Zechariah, 84, 97–98, 196
Zen, 30
Zephaniah, 148
Zoroastrianism, 86, 112